STUDYING GERMAN CINEMA

STUDYING GERMAN CINEMA
BY
MAGGIE HOFFGEN

auteur

First published in 2009 by
Auteur
The Old Surgery, 9 Pulford Road, Leighton Buzzard LU7 1AB
www.auteur.co.uk

Copyright © Auteur Publishing 2009

Designed and set by Nikki Hamlett at AMP Ltd, Dunstable, Bedfordshire

Printed and bound in India by Imprint Digital

Cover: *Das Leben der Anderen* (*The Lives of Others*) © Bayerischer Rundfunk / Aquarius Collection

British Library Cataloguing-in-Publication Data
A catalogue record for this book is available from the British Library

ISBN 978-1-906733-00-1 paperback
ISBN 978-1-906733-01-8 cloth

CONTENTS

ACKNOWLEDGEMENTS AND THANKS

To the Goethe-Institut libraries in Manchester, London and Munich that I scoured over the years and that gave me access to a wealth of German films and related literature which I would not have been able to find anywhere else.

To Cornerhouse, Manchester, especially to Linda Pariser and Rachel Hayward, for the opportunities they gave me as well as their help and support, and to Dave Petty for his invaluable technical advice.

To friends and family who have lent me their ear during the project, especially to Jane for her emotional and professional support, and to all those who have discussed, read and commented on and thus helped to improve the manuscript.

To lecturers and friends in the School of Linguistics and Cultures at Manchester University for their inspiration and encouragement during my MA studies and beyond.

STILLS INFORMATION

Nosferatu (page 15), Aquarius Collection; *Der blaue Engel* (31), Joel Finler Archive; *Triumph des Willens* (45), BFI; *Die Mörder sind unter uns* (61) DEFA/Kobal Collection; *Spur der Steine* (75), DEFA-Stiftung/Klaus D. Schwarz; *Aguirre, der Zorn Gottes* (89), *Angst essen Seele auf* (105), *Die Blechtrommel* (199), BFI; *Heimat* (133), Aquarius Collection/Westdautcher Rund Funk; *Der Himmel über Berlin* (147), BFI; *Lola rennt* (161), Joel Finler Archive/Columbia TriStar; *Der Untergang* (175), *Gegen die Wand* (189), BFI; *Das Leben der Anderen* (201), Bayerischer Rundfunk / Aquarius Collection. Framegrabs within each chapter are taken from the respective Region 2 DVDs of the films.

INTRODUCTION

Every chapter of this book has as its starting point one key German film which is then used to discuss wider issues and implications, be they historical, cultural, or industrial. Each individual chapter has its own particular emphasis depending on the film selected.

Selecting the films was not an easy task. The more research you conduct into possible candidates for a book such as this one, the more you discover just how many German films worthy of close study there are. Our final selection was made according to a number of criteria.

Our aim is to provide a cross-section of significant German films from the 1920s to today, while at the same time keeping the book within a manageable scope. We deliberately did not include films from before that time, mostly for reasons of availability. You will notice that in our first chapter we have expanded our discussion to more than one film. We did this in order to do some justice to this very important decade of film-making in Germany: the 1920s represent the peak of the formative period of art film in Germany and abound with significant films. Fortunately, many later film-makers quote among their influences films and film-makers from the twenties, which allowed us to reference some of them within other chapters. At the other end, historically speaking, the more contemporary the films are the more difficult it becomes to assess their relevance because they have not yet stood the test of time. However, we think that our approach to selection is stringent.

We have assessed the significance of the individual films in a variety of ways: socially, politically, (film) culturally, asking how influential the films and/or their makers have been. At the same time we have aimed for a wide range of issues, genres and styles. We have included: films that deal with contemporary or historically relevant issues; a variety of genres and styles in our films, including two early groundbreaking genre films which have remained influential right into the twenty-first century; drama; melodrama; a film in which music takes centre stage, a literary adaptation; a 'Heimat' film (albeit an alternative one); as well as a propaganda and an anti-propaganda film.

The text availability or accessibility mentioned above has been a consideration for us in two ways: we have chosen films that are available either commercially or from lending libraries. We have also considered the accessibility of films in terms of interest to a wide range of viewers. This book is meant to take you on a journey of discovery via a broad selection of films, some of which you would never otherwise have encountered or thought you might be interested in. Each film is an important example of German cinematic representation and lends itself particularly well to discussions that go beyond the film itself. Therefore each chapter has a certain 'added value' and can be studied individually. Together the 14 chapters provide a comprehensive overview of titles, names, themes, styles and context of German film since the 1920s.

German film history proper began in 1895, with the first public showing of short films by the brothers Skladanowsky at the Wintergarten in Berlin. For about 20 years film was not taken seriously as an art form, but rather as entertainment for the masses. However, from about 1910-1919 film went through a process of experimentation and innovation. Films such as *Das Cabinet des Dr Caligari* (*The Cabinet of Dr Caligari*, Robert Wiene, 1919) started to employ the recognised artistic style of Expressionism. This quintessentially German style originated in painting, sculpture, literature, and in the theatre. In film it was to dominate the first half of the 1920s. As the term implies, Expressionist artists sought to express through their works of art such psychological states and emotions as passion, fear, horror, and dreams. The expression was meant to be entirely subjective. Hence, in painting, the visual style was characterised by vibrant, non-naturalistic colours and bold lines; theatre was dominated by deliberately artificial looking sets, jagged lines, and exaggerated acting; while in film similar devices were used plus extreme camera angles and the famous chiaroscuro lighting, intensifying the differences between darkness and light.

Expressionism was well suited to the turbulent times of the early twenties in Germany – in the aftermath of World War I the country suffered economically, politically and socially. There was a general sense of insecurity, a feeling amongst Germans of having been collectively betrayed. Economically, horrendous inflation increased the suffering of the German nation. Creatively, however, and particularly in the new art of film, the twenties are generally regarded as the period in which German cultural production in all the arts was at a peak. Films such as the *Caligari*, *Nosferatu* (F.W. Murnau, 1922), and the *Dr Mabuse* films (Fritz Lang, 1922) were proof of the artistic merits of the new art form, and at the same time expressions of the 'uncanny' (Freud) and of the impossibility of differentiating between reality and dream, truth and lies.

From this period of film making in Germany we have selected one key film, *Nosferatu*, and one 'subsidiary' film, Fritz Lang's *Metropolis* (1926) and set them both against the purest example of German Expressionism, *Caligari*. We grouped *Nosferatu* and *Metropolis* together because they were arguably the very first films in the genres of horror and science-fiction/fantasy and had an enormous influence on later generations of film-makers, especially in those genres. Our first chapter also includes information about the gradual concentration of cinematic production in the famous UFA studios.

UFA (Universum Film AG) was the largest film production company in Germany at the time. Founded in 1912, it was responsible for a German film industry that in the early to mid-twenties rivalled Hollywood. You will find information on UFA, its history and its successor, DEFA (Deutsche Film AG) studios, in relevant chapters of this book. Suffice it to say here that in its long history UFA/DEFA went through a series of ideological changes, and as such bears testament to the importance that was attached to film as a medium to influence and control the population in the two totalitarian regimes experienced within Germany in the twentieth century.

The second half of the 1920s brought more stability to Germany. Inflation had been defeated; a currency reform had taken place. There was a more upbeat mood in the country, and this can be traced in the artistic output at the time. A new style began to manifest itself in the arts: 'Neue Sachlichkeit', which is usually translated into English as 'New Objectivity'. Film-makers began to turn their attention to ordinary characters and stories, away from the monumental, the allegorical and the fantastic. Up until the advent of sound film (and beyond), new genres were created and old ones were given more realistic content. The ever popular crime film, for example, now dealt with issues of 'the street', i.e. social and psychological issues, a trend that culminated in 1931 in Fritz Lang's *M* (an early sound film).

The new realism in film continued into the technological innovation of sound film. The transition from silent to sound film was fraught with problems. One of them was the issue of speaking voices. Many of the film actors of the silent era did not have 'good' voices. However, our next film choice turned its lead actress into a star literally overnight - and this was in no small measure due to her voice. The actress is Marlene Dietrich, the film *Der blaue Engel* (*The Blue Angel*, 1930, directed by Josef von Sternberg), a very early example of a German sound film. With her unusual singing voice and rendition Dietrich made the film's songs famous.

To devastating effect, this prolific period of cultural production in the Weimar Republic was interrupted by the Third Reich, before and during which many cultural icons of the twenties left Germany. Many film personnel (such as writers, cinematographers, directors, actors and craftspeople) emigrated to Hollywood, where they made new careers. Among them were Ernst Lubitsch, Fritz Lang, Billy Wilder, Josef von Sternberg, Robert Siodmak, Detlev Sieck (Douglas Sirk), Marlene Dietrich and Peter Lorre.

Some stayed in their native country, either working in the services of the Nazis or managing to eke out a living without compromising their integrity too much. One of the (if not the) best-known and most controversial film-makers of the Nazi period is Leni Riefenstahl. Two productions stand for both her talent and the controversy surrounding her support of Nazi ideology, *Triumph des Willens* (*Triumph of the Will*, 1934), which we have selected for this book, and *Olympiad* (1938), her depiction of the 1936 Olympic Games in Berlin. Josef Goebbels, the Third Reich's propaganda minister, recognised and used immediately the power of film to transmit ideological content, not just in documentary propaganda films, but also in feature films such as war films, historical drama, musical film, melodrama, and comedy. There will be more detailed discussion of Nazi films in our chapter on *Triumph des Willens*.

After World War II, Germany was occupied by the Allied forces: the USA, Britain and France in the West and the Soviet Union in the East. In 1949, the growing Cold War climate between East and West resulted in the division of Germany into two states. This division cemented the ideological lines between capitalism and democracy in the West and socialism in the East. East Germany, or the German Democratic Republic, became a satellite state of the Soviet Union, while West Germany, or the Federal Republic of Germany, was shaped by Western democratic principles and received strong financial support from the West, in particular from the United States.

There was only a brief time immediately after the war when a couple of interesting films were made with East and West participation. The only film still available of that time is *Die Mörder sind unter uns* (*Murderers Are Among Us*, Wolfgang Staudte, 1946), whose title conveys its message clearly. Its main significance lies in the fact that it was filmed in bombed-out Berlin, in extremely difficult conditions, and that it dealt with the immediate post-war situation in Germany, and began to assess the legacy of the Nazi regime critically. It was the first anti-fascist film, made 'between' East and West. In East Germany anti-fascist films would become a very important means of appraising the Nazi past.

Within a few years the two very different ideologies had produced two very different Germanys, not just in political and economic terms, but also socially in the two peoples' value systems. West Germans were busy reconstructing their country in the Western Europe model; they enjoyed renewed wealth relatively quickly, and became avid consumers, but generally speaking there was no conscious psychological complete ideological break with the recent past. Real discussion and confrontation with their own identification with the Nazi regime were buried under the 'economic miracle' and a consumerist society which brought about a sense of superiority and complacency.

In East Germany a complete break did take place, in political, economic, and social terms. Socialist ideals were going to be put into practice, and this led many dedicated left-wing Germans to leave the West for the East. This is ironic really, because not much later, during the fifties, the stream of people in the other direction (leaving the East for the West) gathered in strength. The reasons for this were disillusionment with socialism, its growing ideological dogmatism and the stifling of any opposition; as well as also the lure of consumerism. Cinematically, the complete break in the GDR with the fascist past manifested itself in anti-fascist films that became a mainstay from now on. We shall pick up on the East German context later in this introduction.

In West Germany in the 1950s, film production was at an unprecedented low, not with regard to quantity, but concerning artistic quality. The country seemed to be in the grip of a disease which was later described and analysed as an 'inability to mourn'. Social psychologists described it as a form of numbness which ensues when the loss of a beloved person is not mourned appropriately. What Freud had identified before as the melancholy of the individual was applied to explain the behaviour of a whole society. At the same time consumerism blossomed. The economic miracle of West Germany was in full swing in the fifties. Only a handful of interesting films were made during that time. The majority of films consisted of comedies, musicals, and the most German film genre of all, the so-called 'Heimat' films. These feel-good genres represented more or less a continuation of genre films made during the Third Reich, a fact that was criticised by a new generation of film-makers who appeared on the scene in the early sixties.

Twenty-six of those young German film-makers signed a manifesto at the 1962 Oberhausen Short Film Festival in which they declared the 'death of old cinema'. Their approach to film-making was to be radically different in both narrative and style. However, this did not mean that they formed a coherent movement. In order to describe the common thread that runs through the films of both Young German Cinema of the sixties and its continuation in New German Cinema in the following decade, Thomas Elsaesser, the most eminent of German film scholars coined the term 'cinema of experience'. If we view some of the new film-makers' output in the light of this expression we can see that there is indeed commonality between them, notwithstanding their significant differences.

Of the first generation of German film-makers from the sixties (Young German Cinema) that have remained true to their principles only Alexander Kluge, Edgar Reitz and Volker Schlöndorff are still active film-makers today. In the late sixties and seventies they were joined by a second and third generation, the main protagonists of which are Rainer Werner Fassbinder, Werner Herzog, Margarethe von Trotta, and Wim Wenders. The best-known, most notorious and influential film-maker of the seventies, Fassbinder, died in 1982. He even achieved commercial success with his later films (unlike some of his colleagues).

From the prolific years of New German Cinema we selected Werner Herzog's first international success, *Aguirre, der Zorn Gottes* (*Aguirre, the Wrath of God*, 1971), Fassbinder's *Angst essen Seele auf* (*Fear Eats the Soul*, 1974), and Volker Schlöndorff's *Die Blechtrommel* (*The Tin Drum*, 1978), which won Germany's first Oscar. It is also interesting as a literary adaptation. Also within New German Cinema the genre of 'Heimatfilm' received new treatment. It was Edgar Reitz who made a new type of 'Heimatfilm', an internationally famous and popular 12-part film epic which bore the simple title *Heimat* (1984).

In the 1980s, there was another hiatus in West German film-making, coinciding with a return to conservativism in West Germany (and elsewhere in the Western world). Once again, West German film-makers produced little of note, with the exception of a good comedy here and there. The most successful 'lifestyle comedies', which incorporated feminist issues, were directed by Doris Dörrie, one of the few popular female film-makers in Germany.

Other exceptions to this lull in film-making were *Heimat*, and Wim Wenders' *Der Himmel über Berlin* (*Wings of Desire*, 1987), to both of which we have devoted a chapter. *Der Himmel über Berlin* is significant in that it marks Wenders' return to Germany after several years of filming in the United States. He was more successful in continuing a career that spanned the US and Europe than most other German film-makers who have undertaken this difficult split. *Der Himmel über Berlin* is also the last important film to have as its setting the divided city of Berlin, which was reunified only a couple of years later.

Coming back to the development of the film industry in East Germany we notice that a strong tradition of anti-fascist film-making developed there. The very first DEFA film was an anti-fascist film, *Die Mörder sind unter uns*, mentioned above. After Stalin's death it became possible for new East German directors to make less dogmatic, more diverse, and in particular more stylistically interesting anti-fascist films than before, although the genre itself was always regarded as politically desirable.

Later political turbulences in East Germany were reflected very closely in film production and censorship measures. The years 1965 and 1966 were characterised by an unprecedented wave of political dogmatism which resulted in repressive measures against cultural production. The 11th Plenary of the Central Committee of the Socialist Unity Party (SED) marked a low point in curtailing freedom of artistic expression and resulted in bans of a large number of films. *Spur der Steine* (*Traces of Stones*, Frank Beyer, 1966) is one example of just such a film.

As outlined above, during the years of the division of Germany into two ideologically very different countries, film production in the GDR also took a very different turn compared to that in West Germany. Production started in East Germany very soon after the end of World War II and the division of Germany, and much sooner than in the West. The main GDR film production company was DEFA (Deutsche Film AG), which was based at the old UFA studios in Potsdam-Babelsberg. Their first production was *Mörder*. This film is the first example of dealing with a topic that was very close to the heart of the new communist state: anti-fascism. Throughout the history of the GDR anti-fascism played a major role in the political, social and cultural life of the republic, in sharp contrast to the situation in West Germany at the time, as described above.

During the 41 years of its existence the GDR went through a number of phases, usually dictated by the current political climate in the Soviet Union. Accordingly, film production in the GDR was closely prescribed and monitored by the communist apparatus. Strong ideological content dominated in every film genre and form. This does not mean that the films themselves were of low quality. On the contrary, there was a particularly strong tradition in documentaries, anti-fascist films and children's films, made by people such as Konrad Wolf, Kurt Maetzig, Heiner Carow, and Frank Beyer. Apart from their intrinsic artistic merits these productions are interesting as evidence of a highly controlled and heavily censored film production machine. Again and again, though, film-makers (and other artists and writers) were critical of the 'real existing socialism' of the GDR. Depending on the dominant political climate they were able to express their views more or less directly.

Since the turn of the millenium or so many GDR films have been re-discovered. Quite a few of them were works that had been banned by the East German authorities and locked away in cellars and other inaccessible locations. Fortunately they have not been completely destroyed. In this book one film stands as an example of GDR film: *Spur der Steine*, an anti-propaganda film with a remarkable history. Upon its premiere it was taken out of distribution immediately, a fate that befell nearly all the films produced in the GDR in 1966, a particularly repressive year. When discussing *Spur der Steine* we place particular emphasis, as with some other films, on its wider historical and political context.

The Berlin Wall fell in November 1989; German economic and political reunification was completed (at least organisationally) in 1990. The psychological consequences for film culture were in some respects not dissimilar to those at the end of the Nazi regime. The momentous political and social changes had to be digested by East and West German film-makers alike. They are reflected in many films of the 1990s, especially in the first half of the decade. Some of the new themes and subject matters were darkness, night, Berlin, borders, stirrings of (re-)addressing the National Socialist past and GDR history. One strand of the latter concern developed around the turn of the millennium. There was a wave of 'Ostalgie' (nostalgia for the East), which manifested itself in 'GDR tourism', re-enactments of GDR traditions, rediscovery of GDR consumer products, etc. Part of this nostalgia was the release of a number of 'Ostalgie' films.

Before that, a new wave of German film-making can be said to have started with *Lola rennt* (*Run Lola Run*, Tom Tykwer, 1998), our next film choice in this book. Its unprecedented critical and commercial success made people take note of German films once again and paved the way for the international release of new German productions. Since 1998 new synergies between the eastern and western parts of Germany, growing confidence and the desire and ability to articulate new issues have put German film back on the international map. This revival justifies our inclusion in this book of three more films with very different subject matters that are, however, treated with similar confidence and were made within just three years of each other. *Gegen die Wand* (*Head-on*, Fatih Akin, 2004), a Turkish-German film, represents the growing number of depictions of immigrant culture in Germany by those directly involved: the immigrants and their descendants themselves. *Der Untergang* (*Downfall,* Oliver Hirschbiegel, 2005) tackles the subject of Hitler's last few days in his bunker and dares to portray him as a normal human being, thereby breaking a taboo in German film history. The final film in this book is *Das Leben der Anderen* (*The Lives of Others*, 2006), the first portrayal of the dark side of East Germany's history in the ruthless surveillance of its people by the Ministry for State Security (the Stasi).

Within every chapter we make suggestions for further viewing, and our bibliography provides titles for further reading.

NOTES ON SPECIALIST TERMINOLOGY OF FILM ANALYSIS

In order to study and discuss film some basic understanding of film analysis terminology is necessary. We will therefore briefly explain here the most important terms that are used in this book.

Before any filming can take place the film-makers need to decide what exactly to put in front of the camera, including where and how to place it. This act is referred to as '**mise-en-scène**', a French expression which literally means 'placed on the stage', a term with clear connotations of the theatre[1]. Nowadays, of course, the vast majority of films do not remind us of theatre any more. Mise-en-scène comprises mainly setting (e.g. indoors or outdoors, urban or rural, day or night, etc.), the actors (including where they are placed, whether and how they move, their facial expressions), and their costume and make-up (which tell us a lot about historical background, social status and development of the characters).

The lighting of the scene to be filmed can also be included in the mise-en-scène, given that it needs to be in place before a scene can be filmed. However, lighting provides the link with **cinematography**: without sufficient light there cannot be film at all! In fact, cinematography literally means 'writing with light in movement'. Therefore, and expressed in basic terms, the less light there is, the darker the image becomes. Within the image there may be areas that are darker than others. The effects can be quite startling.

The camera captures images which are then viewed by us at roughly 24 frames per second. These images can be taken from different angles, heights and distances. This aspect of film-making is very intricate and technical. For our purposes it is sufficient to know that the 'normal' height of the camera is eye-height and the 'normal' angle is level. This produces the most 'objective' shots. Low-angle shots film the scene from below, high-angle shots from above. In both cases the camera is tilted vertically. Horizontal tilting ('canting') is also possible. This gives us the most 'subjective' shots, used for example to represent drunkenness, or disorientation. There are three basic distances from which an event may be filmed: **the long shot**, **the medium shot**, and **the close-up**, with many more possibilities in between. A long shot will privilege surroundings over individual figure(s), a medium shot will typically show us the whole figure(s), and a close-up can range from a 'head-and-shoulders' shot to an extreme close-up of an eye, a mouth, etc. When filming the camera can be stationary or moving – again in different ways.

Normally a film does not consist of one continuous shot: Shots are put together by means of **editing**. This device allows the film-maker to jump in space and time. There are different ways of putting shots together, the main ones being cuts, fades and dissolves. A cut is simply what it says, an abrupt change from one image to the next. A fade is a more gradual 'fading away' of the image, usually to black. In a dissolve the first image seems to 'dissolve' into the next one, i.e. the next image superimposes itself briefly on the preceding one.

Editing is often done in a way that produces a continuous, seemingly realistic story. This so-called 'continuity editing', although complex and highly accomplished, does not draw attention to itself. Another way of putting images together is by 'montage'. Here, different, sometimes seemingly unrelated, images are juxtaposed in quick succession. This is done in less 'realistic' films or scenes, and produces quite different effects, whether shock, disorientation, or questioning.

Sound is another essential aspect of film, even though this was not always the case. In silent films there was no sound, or at least no sound emanated from the scenes. In most cases there was accompanying sound, though, i.e. a live piano or even an orchestra, or a gramophone record. The distinction between the sound that can be heard by the characters and that which can only be heard by the audience is made by the terms 'diegetic' and 'non-diegetic' sound respectively. In sound films the role of the accompanying piano or orchestra has been taken over by the soundtrack on the film itself, but it is still non-diegetic, since it does not emanate from the scene itself, and thus the characters cannot hear it.

In a fiction film the above elements make up the **narrative**, they work together to tell the story: beginning, middle and end. A classic narrative begins with an introductory depiction of a certain situation, called the exposition, which represents a state of order. Then some kind of conflict is introduced, the conflict is worked through, and the resolution of the conflict and with it a new order tends to be the end of the narrative. The term 'conflict' already points to the fact that it is usually characters that are the agents. The plot focuses on the main characters, or protagonists, who are the film's heroes (less often heroines!). They are the ones that drive the action forwards and bring about change and resolution. Then there are the minor characters, and eventually the extras.

Many film narratives have become conventionalised, i.e. they follow certain patterns that audiences recognise and look forward to. These narratives have developed into certain types, or **genres**, such as Westerns, musicals, or comedies. Genres use certain codes and conventions that have been established over time and that are known to be successful with audiences. Codes are visual signals that provide shortcuts to the interpretation of a narrative by the audience. Genre conventions are very specific ways in which the story unfolds. These generic conventions do not simply exist, they develop. If you follow the development of any genre through the decades you will notice that there are similarities, but also differences over time, through to new perspectives and even subversion.

FOOTNOTES

[1] The earliest film mentioned in our discussions, *The Cabinet of Dr Caligari*, illustrates very well the theatrical legacy of theatre on film.

CHAPTER 1: MASTER NARRATIVES: *CALIGARI* (1919), *NOSFERATU* (1922) AND *METROPOLIS* (1926)

In this first chapter we explore the beginnings of film as art in Germany round about the first half of the 1920s. We will look at the historical, cultural and artistic context that brought about such iconic and influential films as *Das Cabinet des Dr Caligari* (*The Cabinet of Dr Caligari*, Robert Wiene, 1919), *Nosferatu* (F.W. Murnau, 1922) and *Metropolis* (Fritz Lang, 1926). Our main focus is *Nosferatu*, its indebtedness to German Expressionism, and its genre-building iconography and narrative. It is acknowledged as being the first true horror film, totally innovative and much-copied. *Metropolis*, as a science fiction/fantasy film, is the other original German contribution to genre film-making of the twenties. Both films were ground-breaking and have been enormously influential in that their visions have formed a legacy that is still detectable in vampire films and science fiction films today.

Together with *Das Cabinet des Dr Caligari*, *Nosferatu* and *Metropolis* are often thought of as the definitive examples of Weimar cinema. However, the second half of the Weimar Republic produced different types of film, less demonic, less spectacular, and more intimate, with differences in themes and style. It would therefore be more appropriate to say that *Caligari* and *Metropolis* bracket a period of German film-making that is usually associated with Expressionism, of which *Caligari* is the purest example, and that *Metropolis* is Weimar's last monumental film with clear references to Expressionism. In *Metropolis* we can detect elements of a new approach. From about 1926 onwards, Expressionism gave way to a new interest in reality as opposed to fantasy. This 'Neue Sachlichkeit' (New Objectivity) was grounded in social and political reality, and it was prevalent in all the arts, including film. Our focus film of chapter 2, *Der blaue Engel* (*The Blue Angel*, 1930), is an example of this new trend.

Before we turn to the first half of Weimar cinema let us familiarise ourselves with the historical situation of Germany in that period. As mentioned in the introduction to this book, World War I and the years following the war were turbulent times for Germany. At the end of the war the relatively new state of Germany (the country had only been united since 1871, before which it consisted of several kingdoms and principalities of varying sizes and spheres of influence, of which Prussia was the strongest) collapsed completely, not just because of the devastation wreaked by war, but also on account of the political and economic situation. The monarchy was abolished, and a republic was formed in 1919, a new political system that Germany was not very comfortable with. The name Weimar Republic was taken from the east German town of Weimar in which the constitution-forming assembly met.

The next few years were characterised by enormous problems for the new republic in terms of its legitimisation, and brought with them political instability, not least because the new government was inexperienced and weak. There were violent clashes between right and left wing extremists in cities across the nation, most notably in Munich and Berlin. Economically, extortionate war reparations were responsible for the galloping inflation that plagued the German economy in the early years of the new republic. The German people experienced insecurity and loss of control in their daily lives and at national level. If you add to this the loss of thousands of lives during the war and the traumatic experiences that those who survived it brought back with them, you have a nation in turmoil. This extreme state of affairs continued until around the mid-twenties, by which time normality had gradually returned.

If we accept the premise that cultural and artistic expression reflects (at least to some extent) actual social and political developments, then you will understand how the experience of war and subsequent revolutionary action, the excitement and frustrations of a young democracy, plus technical progress and changed labour relations all fed into a radical cultural change during the early Weimar years [1]. Nor should we forget the increasing American cultural influence in Germany. Parallels between politics and art were observable in the predominance of Expressionism up until the mid-twenties and the subsequent development towards 'Neue Sachlichkeit'. This is not to say that avant-garde Expressionist ideas vanished completely in the late 1920s; in fact their influence was felt in one way or another all through the twentieth century. Expressionism is recognised as the first truly modernist art movement. In the following paragraph we will explore what this means.

In European art history, the beginnings of Expressionism can be traced back to artists in Dresden who, in 1905, formed a group called 'Die Brücke' (The Bridge), mainly around painting. From painting, the new movement spread to the other arts and literature, and eventually to the new art form of cinema. The artists called themselves Expressionists, thereby deliberately placing themselves in opposition to Impressionism (mainly a French phenomenon), which they considered to be merely 'representative' and superficial. As Lotte Eisner says in her excellent book *The Haunted Screen*, 'The Expressionist does not see, he has visions.'; and 'Facts and objects are nothing in themselves: We need to study their essence rather than their momentary and accidental form'. By extension Expressionists were essentially anti-authoritarian, rejecting bourgeois values, questioning the new values that an industrial age had brought about and reflecting on the effects of technological advances and industrialisation. Their political tendency was towards the left, but the principle of Expressionism lent itself to radicals of other extremes as well, even towards National Socialism. (For their formal experimentation Expressionist works were eventually banned by the Nazis, though.)

Expressionists were in search of the 'new man' who could only be found through the subjective expression of the artist, through which a deeper meaning of life was sought. For them truth lay in the projection of deep emotion, of extreme mental states (Edvard Munch's painting 'The Scream' can serve as a prime example). The logical consequence for painters and sculptors was that they rejected conventional form and colour and worked towards abstraction. Expressionist literature was characterised by a style of writing in which exclamations and short statements predominated. Narratives included restless, rebellious characters who often represented types rather than individuals. Rebellion against authority figures, generational conflicts, notably between father and son, were major topics. (In this the ideas of the discipline of Freudian psychoanalysis, which was at the time relatively recent, and which was interested in the same issues, namely sexuality, the transition from childhood to adulthood, and expressing repressed traumatic experiences in order to cure mental illness, found their way into the arts.) Expressionist ideas were extended into theatre, where elements of painting and literature were combined and elevated to a new, complete experience. Symbolic, even archetypal visions were translated onto the stage. We must not forget that 'expressing' also means 'distilling'. The acting was pared down, reduced to exclamations, essential gestures. The actor became part of the set design. In accordance with extreme emotions the lighting consisted of extreme contrasts between darkness and light, called chiaroscuro (Italian, literally light-dark). The stage sets were accordingly reduced to basic shapes, and oblique lines dominated. We will see how these elements found their way into the first Expressionist films, the most famous example being *The Cabinet of Dr Caligari*.

Before we do this, there is one other important question to explore: Why was Expressionism a specifically German phenomenon? According to art historians and film theorists (notably Lotte Eisner and Siegfrid Kracauer), there is a certain predisposition of the German imagination towards the irrational. This harks back to Goethe and Schiller's early rebellious years of 'Sturm und Drang' (conventionally translated as 'Storm and Stress', but maybe better conveyed as 'storm and urge or longing') and German Romanticism, art movements from the latter part of the eighteenth century, which stressed subjectivity against the dominance of science and logic in the (previous) era of the Enlightenment. In writing, this included Gothic stories: ghost stories, stories of the uncanny, of nightmares and death. All these predispositions were renewed and intensified by the social, economic and political turbulence brought about in Germany before and after World War I. This background information will help us in our understanding of *Nosferatu* in particular, but also of *Metropolis*.

Towards the end of the 1910s and the beginning of the 1920s cinema gradually established itself as a new art form, as opposed to the fairground attraction that it had been until then [2]. In Germany this transition was not smooth. Traditionally there had always been a clear distinction between high culture (such as theatre, painting, architecture, the concert hall), the domain of the 'Bildungsbürgertum' (the educated cultural establishment), and low or popular culture in pulp fiction, the music halls, the fairground and on the radio, which provided entertainment for the masses.

This is a division that still exists to an extent in present-day Germany, where, unlike in France for instance, 'art films' are not embraced by the majority, and where theatre and opera are still regarded very much as the prerogative of the educated middle classes. Partly in order to overcome the prejudice and contempt which the bourgeois elite felt for the new medium of film and to raise its cultural standing, the ambitious film-makers of the time embraced Expressionism. In its initial and partial extension of theatrical practices, film was well suited to Expressionist ideas. Expressionist cinema is really a cinema of mise-en-scène. Sophisticated camera work and editing did not yet play a major part.

Expressionist cinema is interested in the way in which individual and extreme mental and emotional states and situations can be expressed – by non-naturalistic means. The films were made entirely in the studio in order to achieve total control over mise-en-scène and lighting [3]. Reminiscent of Expressionist theatre, the visual style is characterised by sets full of artificial looking props and décor in geometric shapes, and sharp contrasts, including extreme chiaroscuro lighting – anything that reinforces the expression of intense states of mind and extreme situations. The exaggerated acting style was another way of externalising the characters' mental states.

These devices can be seen very clearly in *Das Cabinet des Dr Caligari*, the purest surviving Expressionist film. The sets remind us of a theatre stage, full of labyrinthine paths, jagged, bizarre, canted, lines and angles, and extremes of black and white, emulating the way the mind works. These sets express the nightmare vision, the madness of the 'master' Caligari, who controls his somnambulist medium. The idea of a 'master' with power over other human beings is an Expressionist narrative device. It runs through all our three films in a variety of manifestations: There is the madness of Dr Caligari; in *Nosferatu* we encounter

Graf Orlok, the vampire; and Metropolis, the city, is controlled by Joh Fredersen who is the master of all he surveys, and who instructs the mad scientist to create a robot. The scientist is himself the master of his creation. However, these masters are not to be trusted. The Expressionist world is a world out of kilter, a threatening, unfathomable world.

Nowhere is this more evident than in *Nosferatu*. Where *Caligari* was probably too stylised to be truly frightening, *Nosferatu* achieves real menace. The film is to this day credited with being the most disturbing horror film ever made. Roger Ebert, the film critic of the Chicago Sun-Times, expresses best what *Nosferatu* does to us: "It doesn't scare us, but it haunts us". The name alone evokes horror: *Nosferatu*, literally 'the un-dead' [4]. Let us explore a little further the provenance of the film and how it achieves its extraordinary effects.

Nosferatu is the first cinematic adaptation of Bram Stoker's gothic novel *Dracula*, written in 1879. Murnau followed Bram Stoker's original story quite closely, but made some significant changes, of which the Count's name is just one: The name was changed from Dracula to Orlok. Count Dracula is a well-educated aristocrat, a seducer who mixes with the best in society and works his charm on unsuspecting victims who cannot help falling for him. At night he turns into the fang-toting vampire who spreads his cloak like a bat's wings and descends upon his victims. Orlok's appearance and demeanour are completely different, much more evidently evil. Where Dracula moves around with ease in daytime, Orlok cannot be exposed to sunlight – he is a true creature of the night, situated somewhere between human and animal, between life and death [5]. As such he provokes strong visceral reactions from his victims (and from the viewers of the film), a far cry from the suave seducer that is the original Dracula. This is compounded by the fact that Nosferatu brings with him the plague in the form of contaminated soil and accompanying rats. Where the vampire Dracula does not cast a shadow and has no reflection, Orlok, in the most frightening scenes of the film, casts a long shadow. The ending of the film marks a complete change from the novel: A woman sacrifices herself in order to save the world from Nosferatu. By contrast, in Stoker's novel the vampire is chased back to Transylvania, where he is caught and killed by the stake. The victims of Nosferatu's spread of disease are the citizens of Wisborg (a fictional town in North Germany, based on the Hanse town of Wismar); the catalyst is the estate agent Hutter; the woman who sacrifices herself is his fiancée Ellen.

In the first instance, and on the surface, then, *Nosferatu* is the antagonist, the 'other' in a literal sense: something frightening outside us, something that represents extreme danger against which we must protect ourselves in order to keep family, friends and society intact. At second glance, and under the surface, though, the vampire can be seen as a representation of something that is part of us, but relegated to our subconscious because it is too frightening to deal with: the 'other' aspect of ourselves. Nosferatu can be read on these two levels [6].

The motif of Nosferatu as Hutter's alter ego is set up early on in the film and brought to its fatal conclusion. On this metaphorical level, Nosferatu serves to externalise Hutter's unacknowledged fears and premonitions that the latter cannot fathom, let alone express. It has been suggested that Nosferatu stands for Hutter's repressed sexuality, and, by extension, becomes involved in his and Ellen's life. Many instances in the film, both in the story itself and in the visuals, suggest such connections between the three protagonists. From the beginning of the story, Hutter is characterised as a cheerful and somewhat naive young man who seems to be more like a brother to his wife than a husband-to-be. He does not comprehend women, who are perceived as having much deeper feelings, longings, intuitions, and a bond with the world beneath the surface of reality. Hutter has only a literal understanding of the world. Even later, when he does indeed experience the utmost horror, he does not comprehend the wider implications and deeper meanings of it.

The very first scene introduces a dark note into the cheerful world of the Hutters at home. With youthful enthusiasm Hutter picks a bunch of wildflowers for Ellen and presents them to her. 'You killed them!' she says. A sense of foreboding is introduced, of which he is blissfully unaware. When he is given his assignment to travel to Transylvania in order to secure a house purchase deal with Count Orlok and tells his fiancée of this unique opportunity to earn good money, she alone senses the danger that might be attached to this journey.

Orlok's connection with Ellen begins in earnest when the Count, during Hutter's visit at his castle, sees a photograph of her in her fiancé's fob watch and is immediately attracted to her. This seals his determination to buy a deserted house opposite that of the Hutters. And although Hutter feels that something uncanny is happening, he does not comprehend the magnitude of the effect of Orlok's signature on the house purchase contract: Orlok has been invited to Wisborg, the important prerequisite to his being able to leave his grounds (see also below). When at midnight Orlok visits Hutter in his room with the intention of drawing precious blood from him, it is Ellen's intervention from a thousand miles away (she calls out in her sleep) that causes Nosferatu to stop in his tracks. At one and the same time Ellen's friend Nina saves her fiancé and responds to the connection that Nosferatu has made previously. Later on, when she waits by the seaside for 'his' return, it is by no means clear who is meant by this – is it really her betrothed, or might it be Nosferatu himself?

We know that ostensibly it is her fiancé that she wants to return, but why does she wait for him in the windy, deserted dunes? After all he travels on horseback. Nosferatu is the one who approaches by sea, and we remember that she has connected with him previously. Visually, the ambiguity is intensified by her black dress, and by the

black crosses dotted about incongruously and higgledy-piggledy on the beach: obvious references to death.

Eventually Nosferatu arrives on his ship, alone, after the rats from his coffin and Nosferatu's need for blood have done their work, killing the whole crew. The ship is the harbinger of death, gliding into the port of Wisborg unaided, obscuring the cathedral as it arrives. This is one of the most frightening scenes of the film: a ghostly representation

of evil about to be unleashed on the unsuspecting citizens. Carrying his own coffin, Nosferatu scurries from the port across the cobblestones, surreptitiously, undetected, and moves into the house directly opposite Ellen's. There he waits patiently behind the window directly opposite Nina's bedroom for Nina to call him. In the meantime the rats overrun the town, and kill one citizen after another through the plague that they are carrying.

It is night. Ellen is filled with horror, fully aware of the situation, and battling to come to a decision which would kill her, but save those who are still alive, while her fiancé still does not comprehend his own involvement in the horror that has been unleashed. He sits by her bed, holding her hand, distraught, but ineffective. Ellen decides to act: She sends Hutter away on an errand and moves to the window to beckon Nosferatu. In a gesture that resembles a lovers' embrace he descends on her and draws blood from her neck. In her final hours she has enough power over him to keep him till morning. The sun

rises. Nosferatu realises too late that he is doomed, but moves closer to the window and accepts the sun's rays which destroy him. He turns to dust. We cannot imagine the effect that this scene must have had on contemporary audiences who had never seen anything like it before.

Let us now look more closely at the representation of the male protagonist and his adversary. Hutter is an example of the ineffectual hero, a type that often crops up in films in the Expressionist tradition. In *Caligari* the good guy goes mad; in *Metr*[...] through a series of dizzy spells, fevers and hallucinations and is thus unable to control the action; and Hutter unwittingly brings the plague to his hometown and therefore causes the death not only of his fellow Wisborgians but even more tragically that of his own wife. These types of protagonist were of distinctly German origin. They would not have been found in Hollywood with its tradition of the 'conquering hero'. Indeed, contemporary American audiences found them off-putting and did not respond well to German films with weak protagonists.

Count Orlok as the anti-hero owes most of his impact to his visuals. There is first and foremost his appearance, particularly his bald head, his ghostly white face, his hooked nose, his huge rat-like ears, his rodent teeth, his fingers with claw-like fingernails, and then his demeanour with slow, stylised movements. The characteristics of his 'un-dead' status are expressed through his association with the night, and with death in the form of coffins, biting, blood, rats, and the plague. In the course of the narrative he is established as the 'master' who controls creatures and humans alike, but who needs to be invited in order to leave his grounds.

Max Schreck's acting is a master class of Expressionist acting, reduced, formalist, essential: Consider for example, his visit to Hutter's room at midnight, after his attempt to draw blood from his helpless victim - the way he turns his head with deliberate slowness, in the same way that his eyes move and focus on a distant place from where he hears Ellen's cry [7]. The chiaroscuro lighting intensifies the whiteness of his face, his heavy makeup, the dark shadows around his eyes which in turn emphasise the whites of his eyes. In this and other interior scenes the mise-en-scène is extremely stylised, as demanded by Expressionist dictum – 'The film image must become graphic art': It is the mise-en-scène that is foregrounded, rather than the cinematography and editing.

The visual language of the film also includes outdoor scenes, most notably Hutter's travels towards Transylvania, and here Murnau departs from the studio filming of previous Expressionist productions, thereby extending the Expressionist vocabulary: His outdoor scenes really are shot outdoors (in Czechoslovakia), which was very unusual at the time. Murnau took great care with the selection of his locations. The camera is used to emphasise the essential nature of the landscapes that Hutter travels through, reality is stylised. This is how Murnau achieves genuine expressions of Hutter's fear in the natural world: the mountains, the ancient castle on the jutting cliff, the likening of a vampire to a hyena, the wind that shakes the trees. At night, after Hutter has been met by Nosferatu's carriage, which turns out to be driven by Nosferatu himself at great speed, he has his first experience of unspeakable dread. At that moment, and only very briefly, the image is inverted from positive to negative. You might be forgiven for thinking that it is a flaw in the photography. Later on we are confronted with Orlok's 'home ground': contaminated soil, rats escaping from coffins. Orlok himself appears to be part of the extreme manifestations of the natural world.

'Every shot has its precise function' (Lotte Eisner). Murnau selected his mise-en-scène (particularly astonishing when filming on location) and his shots so precisely that he did not need to create distorted perspectives or any other extreme effects. The supernatural force of the landscapes in particular is captured in a way that expresses

the protagonist's state of mind. Here it is worth mentioning a German painter of the late eighteenth century who influenced Murnau greatly with his visions of natural landscapes that are recognisable as such, but stylised just enough to evoke mental states: Caspar David Friedrich. In his paintings we often find a human figure (sometimes two) in the foreground, looking over a vast landscape. The Romantic painter Friedrich thus provides a link with Expressionism via Murnau's *Nosferatu*.

However, over and beyond previous Expressionist cinematic tradition, Murnau employs new editing techniques to great effect, no more so than in the way in which he conveys *Nosferatu*'s supernatural power of movement (in deliberate contrast to his otherwise slow movements) – we have already mentioned the speed at which his carriage travels. On the night of his visit to Hutter's room, jump cuts transport him from the far end of a corridor directly to Hutter's door. The horror is here created by Nosferatu's forward movement towards the camera. Later on, when he loads his coffins full of contaminated soil onto a carriage in preparation for his departure, he again moves with great speed.

Much of *Nosferatu*'s iconography and narrative became coded in future vampire films. The trademarks of the horror (and fantasy) genre are, even today, recognisable as owing to *Nosferatu*'s use of Expressionist techniques towards the creation of stylised situations. The link to sexuality, to the 'other', the subconscious, is a defining characteristic of horror films. Point-of-view shots emphasise the subjective and visceral nature of the experience of the 'other', which includes the expression (or projection) of fear of our own subconscious. Vampire movies in particular still follow *Nosferatu*'s conventions: The 'un-dead' tend to live by night; daylight destroys them. *Nosferatu*'s highly stylised approach has made a strong impact on generations of film-makers. Audiences world-wide still discuss its merits today, even though it does not make for easy viewing: It is not as populist and entertaining as many of its successors.

Nosferatu's immediate successors in the genre of vampire films were *Vampyr* (Carl Theodor Dreyer, 1932), and *Dracula* (Tod Browning, 1931). Many film adaptations of the Dracula myth have been made; the interest in filmic vampires in general persists unabated. In 1979 Werner Herzog remade *Nosferatu,* faithful to Murnau's original [8]. More recently, the film-maker and producer Tim Burton has carried on the tradition of the Gothic film from *Edward Scissorhands* (1990) to *Sweeney Todd* (2008).

Much more complex and confusing than *Nosferatu* is *Metropolis,* in both its visual style and its narrative. The confusion results partly from the fact that very different versions of *Metropolis* have been in circulation over the decades. The enormous variations are due to vicious cuts made initially and to a variety of restorations, later ones encompassing reinserted scenes, new explanatory intertitles, different musical scores. However, to this day all these versions are incomplete. [9]

The chief significance of *Metropolis* lies in the fact that its vision of a dystopian future provided the foundation for a new genre, the science-fiction or urban fantasy film. Therefore, in the context of this chapter we will concentrate on the film's salient features of employing Expressionist means (but also going beyond Expressionism) to create a new genre.

The plot of *Metropolis* is basically very simple. The 'Metropolis' of the title is a city and at the same time a vision of a future in which only two strata of society exist: the rulers and the workers. The connection between them is the giant 'heart' machine in the bowels of the city, which is operated constantly by the workers and which in turn keeps Metropolis going. Joh Fredersen, the head of the ruling class that lives in the upper regions of a vertical city, has a ruthless grip on the workers, who live and work below ground, out of sight and out of mind of the masters of Metropolis. However, one day the lower class intrudes into the lives of the upper class through the appearance of a young woman, Maria, and a group of children. She has climbed the stairs to the 'pleasure garden' and shows the children how the upper class lives. She also points out that the two classes are both human: 'These are your brothers,' she says. Freder, Joh's son, is intrigued by her and follows her into the lower regions of Metropolis. There he encounters the horrendous conditions in which the workers live. Freder experiences the inhuman conditions for himself by standing in for a worker. Meanwhile, Maria tries to unionise the workers in order to create better working conditions and to communicate with the masters. Joh Frederson realises that his son has fallen in love with Maria and that this poses a potential threat for the social order of Metropolis. He meets the inventor Rotwang who shows him his nearly-finished creation, a robot, which can take on the features of Maria. The real Maria is captured and used to create the robot. The finished robot is then sent out to stir up trouble. However, the plan goes awry, the susceptible workers are worked up into a frenzy, and Metropolis ends up being all but destroyed. Freder and the real Maria manage in the end to save the city and to reconcile the two opposing forces of 'hands' and 'head' by invoking the 'heart'.

We mentioned before that *Metropolis* stands at the end of the period of film-making that is generally associated with Expressionism in Germany. It still carries many of its features, albeit in different ways to *Nosferatu*. The theme of the 'master', who is often a father figure against whom the son has to assert himself, can often be found in Expressionist art, notably on stage and screen. In *Metropolis* we find Freder, the son of Joh Fredersen, rebelling against the social order that his father has created, an order that works on the principle of total control over the workers in the city of Metropolis. Another 'master' appears in *Metropolis*: The deranged and megalomaniac scientist Rotwang, who lives in the shadowy world of his laboratory, is the creator of a robot – a monster in effect.

These few statements point to another issue close to the heart of Expressionist artists and writers. In the wake of more and more sophisticated industrialisation and the development of new technology, many questions relating to social and scientific issues were discussed critically at the time: was technological change always a change for the good? To what extent was technology able to improve the lives of working people? The answer given in *Metropolis* is conditional: Technology and control without humanity lead to disaster; brain and hands need to be mediated by the heart. All this comes to fruition at the somewhat naive happy ending of the film.

The impact of *Metropolis* is strongest in its visuals. Let us first take a look at its representation of 'visions' and then at Lang's monumental vision of the city of Metropolis itself. In order to mobilise the workers Maria conjures up a vision of Babel in a parable in which the symbolism of hands features strongly. Slaves converge on the site where the

tower of Babel is to be built. They progress in their thousands, in five streams, in the shape of a hand and fingers. There is no communication between the rulers (the brain) and the slaves (the hands), just like in the social order of Metropolis itself. Maria's message in this parable is that understanding (the heart) has to be the mediator between different social spheres.

This vision is one of the most startling scenes in the film. In Freder's feverish vision the huge machine at the heart of Metropolis is transformed into a man-eating moloch. This image is instrumental in making him empathise with the plight of the workers.

Hearts and hands pervade the symbolism of *Metropolis* elsewhere: The scene in which the robot Maria is created from the real Maria is a sight to behold, even today, in an age of computer generated images. Her heart is given great prominence visually, we see it beating, giving its life-force to a robot with no heart. Maria's transformation into a robot is conveyed by innovative editing techniques, the principles of which were applied to

'creation' scenes in subsequent films. This is the most famous and influential scene of the film, evoking horror in us because it violates the distinction between human and machine.

Fritz Lang was an accomplished and fastidious editor. In *Metropolis* the most striking editing technique is the dissolve: Freder's dreams and visions, amongst them the frightening scene in which the central machine in the bowels of Metropolis is transformed, are rendered as dissolves, signalling their subjective nature. The creation of the robotic Maria is a feat of editing, again with dissolves, and became a direct model for the first *Frankenstein* film (1931). For contemporary audiences the slow change from metal shell to fake human being must have been a terrifying sight.

Let us now concentrate on the representation of the city of Metropolis. The opening sequence introduces us to the city architecture of Metropolis and its workings. It is represented as a graphic interplay of the vertical lines of tall, futuristic-looking buildings above ground and the pistons and circular movements of machines below ground. This montage is so suggestive that you can almost hear the sound of the steam whistles that announce the change of shifts for the workers of Metropolis. We then see the faceless army of workers ascending and descending, imprisoned behind the bars of a lift, as if on remote control. The insertion of the intertitles matches their movement. The crowds underground are represented in geometrical arrangements. This is contrasted with a sweep upwards towards the upper regions of Metropolis in order to show the way the master race lives.

The mechanical, dystopian world in which *Metropolis* unfolds required a huge production, involving unimaginable human resources, technical finesse and special effects, an effort hitherto unseen in German cinema (or elsewhere for that matter). A new special effects technique, the 'Schuftan process' (named after its inventor), was employed to build the sets in miniature and to then integrate them with the actors. The exceptional technical achievements of Fritz Lang's team are still recognised today as the definitive standard in hand-crafted special effects. The animation sequences had to be made by laborious single-frame camerawork, otherwise the craftsmen would not have been able to keep tabs on all the movements at the same time. Aeroplanes, railways, pedestrians had to be shifted by different distances between shots in order to achieve the effect of flowing movement – one thousand five hundred individual shots. The production costs soared and overran the original estimate considerably, mainly because the special effects consumed much more time and effort than originally calculated.

In order to enhance the impact of the breath-taking visual effects, Lang used complex lighting arrangements. In *The Haunted Screen*, Lotte Eisner expresses very well how this was done: 'As in all his films, Lang handles the light in *Metropolis* with mastery: the city of the master race towers up as a shining pyramid created by the skyscrapers, surrounded by rays of light. Model buildings have been lit so that their seemingly enormous mass, their chess-board pattern of illuminated windows and dark squares of walls, sends light and steam cascading down to burst apart as a luminous rain of dust. The models, with their suspended streets and bridges, seem vastly exaggerated. And the "trick" to it can scarcely be sensed any more amid this symphony of light.'

The influence of *Metropolis* on genre film-making does not lie in its story, unlike *Nosferatu*, whose iconography and narrative have become staples, as mentioned before. It is *Metropolis'* visuals that have been used and developed further by future generations of genre film-makers. Futuristic and action/adventure films especially of the 1980s make more or less explicit references to *Metropolis*, in particular to its iconography and to individual scenes. One of the most famous dystopian visions that recalls *Metropolis'* iconography and message is *Blade Runner* (Ridley Scott, 1984), in which the Los Angeles of the future becomes a 'corporate state, driven by the globalising forces of migrant labour, mass entertainment and cult religion' (Thomas Elsaesser). Steven Spielberg used *Metropolis* ideas in his action/adventure series *Indiana Jones* (from 1981 onwards), George Lucas in *Star Wars* (from 1977 onwards), Terry Gilliam must have been aware of it when he made *Brazil* (1985). More recently *Dark City* (1998) owes a lot to *Metropolis* visuals. Tim Burton references both *Nosferatu* and *Metropolis* in his work (see also above).

Returning to the cinematic context of the Weimar Republic, a comparison between the circumstances surrounding the production of *Nosferatu* and *Metropolis* provides interesting insights. The differences between them point to a lively and varied film industry in Germany, with small and medium-sized film production companies in the early Weimar years and gradual centralisation in the mighty UFA from then on. They are also examples of the great financial risks that dedicated film-makers sometimes take when realising their projects.

Nosferatu was made by what we would nowadays call an independent film production company. A project of Prana Film GmbH, a partnership between F.W. Murnau and artistic director Albin Grau, *Nosferatu* was made on a low budget and was Prana's only film. For reasons of limited finance, Prana had not sought the rights to film the original *Dracula*, merely crediting Bram Stoker's source novel in the original titles of the film, changing the Count's name to *Nosferatu*, and locating the story in Germany. Ironically, this attempt at saving money led to bankruptcy of the company because of the ensuing dispute with Bram Stoker's estate: Stoker's widow successfully sued Prana; the court ordered that all prints of *Nosferatu* be withdrawn. However, and fortunately for later generations, a couple of prints survived, otherwise we would have been deprived of one of film history's most important works. However, because of the legal issues the film was not seen for nearly 40 years, apart from a very small audience at its premiere.

Metropolis makes a good case study for exploring the institutional context of Germany's key film production company, the UFA (see also the introduction to this book). In the 1920s the UFA studios rivalled Hollywood in size and in their special effects capability. Unlike Hollywood, UFA productions gave individual directors a large amount of creative freedom and therefore responsibility for their projects. This meant great attention was paid to detail, a great deal of time was taken, and the personnel for each film were carefully selected. Within UFA, Fritz Lang and F. W. Murnau enjoyed a special status in that they were the only ones allowed to work within the so-called 'director-unit system'. This meant that a large number of highly experienced crew members were allocated to a single project. Great team spirit was fostered among the supremely trained and experienced personnel. All this meant that there was sustained creative input from a wide range of top professionals and close cooperation between set designers, cameramen, art directors and many other skilled specialists, who, incidentally, had been recruited mainly from the theatre. UFA did not keep its own special effects department; such effects were produced on a project-to-project basis.

Significantly, and disastrously in the case of *Metropolis*, the directors were also given free rein with the budget. This monumental film with unheard-of production values turned out to be a flop at the box office. It contributed to the financial disaster that befell UFA. Erich Pommer, who was the head of UFA around the making of *Metropolis*, and Fritz Lang were the most famous figures in German cinema at the time. However, for Pommer the fact that *Metropolis* lost nearly 4.2 million Reichsmark, which amounted to nearly half of UFA's entire production cost of 1925-26, led to a professional change of direction: The risk he took in realising this film cost him his job at UFA, and for a while he went to Hollywood (more on UFA in chapter 2).

New for *Metropolis* was the extensive publicity given to the film before its release. This was comparable to today's marketing of blockbusters, when pre-release publicity raises expectations. When *Metropolis* did not meet with universal acclaim, the disappointment was all the greater – again a parallel with many of today's aggressively promoted Hollywood films that disappear soon after their release.

Considering these difficulties, nobody would have thought at the time that both *Nosferatu* and *Metropolis* would turn out to be classics. By the way, the differences in their production costs are still relevant today in their respective genres: very effective

hor   " be made on a low budget (just think of *The Blair Witch Project*, 1999),
whe   n films tend to rely on spectacular sets and expensive special
effec

As mentioned before, the influence of both *Nosferatu* and *Metropolis* can be traced in many subsequent genre films. The influence of German Expressionism in general can be traced across a large number of films in which extreme psychological states are explored. In this context, a differentiation between expressionism with a small 'e' in general and German Expression in particular is useful: The former can be described as a mind-set or 'Zeitgeist' which can emerge at any time as a particular response to a given number of socio-historical factors. The emergence of film noir, in which expressionist techniques have been used to great effect, would be a famous example. Expressionism with a small 'e' can therefore be applied to a number of visual styles and narratives other than the strictly defined German Expressionism which, in its pure form, only exists in very few films, such as *Caligari*.

We would recommend watching *The Cabinet of Dr Caligari*, *Nosferatu*, and *Metropolis* as companion pieces. It is also worth tracing their legacy in horror films, science-fiction films, and urban fantasy films, the most recent of which is the latest Batman film, *The Dark Knight* (2008). Christopher Nolan, the director, must have seen the two classics: He sets up the Joker as Batman's alter ego, battling it out in a city in social and political turmoil – *Nosferatu* and *Metropolis* combined in one very dark film indeed!

FOOTNOTES

[1] Albin Grau, the set designer and overall artistic director of *Nosferatu*, linked the experience of war to this film. According to him the horrors of war were no longer visible in people's daily lives, but something of those horrors remained - something that could not be conceptualised, like a "cosmic vampire".

[2] Interesting: *Caligari* takes up the topic of the fairground, which is where Dr Caligari plies his trade. Is this a conscious reference to the changing status of cinema in Germany?

[3] There were other reasons for studio filming, namely unwieldy camera equipment and slow film stock which necessitated artificial lighting.

[4] The original musical score intensifies this horror by assigning a musical motif to the name which functions like an invocation of the vampire. On DVD only on the Masters of Cinema edition.

[5] His long shadow has (literally) been cast into the 1940s, when film noir anti-heroes are represented in a similar way...

[6] The two aspects of human nature had been explored previously in the first film adaptation of R.L.Stevenson's morality tale *Dr Jekyll and Mr Hyde* (J.S.Robertson, 1920).

[7] An aside: The name Schreck means fright, terror, horror, a fact that was deliciously referenced in *Shadow of the Vampire* (Merhige, 2000), a homage to the original and to Murnau as a film-maker.

[8] There is a direct link between Expressionist film-making and Herzog's approach, to be found in terms such as 'essential nature', 'deeper truth', 'manipulation', 'the subjective artist as creator', etc. See chapter 6 of this book.

[9] The recent significant find of long-lost reels in Argentina has caused tremendous excitement amongst experts. The insertion of these new finds will, after restoration, surely result in an 'ultimate version' of *Metropolis* – but it may still not be complete, at least not as the director intended.

CHAPTER 2: THE SOUNDS OF LATE WEIMAR: *DER BLAUE ENGEL* (*THE BLUE ANGEL*, 1930)

Der blaue Engel is our second offering of Weimar cinema. The film was released in 1930, four years after *Metropolis*, but it seems to be from a completely different era of film-making. This is due mainly to two factors. The first one is its very different subject matter and treatment, which we will look at more closely in this chapter. The second factor is the advent of sound. *Der blaue Engel* is the first major sound film produced in Germany. It makes for a good case study for exploring early sound cinema. *Der blaue Engel* may also serve as an example of late Weimar film production with regard to its main collaborators and their decision either to stay in Germany or to become émigrés to Hollywood. We will therefore take a look at their biographies.

As mentioned in chapter 1, Weimar cinema after *Metropolis* took a turn away from Expressionism and the telling of monumental and fantastical stories towards more introspective, psychological, and realistic narratives. 'New Objectivity' was the key term, not just in film but in all the arts. Attempts were made to represent social and economic reality: the daily lives and work of people, mainly in the cities, became the focus of the new style. In cinema this conscious departure from Expressionism was not only marked by a change in narrative focus but also in visual style. Whereas Expressionism favoured the representation of the subjective and irrational by distorted and disorientating mise-en-scene, especially in terms of studio sets and 'distilled' acting (see also chapter 1), New Objectivity employed a much more restrained visual style. It was factual and informative, consciously avoiding political comment and exaggerated emotional impact. An early film in the New Objectivity style is F.W. Murnau's *Der letzte Mann* (*The Last Laugh*, 1924). The most pared-down example of this style is the semi-documentary *Menschen am Sonntag* (*People on Sunday*, 1930), which premiered in the same year as *Der blaue Engel*.

In this new style women characters were given a much greater prominence than ever before. One film-maker who put women in lead roles is representative of this new trend: G. W. Pabst. Towards the end of the twenties he made two seminal films that may stand for the best of New Objectivity: *Die Büchse der Pandora* (*Pandora's Box*, 1928) and *Tagebuch einer Verlorenen* (*Diary of a Lost Girl*, 1929). What both those films, although silent, have in common with *Der blaue Engel* is that they demonstrate the changes that happened in the 1920s, not just in Germany, with regard to the position of women in society.

Every film reflects to some extent the social conditions prevalent at the time of its making, even if it does not do it directly, sometimes even deliberately rebelling against them. Since the end of World War I the role of women in society had changed significantly. During the war, women had taken on roles that had traditionally been reserved for men, and when the war ended they were understandably reluctant to give up the freedoms and the extended responsibilities that had come to them with their 'male' roles. This explains why, in line with the development of more sophisticated and psychological film narratives, the representation of women in cinema became more diverse than it had been before. The 'new women' had jobs, for example, which made them economically independent from men. They were liberated in many ways, which was also shown in the more stylish and less constraining fashions for women that developed during the twenties. They also began to take more time to decide whether they wanted to get married and have children. If they decided against a family, there was no longer such a strong stigma attached to it.

By and large this was a positive development, since it gave female film viewers the opportunity to see a variety of role models away from the traditional ones. However, there was a backlash, too. We need to remember that films were generally made by men who, of course, pursued their own interests and represented women from their own, male, perspective. Therefore, and possibly because of the threat that liberated women posed to male egos, quite often less than complex female characters were portrayed, and quite a few actresses became type-cast. Louise Brooks, the lead actress in *Die Büchse der Pandora*, for instance, became somewhat type-cast as the 'flapper', a 1920s 'invention', the young woman who is constantly in a state of excitement, bubbly, lively, irresponsible, and who is the centre of attention everywhere. Men cannot help falling for such women, especially since they quite obviously project the need for male protection. However, to give the director, Pabst credit, his male characters bear a certain amount of responsibility: Ultimately they act out of self-interest and thus are implicated in their own (and the women's) downfall.

Another type of woman that emerged in films of the 1920s, personified among others by Greta Garbo, was the 'vamp'. Unlike the flapper, she is aware of her power; she quite consciously seduces men in order to gain advantage. She is the personification of all the strong female traits that men feel threatened by. She is self-assured, cold, merciless – as viewed, it needs to be reiterated, from a male perspective. Men are not well-equipped to get to grips with her sexual liberation and her economic independence. Marlene Dietrich as the singer and entertainer Lola Lola in *Der blaue Engel* portrayed such a vamp. Even such stereotypical female representations of women, however, gave female audiences the opportunity to see and identify with strong women on screen.

Der blaue Engel is a loose adaptation of Heinrich Mann's novel *Professor Unrath*, one of the acknowledged examples of New Objectivity literature. Interestingly, the novel's title, which foregrounds the male protagonist, was changed to the name of a nightclub, the most important location of the film, thereby shifting the focus away from the professor and closer to the female protagonist. In the film the novel's strong social comment is down-played, but the focus on the downfall of one individual, strongly psychologised, is in line with the aims of New Objectivity. The satire present in the novel is converted to the screen by a multitude of aesthetic devices, in particular the interplay between visuals and sounds. We will analyse some of those synergies later. *Der blaue Engel* tells the story of Professor Immanuel Rath who is a teacher at the college in his hometown, with high social status but leading a lonely existence [1]. He is unloved and feared by his students, not least because of his authoritarian behaviour. One day he discovers that some of his students frequent a nightclub, Der blaue Engel, where the charming Lola Lola makes her risqué appearances. Rath manages to catch his students at the club but himself falls under the spell of the entertainer, whose character, in the course of the narrative, turns out to be more complex than at first assumed. Eventually he even proposes to her. Surprised and flattered she accepts. This fact and a revolt in the classroom lead to his dismissal from the school and his disgrace in the eyes of the town. He becomes a member of the group of travelling artistes to which Lola belongs. More and more he falls under the influence of the troupe's director (the magician) who forces him to earn his keep by becoming his assistant as a clown – a terribly undignified role.

This existence reaches new depths of humiliation when the troupe once again performs in Rath's hometown, at Der blaue Engel. He is forced to play the stupid clown in front of a crowd of people who want to see him embarrassed. At the same time, Lola has started giving in to the advances of Mazeppa, a young, dashing artiste. This combination proves too much for Rath to bear. He loses his sanity, begins to strangle Lola, then leaves the nightclub and returns to his old school where he is found the next morning at his desk, dead.

This synopsis already hints at the fact that the roles of Lola's 'vamp' (wicked) and Rath's 'trapped man' (innocent) may not be quite so clear-cut: Lack of self-awareness and a subsequent inability to deal with a liberated woman make Rath more the victim of his own repressed personality and the resulting inappropriate flaring-up of his sexuality than simply the victim of Lola's seduction alone. In the course of the film the two erstwhile pillars of his existence, Prussian discipline and authoritarianism in the classroom, are shown to be as flimsy as a house of cards. It could be argued that the woman here is to some extent the victim of a man who struggles with honest sexuality, and who misunderstands and mystifies it.

After living in his own authoritarian world and being allowed to act out his own sadistic tendencies in the classroom, Rath is ill-equipped for life outside this narrow world, even though he is clearly drawn to it. His world is the classroom; here he exercises control. Here we encounter his meticulousness, his excessive sense of order, and his distant and authoritarian manner. His teaching methods are disastrously ineffective and inadequate, not just by today's standards, but quite clearly by any standards. They are satirised by director Josef von Sternberg (as in the source novel). It is obvious: Rath is not a likeable man. One phrase summarises his character's helplessness. Whenever he is at his wits' end, he utters the empty threat: 'We'll speak again!'

As a well-known silent actor, Emil Jannings was able to convey mood and attitude with the slightest change of facial expression. Von Sternberg directs him very effectively and the story moves along economically. For instance, Rath's fateful link with Dietrich's Lola is first established when he finds compromising photographs of her on his students. One in particular has the fringe of a skirt attached to it, which he cannot resist blowing up to expose her legs. This simple act indicates both his hypocrisy and susceptibility, and marks the beginning of his downward spiral. From this scene the film cuts to the nightclub where Lola performs, singing her song 'I am naughty Lola'. In it she warns everybody not to 'mess with her'; otherwise she will 'punch and kick'.

Marlene Dietrich fills her first major film role with verve, in fact she steals the show. And yet, the film is introduced with Emil Jannings in the lead. This is not altogether surprising if we consider that he was the most famous actor of Weimar cinema and she was a mere theatre student whose first film role this was. Josef von Sternberg had been looking for the right 'vamp' figure for a long time. He knew exactly what he needed, and she had to be able to sing. When Marlene auditioned, there was no doubt in his mind that he had found his Lola. After *Der blaue Engel* became a huge success, and Dietrich was catapulted to stardom, von Sternberg insisted that there was no 'myth' of Dietrich, but that he was the myth behind the camera. By this he meant that her whole star persona was created by the camera [2]. This seems terribly overstated. Dietrich later complained that during filming her legs were the centre of attention. She felt it was quite obscene to have four cameras directed mostly at her legs. So, yes, it is true, Lola does for the most part represent sexuality and glamour. However, without Dietrich's unique characterisation, her almost passive underplaying of the role, and her voice, the image of her alone would not have been enough to guarantee her success, let alone her future stardom. Within the role itself the traditional lines between women as selfish sexual beings and women with caring characteristics were beginning to be blurred.

By commenting only on Marlene's image von Sternberg underestimated his own achievement in the area of sound. *Der blaue Engel* was one of the first German sound films: It was premiered on 1 April 1930. We cannot imagine today just how revolutionary the development of sound film was. And, like any revolution, it was not greeted with unanimous joy. Early film critics whose prime concern it had been to establish the new medium of film as art were worried about the merits of film sound; they even rejected it initially as 'not artistic'. They felt that the silence of film was its special and richest expression. Music accompanying silent film (non-diegetically) was acceptable, but diegetic sound was not. Communication in silent film was perceived to be direct; reality was unfiltered by words and linguistic concepts. Where language could be a means of oppression, cinema offered freedom. Therefore, to many contemporary critics the development of sound was a disaster. Even later critics frequently upheld the view that image had primacy over sound, that sound was merely a 'complement' to image. Even today, when we talk about a film we privilege visuals over sound: We 'watch' films, and do not acknowledge that we also 'listen to' them.

However, the most talented film directors used sound to open up completely new dimensions in film, both in space and time. Off-screen space was suddenly accessible without recourse to visual means, because we can now 'hear' what goes on off-screen as well as on-screen. Speech could be used to mark time by talking about the past, for instance, and both could be manipulated through sound editing. Sound and images can reinforce each other, comment on each other, or even contradict each other. *Der blaue*

Engel uses all these innovative devices. Therefore it is one of the most remarkable early sound films, and one that demonstrates very well the tools at the disposal of a good film-maker. By focusing for a moment on the technical and stylistic means employed in the film we shall see how vital sound is to its narrative, the organisation of space and time, and the symbolism of the film.

There are basically three different types of sound in a film: the human voice, music, both diegetic and nondiegetic, and noise. Concentrating on sound while we watch a film is quite difficult: It is elusive, unlike images that we can stop and freeze. Another characteristic of sound and the way we register it is that we are able to hear more than one sound at a time: sometimes sounds compete with each other; sometimes they form a kind of sound carpet. Because *Der blaue Engel* is an early sound film and therefore less 'realistic' than modern films in that respect, individual sounds can be distinguished more clearly than in a 'sophisticated' modern film in which sounds are blended and therefore harder to isolate. Therefore *Der blaue Engel* provides us with a good case study in the interrelationship between sound and visuals.

In *Der blaue Engel* off-screen sounds are mainly those from the nightclub. We become aware of them whenever the door between Lola's dressing-room and the hall that leads to the nightclub is opened. The suddenness with which those sounds intrude into the dressing-room and the way they are 'turned off' with equal suddenness makes us aware of the relatively crude operation of early sound on film. It was technically not possible to achieve a more realistic effect.

The ambient sounds outside the nightclub are deliberately sparse because the small-town setting is not of great importance: Apart from a foghorn sounding on two occasions and the church clock marking time, it is the internal spaces that matter. This deliberate closing-in on the two main characters emphasises their psychological states. Here Rath's lodgings and Lola's dressing-room-cum-lodgings are of particular significance. They are organised aurally in distinctive ways. Rath's lodgings are strictly associated with mornings, with the church clock playing its little tune, and then striking eight times (see below). The only other sound we associate with them is the landlady's voice. No other sounds penetrate Rath's isolated existence. Lola's place is a hubbub of activity, clearly assigned to the night. Her dressing-room at the club has a spiral staircase which leads to her lodgings. In this arrangement the dressing-room is the main setting. However, we are aware of the off-screen spaces by means of sound: the noises of the nightclub horizontally, her voice from upstairs vertically.

The contrast between sound and silence is another very effective device to produce dramatic effects in *Der blaue Engel*. The silent bird in Rath's cage is one such example. It is worth reminding ourselves that before the arrival of sound silence could not be conveyed in film, trite as the statement may seem. For although Rath's and Lola's lodgings are partly defined by sound, by 'noise', there is also silence. We have already mentioned the door that leads from Lola's dressing-room to the nightclub. This door is opened and closed many times during the film. There is a constant stream of performers in and out, which produces an exaggerated effect of noises from the club being admitted to or excluded from the dressing-room. These constant interruptions have a disorientating effect on the action in Lola's dressing-room, which is the centre of the unfolding narrative. They are also a constant reminder of the fact that Lola's life and all her relationships are more or less public: she belongs to her rowdy audience. The short silences provide only brief respite.

The human voice holds a special place amongst all the sounds which we perceive. Apart from our need to communicate through dialogue it bears confirmation and reassurance that we are part of a community. In the days of silent films it must have been quite frustrating not being able to hear the characters speak: Audiences had to rely on intertitles and on facial expressions, movement of the characters and other clues in the mise-en-scène in order to make sense of the story. In *Der blaue Engel*, a whole range of voices is used to express social situations, emotional states, and power relationships in addition to the visual clues. The emotional range of the voices is extraordinarily wide: There is, for example, the contrast of Rath's authoritarian, Prussian tone in the classroom and the childlike voice he adopts with Lola. The most striking use of his voice occurs at the end of the film, which is also the moment when he expresses his real emotions. We will go into details of this final scene set at the nightclub later.

Here is an example of an exchange between Rath and Lola which sets up the power relationship between them. As soon as he has met her he submits himself instantly to her. He is hardly able to speak in full sentences. In her dressing-room she flirts with him: 'Beautiful eyes, right?' and when he is tongue-tied, she says in mock-

disappointment: 'No?' upon which he stammers: 'Yes, yes!' She taunts him by blowing make-up powder in his face, then wiping it off, instinctively realising her dominance over him. This establishes a very unequal (verging on the sado-masochistic) relationship with very few words and restrained acting.

In the course of the film Lola comes across as a rather more complex character than you would at first assume: After he has spent the night with her she makes him breakfast, flirtily counting out the number of sugar cubes he wants for his coffee. He is clearly impressed by this attention. She tells him: 'And you could have this every day!' to which he replies: 'There should be nothing in the way. I'm not married.' When he proposes to her she is genuinely surprised and moved, and accepts. She defends him against some of the outrageous humiliations of the director of the troupe. When he refuses to go on stage in his home town she persuades him to do it – after all, the show must go on – and she cares enough for him to be torn between loyalty to him and her own desire for another man towards the end. This is reflected in her voice which is able to switch from mockery to genuine feeling.

Probably the most distinctive use of her voice, though, is in her songs as she performs on stage at Der blaue Engel. These diegetic songs are an integral part of the narrative, they complement Lola's behaviour off-stage and thus provide important elements of her characterisation, and they comment on the action. The impression she has left by her introductory song – 'I am naughty Lola' – is later confirmed when we hear her sing 'Nimm dich in Acht vor blonden Frau'n' – 'Beware of Blondes', with which she again comments on her own character. This song is juxtaposed with Rath sitting alongside one of her posters, next to her legs. By that time we already know that Rath is doomed, and the song and accompanying image merely underline that fact.

The most famous song of the whole film, and the most famous of Dietrich's whole career, 'Falling in Love Again', is another comment on Lola's character. She cannot help falling in love all the time; it is not of her own free will. Here we catch a glimpse of her status as a victim of her own emotions. At the same time she abdicates responsibility by making it clear that it is not her fault if men 'burn' at the flame to which they are drawn like moths. The song is sad and callous at the same time.

Lola certainly has her fair share of 'vamp' characteristics to taunt and dominate the professor. But is she really his ruin? Is he not also responsible for his own life? Has he not listened to the songs? We mentioned before in our brief synopsis that he contributes to his own downfall by misunderstanding her flirtations and by not being able to handle her 'wild' character, on stage and off stage. We get the first inkling of this fateful misunderstanding when he arrives at the nightclub for the first time. She is heard singing that what she wants is 'einen Mann, einen richtigen Mann' – 'a man, a proper man' – while he is shown entering the club almost blindly, entangled in veils and nets. This scene is another example of the ingenuity of the film, of the way in which continuity is achieved

by means of visual and sound editing – by bringing the two spaces of outside and inside together through sound. Her singing 'seeps into' the outside shot. At the same time the song provides an ironic comment on his arrival through this kind of montage of image and sound. Yes, a man is approaching, but he is not the man of Lola's dreams.

Rath's confusion and disorientation is visually conveyed by nets, curtains, fog, and overstuffed rooms. At one point his reflection in three mirrors simultaneously begs the question: which of three is the real Rath? That he has gone wrong by spending a night in Lola's bed is signified by a cut to his empty bed in the morning, over which we read the inscription 'Do right and fear nobody!' His steady descent into submissiveness and ultimate destruction is represented, again silently, by a pair of hair curlers which Lola has set over a flame in order to heat them up. She orders him to pass them to her and then complains that they are too hot. In desperation, Rath tries to cool them down by using them on paper. They burn through the pages of a wall calendar, one day at a time. He burns through a fair number of them until he reaches the year 1925. Time has passed and he is now a clown – the next image that von Sternberg cuts to. The scene is set for Rath's ultimate humiliation.

This is where sound becomes prevalent again. As described earlier, we constantly privilege the human voice over other sounds. Therefore it is particularly disconcerting when that voice is distorted. Towards the end of the film we encounter a horrific distortion of Rath's voice. Rath's humiliation reaches its climax when he is forced to perform as a clown in his own hometown, on the stage of Der blaue Engel, while his wife is flirting with another man backstage. He goes on-stage only reluctantly and again gets caught in the veil that is spread across the stage. His spectators are getting impatient by his reluctance to perform. They shout and heckle, greedy for entertainment, smelling blood and whipped

up into a frenzy when Rath is about to be humiliated. We see several people writhing with unease; one or two even leave the club. The audience seems to vacillate between revenge and guilt: revenge for Rath's previous authoritarian strutting, guilt for their own voyeuristic tendencies and for feasting on someone else's misfortune.

However, Rath does not seem to notice them. It is as if he were listening to some inner voice. The troupe director does his silly trick of pulling eggs from Rath's nose and smashing them on his head. However, Rath does not react as he is supposed to, by cockcrowing in response, but remains in his stupor. When he finally comprehends the full reality of his situation he lets off several spine-chilling cockcrows which express both his anguish and acknowledge that he has been cuckolded. (The – archaic – German word for 'cuckold' is 'Hahnrei', 'Hahn' meaning 'cock'.) He then proceeds to walk off the stage and attempt to strangle Lola. After that there is nothing left for him to do but to die. The cockcrows are the last (semi-)human sounds we hear from him. Lola's new lover saves her from Rath's desperately violent act. The troupe director shows a certain amount of

pity: 'You are a sophisticated, educated man. I don't understand you. All this because of a woman.' Rath does not speak another word. After being released from his straight-jacket he stumbles out into the winter night and returns to his old grammar school where he sits down at his old desk and dies. In the end

Rath is his own judge and jury.

Various breeds of bird are prominent throughout the film, contrasted by sound and silence respectively. The opening shot reveals images and sounds of a woman herding geese into cages, a portent of things to come. Our first encounter with Rath is in the morning, when he is having breakfast at his lodgings and realising that something is missing: He cannot hear his own little canary singing. He finds it dead in its cage. The complete silence with which this scene is played out is intense – it might be telling us that in such barren, loveless surroundings not even a little bird can survive. In contrast, Lola's canary is twittering happily, as if to say that Lola is alive. This impression is reinforced by her 'noisy' lifestyle. Towards the end of the film, Rath himself is forced to become a bird.

Even his own musical motif is related to birds. We first encounter it as a cheerful little melody played by the church clock at eight o'clock in the morning, signifying Rath's daily routine. Strikingly, it is an aria from Mozart's *The Magic Flute*. In the opera it expresses Papageno's longing for a companion: 'Ein Mädchen oder Weibchen wünscht Papageno sich' ('A girl or a wife is what Papageno desires'). The term 'Weibchen' normally refers to a female in the animal kingdom (in the opera it is a bird). If used within a human context it is somewhat pejorative, since it denotes a distinctly non-liberated little woman. Whether in Rath's case it means that he can only form a relationship with a little bird in a cage or possibly with a 'dumb female', or that he is himself a 'dumb bird' is open to interpretation. The term forms the correlative to Lola's wish for 'a real man'. These two tunes set up the basic and ultimately fateful incompatibility of Rath and Lola.

It is common practice in sound film for non-diegetic orchestral music to accompany films, especially over the titles. This framing device is used in *Der blaue Engel*. However, what is remarkable is the change within the music from the opening titles to the end: At the beginning of the film it consists of a cheerful orchestral mix of 'Falling in Love Again' and the cheerful clock-motif. At the end the same mix is taken up by a full orchestra with more melodramatic impact, and in a minor key, thus emphasising the psychological nature of the narrative. This change of register and separation from diegetic to non-diegetic, not only closes the film, it also comments on the narrative by telling us that 'Falling in Love Again' and Papageno's/Rath's desire for a 'dumb female' ultimately leads to Rath's destruction. The symbolic meaning of the two interlinked musical motifs thus comes together perfectly at the end.

Der blaue Engel is an interesting example of the collaboration, the interrelationships and exchanges of key personnel between Hollywood and Germany. Mainly during the 1920s, it was common practice for producers, directors, actors and other film personnel to shuttle between the two locations. During the Weimar years this exchange happened due to the success of German cinema and the better conditions that Hollywood offered to German technicians. After the financial fiasco of *Metropolis* the Hollywood studio Paramount had bought significant shares in UFA, and from then on even more exchanges between Hollywood and UFA took place. During the rise of the Nazis and in their early years in power, when the dictatorship was being built systematically and when Jews and any political dissenters were persecuted, the direction of movement by film personnel became one-way, away from Germany – the biggest disaster that ever befell German culture. After the end of World War II some of these émigrés returned to Germany. Most of them did not have the success that they had enjoyed in the Weimar years, however.

With this in mind, let us now trace the careers of some of the cast and crew of *Der blaue Engel*. The key players were the director Josef von Sternberg, the producer Erich Pommer, the composer Friedrich Holländer, the lead actor Emil Jannings, and the new discovery, Marlene Dietrich, who is not even credited in the titles to the film. Von Sternberg, an Austrian-American film director, was born Jonas Sternberg in London in 1894, to Austrian parents. He later took 'Josef' as a stage name, and the aristocratic 'von' was added even later by a Hollywood studio. He died in 1969 in California. In 1920s' Hollywood he worked, uncredited, on one of the defining films about the new type of woman that we mentioned earlier in the chapter. The film was *IT* (1927), which defined the new type of the 'It Girl', a term with which we are now quite familiar. The 'It Girl' was played by Clara Bow, one of the icons of 1920s' Hollywood cinema. She had similar characteristics to Louise Brooks, the iconic 'flapper' of silent films, who was initially supposed to play the female lead in *Der blaue Engel*.

Von Sternberg was under contract with Paramount and was sent to Berlin to make *Der blaue Engel* at UFA. He was not happy with Louise Brooks as Lola Lola. He needed someone who appeared less innocent, more knowing, more 'vamp' than 'flapper'. He insisted on having discovered and 'made' Marlene Dietrich. There is, however, an anecdote that tells us how Dietrich, Jannings and von Sternberg got together. This little story involves the famous Hotel Adlon in Berlin, which was in the twenties a place for cultural and political encounters, 'the' place to be seen, the place where deals were made. Apparently Dietrich and Jannings were introduced to each other there, and Jannings saw immediately the potential of this young woman. He subsequently introduced her to von Sternberg, and the rest is film history.

Marlene Dietrich was born in 1901 (she preferred 1904). At first she pursued a musical education and then began working in the theatre with Max Reinhardt, before she became a film actress. Immediately, in fact on the day following the release of *Der blaue Engel*, she left Berlin with von Sternberg. She says that she was not even aware of the phenomenal success of her first film because of her immediate departure. They were bound for Hollywood, where she signed a seven-year-contract with Paramount. In her first film at Paramount, *Morroco* (1930), again directed by von Sternberg, her dinner suit and her generally androgynously provocative demeanour on stage caused a sensation. Her completely novel way of dressing on-screen has been much imitated by other actors, as well as off-screen. Even today we speak of a 'Marlene' outfit. In Hollywood, Dietrich and von Sternberg worked together on several films, in roles where she was always the seductress. Von Sternberg was often accused of privileging appearance over convincing narrative. A journalist wrote in 1931: 'You see she [Marlene Dietrich] has never yet had a real break on a story... Josef von Sternberg doesn't care much about strong stories. If he

has too much story he can't find room for his artistic effects, and these effects are much more important to him than story.' His obsession with Marlene's legs in *Der blaue Engel* is one example of this. She reports that he told her to show off her legs in every scene, no matter how. With regard to artistic effects, he was also the director who claimed that he had found the definitive lighting for Marlene's face.

Back in Germany, Josef Goebbels, the Nazi propaganda minister, tried to lure Dietrich back to Nazi Germany and offered her roles with huge salaries attached. She refused. In 1939 she became a US citizen. After von Sternberg, she worked with Ernst Lubitsch, Billy Wilder and later Fritz Lang (three other émigrés from Germany). She also became famous for the concerts she gave for the American troops during World War II, visiting them at the front in complete defiance of the physical danger in which she put herself. For her contribution to the war effort she received the American Medal of Freedom, and two Medals of Honour in France. After the war, from 1950 to 1975, she made a career as a show star. In 1960 she returned to Germany for the first time, where she was celebrated by many, but also rejected in some circles because of her 'desertion' of Germany before and during the war. She lived more or less as a recluse in Paris from 1978 until her death in 1992. Her family had to fight for her right to be buried in Berlin.

For von Sternberg, Emil Jannings was the ideal choice to play the lead in *Der blaue Engel*. In fact, this film was a milestone for the already very experienced actor, and he was propelled forward to even greater things. Born in 1884, the stage and film actor was one of the best-known faces of German silent film. His first real success on film was *Madame Dubarry* (Ernst Lubitsch, 1919), in which he played Louis XV. He played a few more royal roles until he began working with F. W. Murnau: in 1924 he played the lead in Murnau's masterpiece of German 'New Objectivity', *Der letzte Mann* (*The Last Laugh*). This exploration of the psychological depths of a man and his fateful descent became a Jannings trademark in other films – of which *Der blaue Engel* is another example. Another collaboration with Murnau was *Faust* (1926), where he plays the role of Mephisto. In the same year Jannings went to Hollywood where he worked for Paramount. For his roles in *The Way of All Flesh* and *The Last Commando*, directed by von Sternberg, Jannings received the very first Oscar ever for an actor in a leading role – in 1929, the year in which the Oscar ceremony was held for the first time. As of today he has remained the only German actor to have been honoured in this way. His Hollywood career went very well, until sound film forced him to give up his well-paid career because his English was not good enough. The English-language version of *Der blaue Engel* showcases his English voice.

It is obvious that the quality of his accent leaves a great deal to be desired.

Der blaue Engel was Jannings' first sound film and a triumphant comeback in Germany. From then on his career in Germany took off once again. As an actor he was under contract with UFA; he put himself in the service of the Nazis and became Hitler's favourite actor. The psychologically nuanced roles of the twenties gave way to representations of members of the master race as favoured by Nazi ideology. In 1938 he took over as head of one of the subsidiaries of UFA, and produced his own films, thus cementing his reputation within the Nazi dictatorship. His collaboration with the Nazis led to a ban by the Allied forces after World War II. Jannings died in 1950. He is a major example of the continuity within the film industry from Weimar through to the Third Reich. (Another example is Leni Riefenstahl, whose work we will explore in chapter 3.)

Thus Emil Jannings and Marlene Dietrich not only ended up on opposite sides of the Atlantic but were also diametrically opposed in terms of their political affiliations. The only thing they still have in common to this day is their enormous success in Hollywood, albeit at different times. Never again have there been any German film stars that were able to establish themselves in Hollywood in the same way.

The producer of *Der blaue Engel* was Erich Pommer, another example of personnel exchange along the Berlin-Paris-Hollywood axis. Born in 1889, his career as a film producer began in 1915 and ended in 1955, during which time he produced approximately 200 films. Amongst these were the most important Weimar films, such as *Das Cabinet des Dr Caligari* (see chapter 1), Fritz Lang's Mabuse films, *Metropolis*, Murnau's *Der letzte Mann* and *Faust* (both with Emil Jannings), and, of course, *Der blaue Engel*. He was director of UFA from 1921–1926, then he had a short stint in Hollywood, with Paramount and MGM, after which his contract with UFA was renewed and he worked there until 1933. Like so many other film personnel of the Weimar years he was forced out of Germany because he was Jewish. From Paris he went to America and became a US national in 1944. His post-war success was somewhat mixed, like that of so many of those artists whose careers were fatefully interrupted by the Third Reich.

Friedrich Holländer, the film composer, born in 1896, was a student of Engelbert Humperdinck's in Berlin. When he was very young he improvised to silent films on the piano - he had a great talent for improvising to moving images. In the 1920s he became one of the most creative talents of Weimar culture. His various musical activities included writing musical revues, cabarets and songs. Of his film music the score he wrote for *Der blaue Engel* was his most famous, and the songs subsequently became hits in their own right and helped catapult Marlene Dietrich to stardom. She still sang them when she was in her seventies. And again, like countless other talented people, he was blacklisted by the Nazis for being Jewish. He, too, emigrated in 1933, to Paris in the first instance, then in 1934 to Hollywood. There he wrote for the theatre and for film. In 1955 he returned to Germany. But, again like many others, he was not able to re-establish himself with the same degree of fame that he enjoyed in the Weimar Republic. For Marlene Dietrich he wrote other songs, though, such as her famous 'Wenn ich mir was wünschen dürfte' (If I were allowed a wish). He died in 1976 in Munich.

In the credits to *Der blaue Engel* all the above-mentioned names are given their due, except Marlene Dietrich's, as we mentioned before. In retrospect this is quite unbelievable considering the enormous impact she has on-screen. In an interview (you can find this on the two-disc DVD set of the film released in Britain) she reminds us with her usual cool irony that she was 'not the attraction of the film'. Some films that highlight her further career in Hollywood are *Morocco*, *Rancho Notorious* (Fritz Lang, 1952), and *Witness for the Prosecution* (Billy Wilder, 1957). Her last screen appearance was in *Just a Gigolo* (David Hemmings, 1978). There are two documentaries about Marlene Dietrich worth mentioning: *Marlene* (Maximilian Schell, 1984) and *Marlene Dietrich - Her Own Song* (David Riva, 2001), which highlight different aspects of her life.

FOOTNOTES

[1] 'Rat' means 'advice' or 'counsel' in German; 'Unrat' refers to something useless, a wonderful pun that sets up the satire effectively.

[2] There is a parallel: Louise Brooks wrote in her autobiography that Pabst always had the impression of having created her. 'I was his Lulu!' For other connections between Brooks and *Der blaue Engel* see below.

CHAPTER 3: IN THE SERVICE OF IDEOLOGY: *TRIUMPH DES WILLENS* (*TRIUMPH OF THE WILL*, 1934)

Triumph des Willens is the only non-fiction film in our selection. It has been chosen to represent the period of National Socialist film-making for three reasons: its enormous impact at the time; its technical bravura; and because Riefenstahl was reputedly Hitler's favourite film-maker. In this chapter the film is set in the context of the development of the National Socialist dictatorship and its grip on cultural production. The chapter also explores facts and myths surrounding Leni Riefenstahl, a legendary character who may or may not have been a Nazi. Whatever her direct political affiliations may have been, she was indeed an artist who worked for the Nazi regime. We will show how she did this by analysing the key features of her documentary style.

During the twelve years of National Socialist rule, about 1,000 feature films were made in Germany. However, not all of them were straightforward propaganda films as might be expected. Nor did the (film) culture of twenties' Germany stop and vanish without a trace: There is evidence of continuation in films of the thirties, e.g. Bauhaus¹ style decor and furniture, jazz music (termed 'degenerate' by the Nazis), or iconic American products such as Coca-Cola or Mickey Mouse, but also in the tradition of 'Arbeiterfilme' in the style of New Objectivity. Genre films such as comedies, action films, costume dramas, melodramas often emulated Hollywood productions, even though audiences were not necessarily aware of this. Some German actors and actresses specialised in emulating well-known American film stars. It was not until 1941, when the USA entered World War II, that Hollywood films were actually banned from German screens. The continuing influence of Weimar Germany and Hollywood on National Socialist film-making has often been overlooked.

Josef Goebbels, who was the Third Reich's Minister of 'the People's Enlightenment and Propaganda', saw film as an effective tool to spread the regime's messages and to influence people accordingly. However, contrary to the belief that film production was under the complete control of the Nazis from the beginning to the end of the Reich, research has shown that this was not the case: The film scholar Karsten Witte, by analysing films individually, was the first to argue convincingly that there was a gradual process of 'nazification' of film production and, interestingly, that even then not all films made during National Socialists rule conformed to Nazi ideology. The following paragraphs go into some detail regarding the process of gradual 'integration' of film production in Nazi Germany. These facts and figures are important in that they show this complicated process and make clear how long it actually took the Nazis to exercise something approaching complete control. So please bear with us if you find figures 'boring'!

The process of gradual control over film production began in the same year (1933) that the National Socialists seized power in Germany. Goebbels began the process of 'Gleichschaltung' [2] within the sector of film production. As early as September the 'Reichsfilmkammer' (a kind of professional association for film-makers) was founded, stipulating that 'non-Aryans' and political undesirables were excluded. The purpose of this measure was to ensure that only film-makers who conformed to National Socialist ideology were able to work.

The regime aimed to nationalise all cultural production. To this end, and immediately in 1933, the state-owned Filmkreditbank was founded, which, by 1937, was financing 50% of all feature film production in Germany. With regard to censorship, from 1934 all screenplays had to be approved by the Reich's Screenplay Censor, whose brief stated that all material that was deemed to be against the 'spirit of the time' or against 'National Socialist or artistic sensibilities' should be banned. A new seal of approval for 'artistically valuable' or 'politically valuable' films was introduced. Overall decision on the merits of any film was in the hands of a representative of the Propaganda Ministry. In 1936 film reviews in the media, 'as practised hitherto', were banned. Only reviews written by carefully selected critics and published in politically opportune media were allowed.

The UFA, which, as you will remember, was the largest and most important film production company in the Weimar Republic, was gradually brought under state control, and by 1937 72 per cent of its capital was in the hands of the Reich. Smaller film production companies such as Terra, Tobis, and Bavaria were usurped by the state in clandestine operations. However, it was not until 1942 that all film production companies had been placed officially under the direction of UFA-Film GmbH. In order to secure reliable personnel, a German Academy of Film Art was inaugurated on the UFA estate at Babelsberg in 1938. Needless to say, the film-makers who graduated from this film academy were Nazi-friendly.

It was only from 1942 onwards, though, that all film production was placed under the control of a 'Reich Film Bureau' which was responsible for the 'overall artistic and spiritual attitude of film production'. From now on, film production, distribution and exhibition were under state control. Reception was controlled through the above-mentioned system of 'selective reviews', and audiences were controlled by making viewing of desirable films compulsory for HJ and BdM (the male Hitler Youth and the female Association of German Girls) members and by not admitting latecomers to the cinema. Newsreels were a compulsory part of any film screening.

Nevertheless, complete control was still not achieved. Even within this tightly controlled system there were loopholes of resistance and also of indifference towards the regime among film-makers. There was a 'small alliance of aesthetic opposition' among film-makers such as Helmut Käutner and Wolfgang Staudte (see our next chapter on *Die Mörder sind unter uns*). Even in the final years of the Third Reich some film-makers were able to 'smuggle' oppositional visions into their films and to escape the censors. It has been suggested that there were possibly only three film-makers who actively supported the NS system: Fritz Hippler, Veit Harlan, and Leni Riefenstahl. Bearing this 'incomplete' system in mind makes it possible to put *Triumph des Willens* in context with other, earlier and later, film productions of the Third Reich and puts to rest assertions that there was only one type of artistic expression during those years.

The first feature films made under the National Socialist regime were still in the tradition of leftwing Weimar cinema of the late twenties and early thirties. These films were still characterised by the portrayal of daily life, usually of the proletariat, with a strong sense of community and, as a consequence, a lack of heroes. Visually some of these films still contain avant-garde features such as montage. A good example for this is *Morgen beginnt das Leben* (*Tomorrow Life Begins*, 1933).

Hitlerjunge Quex (1934) is widely regarded as the first feature film with a clear propagandist message. It is also the first to use children in masses as impressionable and susceptible beings, a device that is also detectable in Stalinist and in Italian fascist films. The film depicts the contrast between communist organisations, with their selfishness and disorderly conduct, and National Socialist groupings as representatives of the heart-warming discipline of the Nazi regime. At the end the young hero dies as a victim of communist persecution. His body is covered with flags; the image is accompanied by arousing music. Death for the National Socialist cause is glorified. As an early ideological film it was clearly aimed at the as yet unconverted.

In Riefenstahl's *Triumph des Willens* the masses of children became masses of marching troops as a symbol of German discipline and authoritarianism. The film was an important part of the construction and consolidation of the new Reich. Through it the immense power and allure of the Führer was to be demonstrated and committed to celluloid. *Triumph des Willens* was the first of the elaborate, expensive and spectacular non-fiction films of the Third Reich, ordered personally by Hitler and financed by the state. By the time Riefenstahl made her two-part film about the Olympic Games of 1936 in Berlin, the self-confidence of the state was clearly in evidence and reflected in films.

Closer to 1939 and the outbreak of war, more and more costume dramas were made, many of them with Emil Jannings in the role of 'great men' of history. He had become the most revered actor in Nazi Germany, which makes an interesting contrast to Marlene Dietrich, his co-star in *The Blue Angel*, who left Germany in 1933, and later entertained American troops and boosted their morale during the war.

Gradually, the National Socialists' very own genre developed: that of the anti-Semitic film. *Der ewige Jude* (*The Eternal Jew*, 1940) was ostensibly a 'documentary' which was shown simultaneously in 66 cinemas in Berlin, and was compulsory in all occupied countries on the Führer's personal orders. It provided a model for the most notorious anti-Semitic film of all, *Jud Süß* (1941) by Veit Harlan.

As late as 1943, when Germany lay partly in ruins, the population was suffering tremendous hardship, and German troops were being decimated on the eastern and western fronts, UFA produced its most impressive and technologically advanced film, *Münchhausen*, by Josef von Baky, as an escape from the grim reality of war. Later, in 1945, *Kolberg*, another film by Veit Harlan, represented a final attempt at strengthening the population's morale.

The previous paragraphs have tried to trace the development of the German film industry throughout the twelve years of the Third Reich. This development shows a clear trajectory from the first 'practice runs' of the new regime in 1933 to its disintegration in 1945. It also shows, surprisingly, that there were niches for those who did not wish to conform.

What is Leni Riefenstahl's role in all this? In order to get a measure of the most famous woman film-maker of all time we will now take a brief look at her biography. Riefenstahl was born in Berlin in 1902. She started her career as a dancer, working solo with Max Reinhardt at the prestigious Deutsches Theater Berlin from 1923–1926. This is where she was spotted by Arnold Fanck, a film director who was famed for his 'Berg films' – mountain films in harmony with nature, a genre that, as the name suggests, focused on the romantic spectacle of mountains and the triumph of heroic humans conquering them. Nazi ideology was pre-inscribed in those films with their stress on physical perfection and heroic sacrifice. Fanck was keen to cast Riefenstahl in his next film, *Der heilige Berg*

(*The Holy Mountain*, 1926). Her collaboration with Arnold Fanck was the most important phase in her professional development. Through him she not only became an actress, but also learnt a great deal about film-making. He taught her how to use a camera, how to direct, how to edit. She was a shrewd young woman who was willing and able to learn new skills. Fanck became an ardent Nazi; his (and by extension Riefenstahl's) style influenced Nazi aesthetics greatly.

Riefenstahl's directorial debut was *Das blaue Licht* (*The Blue Light*, 1932), which she made under the tutelage of her mentor and which was financed by her long-term sponsor and lover Harry Sokal, a Jewish (!) banker. She also starred in the film. 'All of them were in love with me. Oh, it was a drama always!' Riefenstahl exclaimed in her memoirs. *Das blaue Licht* was dismissed by the critics. But when Hitler saw it he apparently became convinced that she had to become the film-maker to represent National Socialist ideals on film. He thought of *Das blaue Licht* as the 'sublime manifestation of the German spirit'. As so often in his career his instincts proved right, although before Riefenstahl ever came to Hitler's attention there was *Metropolis*. He saw something in its visuals, particularly the powerful and visually arresting geometric patterns in which Lang arranges masses of people that led him to believe that Fritz Lang was 'his' director – notwithstanding the fact that he was Jewish. Hitler must have been attracted by the obsessiveness, perfectionism and meticulousness of both Lang and Riefenstahl. He seemed to have a very strong sense of how he wanted his ideas to be transformed into images. However, Lang declined and emigrated, which left Riefenstahl to carry Hitler's torch, and Lang's ex-wife Thea von Harbou to write Hitler's screenplays.

In her memoirs, published in 1987, Riefenstahl tells of the first time she heard Hitler speak at a rally. 'That very instant I had an almost apocalyptic vision that I was never able to forget. It seemed as if the earth's surface were spreading out before me, like a hemisphere that suddenly splits apart in the middle, spewing out an enormous jet of water, so powerful that it touched the sky and shook the earth. I felt paralysed.' These few words alone convey to us that she was a very impressionable person and given to hyperbole, two ingredients that, together with her technical skills, made a perfect mix for the creation of propaganda. But we shall come back to this later.

Riefenstahl's first project for Hitler was a short film of the 1933 Nuremberg rally of the NSDAP – the National Socialist German Workers Party. He provided the title for it: 'Victory of Faith'. Riefenstahl's work impressed him so much that he personally commissioned her to make a full length film of the 1934 Party rally, circumventing Josef Goebbels, the propaganda minister. This contributed to the animosity between Goebbels and Riefenstahl – he may have seen in her a shrewdness and perfectionism that rivalled his own.

After *Triumph des Willens* her next film project was an account of the 1936 Berlin Olympic Games, which was supposed to show the world the double accomplishment of athletic achievement and the regime's ability to stage it. This four-hour epic, released in

1938, is generally accepted as less overtly political than *Triumph des Willens* and therefore less controversial. By elevating sports images to art and celebrating the beauty of human motion it breaks new ground and is regarded as her finest achievement. However, her glorification of the perfect human body does come close to, or is, in the eyes of some critics, an expression of fascism.

Both *Triumph des Willens* and *Olympiad* became great successes, not just in Germany, but internationally. They both won awards, including the prestigious gold medal at the Venice Film Festival. *Olympiad* continuously received special recognition by the International Olympic Committee, which obviously focused on the innovative and technically brilliant way in which the film portrayed sports events. They ignored the ideological content.

Riefenstahl once again courted notoriety with her next project, a feature film called *Tiefland* (Lowland). Because of her connections to the Nazi regime she was able to recruit a large number of extras for her film from concentration camps, both Sinti and Roma, who she claimed were necessary for accuracy. After the war she was accused in a court of law for not paying these extras, and moreover for promising them freedom, something she was neither authorised to do nor was able to achieve. At least half of them perished in concentration camps.

Of all the film-makers of the NS regime Riefenstahl enjoyed the most regard and freedom. She was given the best opportunities, lavish financing, and most political protection. The fact that she was never a member of the NSDAP served later as her strongest argument when claiming that she had never been a Nazi film-maker. After the end of the Hitler regime, she was detained by the Allies for almost four years under 'de-nazification' rules [3]. She was exonerated from being an active Nazi for lack of evidence, and because of her own protestations of innocence and her justifications for her actions. Together with Albert Speer, the Nazi architect who worked on the 'sets' for *Triumph des Willens* with her, and Veit Harlan, the maker of anti-Semitic films, she was cleared of being an active Nazi. It was determined that they had been mere sympathisers of the regime. These judgements seem incomprehensible given the important role artists (especially those who produce such publicly visible works as film-makers) play in society in general and in dictatorships in particular. They may have come about partly because of the difficulty of pinning down artistic expression as directly political – after all, the view does exist that all true works of art should be free of political purpose.

For the rest of her life Riefenstahl maintained that she was never a 'political film-maker'. In her memoirs (1987) she goes to great lengths to emphasise her innocence. With regard to *Triumph des Willens* she reiterates again and again how she was forced to make the film against her will. She was adept at turning her own statements around, at 'doctoring' the facts, and at denying her more than willing compliance with the regime.

After the end of the Third Reich several court cases were brought against her for her propaganda activity on behalf of the Nazis. She was cleared every time, but the negative publicity resulted in a kind of unofficial blacklisting. She simply did not manage to secure funding for any more film projects. For more than 25 years she did not achieve anything of note. Her later work as a photographer was greatly admired and received international acclaim, but at the same time it was much discussed and criticised, and described by the influential New York critic Susan Sontag as 'fascist aesthetics'.

The rest of her life was spent under the shadow of her involvement with the Nazis, an involvement which is still debated nowadays, even though Riefenstahl died in 2003. The debate concentrates on whether it is possible to separate her talent from her political views, i.e. whether we can appreciate her work on purely aesthetic grounds. It is certainly true that her revolutionary techniques influenced later generations of film-makers, particularly in the areas of documentary and commercials. When her memoirs were published in 1987, the book was translated into nine languages and proved a great commercial, if not critical, success. Its publication renewed interest in her. A film biography was made in which she maintained again and again that she felt unjustly vilified. She was always prone to contradictory statements, though. The latest, and most insightful and meticulously researched analysis of her life and work is a biography by the American film historian Steven Bach, *Leni. The Life and Work of Leni Riefenstahl* [4]. Bach sets out to dissect her own assertions and to contrast them with authentic historical documents, thereby exposing many of her own statements as half-truths or lies.

When Riefenstahl was interviewed for the influential French film magazine *Cahiers du Cinema* in 1965 she maintained that her *Triumph des Willens* was 'a purely historical film. To be more precise: It's a documentary. It reflects the truth of the history of 1934. It is a documentary, not a propaganda film.' However, what exactly is the difference between a documentary and a propaganda film? In the context of Riefenstahl's 'non-fiction films' it is interesting to take a closer look at the relevant terminology before we set out to explore *Triumph des Willens* in more detail.

First of all, we must remember that documentaries tell stories as well. There is in any film a *selection* of facts that are presented in a certain order; certain shots are selected in production and in post-production, ending with the choices that the editor makes and overlaid by post-production sound. In the 1920s there were three important views and practices regarding documentary films. A politically conservative point of view stated that documentaries should contain 'education', 'information', even 'propaganda', as a 'creative treatment of reality'. Here the term 'propaganda' is not used negatively. A more leftwing view declared that the aim of documentaries should be to portray 'everyday life and sounds of ordinary men and women'. The Soviet film-maker Dziga Vertov focused on reality, using film as an educative tool, employing the Soviet montage style of contrasting editing, which meant placing very different shots next to each other, making new connections between previously unrelated bits of information. This strictly formalist approach resulted in the manipulation of the spectator. The 1960s also saw radical approaches: 'cinéma-vérité' in France, 'direct cinema' in the USA, and 'free cinema' in

Britain. These latter approaches aimed to represent reality as it was, with no manipulation. Other, modified types of documentary continue to be made today, many of which challenge the establishment [5]. This brief excursion shows that there are many different ways of making documentaries, including propaganda films!

Nowadays the term 'propaganda' has purely negative connotations. However, it used to be quite neutral in its meaning: It used to refer simply to the act of persuasion of others in order to put across your own point of view. In World War I the meaning of propaganda for the first time became synonymous with an instrument of the state in order to systematically shape its citizens' positive perceptions of and reactions to the official line of the state. This political propaganda was taken much further by the Nazis in order to cement their ideology in the minds of the German people. In Goebbels' words: 'The essence of propaganda consists in winning people over to an idea so sincerely, so vitally, that in the end they succumb to it utterly and can never escape from it.' [6] In order to achieve this mind control by a dictatorship, propaganda needs to be combined with censorship, the limitation and control of information.

Now we have established that propaganda was indeed at the heart of the Nazi dictatorship. We have also seen that defining 'documentary' is not straightforward, and that there is such a thing as a 'propaganda documentary'. So how do we determine where 'documentary' ends and 'propaganda' begins? Can *Triumph des Willens* definitively and conclusively be assessed as a 'pure' propaganda film? Does it matter that Riefenstahl herself denied this? Can artists exist in a vacuum or do they always have to be aware of the social implications of their work? We cannot answer all these questions. What we can and should do is to take the film on its own terms by considering some of its key aspects as we watch it, thereby reminding ourselves of what the debated issues are.

In her memoirs the 'apolitical' Riefenstahl writes that one of the most nagging questions in conceiving the film concerned the fact that a Party rally was basically a boring, repetitive event. Surprisingly, she did not consider including in her film the preparation of the rally and its grounds. Such an approach would have made for a very interesting introduction indeed. Instead she concentrated on the actual rally. In order to make it more interesting, Riefenstahl came up with the idea of mobile cameras, a completely new approach to documentary film-making at the time. She had rails and tracks built at the rally site. There was even a lift which ran up a flagpole which was so small that it could just about accommodate a cameraman and a camera.

Altogether, Riefenstahl used 16 camera teams and more than 100 crew members. By the end of shooting she had more than 60 hours of footage which she then condensed to around two hours of finished film. On the soundtrack we find original sound (such as speeches, cheers, and some fanfares and other musical contributions) as well as especially composed music, which was added to the soundtrack in post-production along with songs of camaraderie. In addition to this there are opening titles and inserts with the names of the many speakers. This is fortunate not only for those of us who are not familiar with the members of Hitler's government, but also for contemporary audiences to whom such details may not have been known yet either.

In the title section we are informed that the film was produced on the personal orders of the Führer and 'designed' by Leni Riefenstahl. The Party Rally began on 5 September, 1934. We are also informed that this is happening '20 years after the start of the Great War, 16 years after the start of German suffering, 19 months after the beginning of German rebirth'. The 'start of German suffering' refers to the end of World War I and the subsequent peace treaty which forced on Germany extremely tough terms and conditions of making reparation payments to the winners of the war. These harsh conditions led to a breakdown of the German economy, which in turn proved an important factor in the rise of nationalism and fascism and helped Hitler on his way. 'German rebirth' refers of course to Hitler's NSDAP winning the 1933 general election and his seizure of power. It does not need stressing that the wording of the titles already tells us that we are dealing with a patriotic film, to put it mildly.

In the first sequence, which we could term the 'God-like Hitler Descending' sequence, we are in the air above Nuremberg with his plane flying through clouds (the clouds of past sufferings?) into the light and descending on the city of Nuremberg, where the Party Rally is to be held and whose beautiful historic centre would be completely

destroyed in World War II. The images are greatly intensified by the overture to Wagner's *Mastersingers of Nuremberg* that is being played on the soundtrack, a real stroke of genius by Riefenstahl. When the clouds are finally behind us we see, from Hitler's viewpoint, troops on the ground that are already marching into the city. As we get closer we can make out crowds of people of all descriptions, waiting for their Führer, smiling, waving, and cheering. When Hitler is being taken along the rows of thousands in his car, the camera travels along with him.

The camera work, even just thus far, is astounding. It seems likely that the scene of the landing plane was shot later. It is a matter of record that some scenes were shot subsequently and inserted into the film later, a fact that Riefenstahl nonetheless denied. However, this does not diminish the technical feat of moving the cameras, mounted on tracks, something we will see more of later. How spectacular this was is hard to imagine now, but we need to remind ourselves that this had never been done before. There are quite obviously cameras high up on or in buildings. All through the film Riefenstahl uses striking high-angle and low-angle shots, close-ups, extreme close-ups and detail shots.

During Hitler's entrance into the city much is made of the medieval beauty of Nuremberg (German architectural achievement at its best). The whole town is decorated; every single window is copiously peopled and flagged. Hitler arrives at his hotel. This is the end of the first sequence. It would be an interesting exercise to analyse this sequence by trying to separate the purely 'recording' elements from the 'propaganda' ones. This could be done by trying to think of other ways of doing it, or comparing the footage with the modern coverage of, say, the arrival of key politicians at a party conference.

Riefenstahl took liberties with the time frame. Not all sequences as presented in the film correspond to those of the actual Rally. In addition to this some scenes were shot retrospectively. This means that we cannot be certain that the first daybreak shown is actually the next day of the Rally. However, we are meant to assume so. It is another very striking scene, opening onto the dark roofs of Nuremberg as they are gradually lit up by the rising sun. Again we hear Wagnerian music, and it is apparent that this sunrise has metaphorical meaning. Again Nuremberg buildings are shown in all their beauty. The film then cuts to a camp of tents which seems to be out of town. We see happy, smiling boys beating the drums, presumably as a wake-up call to their mates. There is washing, having fun, working together to get the fires going, there is breakfast, playful wrestling – in short, male bonding. These scenes without spoken words, without commentary, embody (in the true sense of the word) the National Socialist ideal of healthy bodies working towards a common goal. That this bonding was not necessarily always voluntary (both boys and girls were forced to join their respective youth organisations according to the principle of 'get them young') does not figure in this representation.

Hitler is shown in a variety of poses and moods, with different facial expressions: sometimes smiling, sometimes pensive, sometimes shaking hands, chatting, then in leader mode, making speeches. He is shown as a well-rounded human being, approachable if appropriate, remote if necessary. He is shown to be genuinely interested in all his subjects, whether it is little children or the row upon row of military personnel. Women appear rarely, and then only as waving, smiling faces or clothed in traditional costume.

The Rally proper is opened with the words: 'I declare this 6th Party Rally open with the commemoration of Reich Field Marshal and President Hindenburg'. Hindenburg died in

1934, thereby removing the final obstacle for Hitler to extend his powers from Party leader and Reich Chancellor to Reich President. This was the final instalment of Hitler's path to dictator. Now the Wehrmacht (the German Army) was directly under his orders. 'My Führer, you are surrounded by flags and standards of this National Socialism. You are Germany. When you act, the nation acts. When you judge, the people judge.' Every utterance is greeted with cheers from the crowds. 'You were the guarantor of victory. You are the guarantor of peace. Adolf Hitler! Sieg Heil!'

There are various speakers who all praise the achievements of the regime so far, who stress peace and promise continuing development for the betterment of the German people. We do not hear the complete speeches; well-chosen snippets (probably the first instances of 'sound-bites' on film) are cleverly edited together, linked by ghostly intertitles of the name of the next speaker. Soldiers, farmers and workers are addressed in turn.

A truly totalitarian regime relies on careful and unified use of language. In order to convey and manifest its ideology the development of such a language taps into well-known words and phrases that have emotional resonance among the people. These stock phrases are established and used over and over again; new meanings for existing terms are created; similes, metaphors and neologisms further cement the ideas of such a regime into the minds of its people. There are many such instances in evidence in *Triumph des Willens*. We must remember that this Party Rally of 1934 was part of the formative period of National Socialism. This means that we, the audience, are witness to fresh indoctrination. In fact, some of the phrases we hear might be used here for the very first time.

Here are some examples: Goebbels emphasises the 'bright flame of our enthusiasm', he wants to 'win the hearts of the people' through 'modern political propaganda' which works 'better than the might of weapons!'. Riefenstahl's images of real burning fires and cheering crowds underscore these words, even though most of the addressees of the speeches are in uniform! The assurance of 'peace' instead of 'weapons' in several later speeches was most likely not only directed at Germans, but must have served to reassure the rest of the world of the peaceful intentions of the regime.

The new phrase 'One Volk, one Führer!' is reinforced by a staged scene of men pretending to be from all manner of geographical regions of Germany. (It is obvious that they are not from those regions, because their accents quite blatantly do not match their presumed provenance.) This is a very clever device, since it  demonstrates the reach of the Reich from Bavaria to Frisia, from the Black Forest to Silesia, and at the same time emphasises the collaborative effort of all Germans to build a new Germany, with Hitler (in medium close-up) providing work for everybody. And we are left in no doubt that those well-built men with their strong profiles (in close-up) will be able to build a new Germany.

Through her choices of shots, angles and perspectives, through her mobile cameras and her editing, Riefenstahl makes sure that the audience gets the message. She explains (in her memoirs) that for Hitler's own speeches, the culmination of the Party Rally, 'I had circular tracks built around the podium [from which Hitler was supposed to speak]. The camera could circle Hitler at a suitable distance while he spoke. This resulted in new and lively images.' It certainly does that. We even see Hitler from behind and from a high angle, shots that must have been taken by the camera on the aforementioned flagpole.

Hitler's four speeches address different audiences at different times of day. In his first speech he sets out his programme of work for all, community, and the role of the young in his vision of Germany. At night searchlights roam among '200,000 men' who have been 'called by their hearts, their loyalty'. In this speech Hitler emphasises the suffering of the German people which has brought about their unity and by extension his regime. He

stresses that none of this has happened through an 'order by the state', but through a 'movement', the free will of his fellow Germans. 'It is not the state that has created us, but we who are creating our state.' Anybody who thinks otherwise is 'mistaken'. In this central speech, Hitler's exalted gestures, his passionate, almost

breaking voice, his careful choice of words, are particularly evident. All of this is underlined by Riefenstahl's use of travelling shots and close-ups from a very low angle, which elevates Hitler to a god-like figure. There is one particularly striking shot taken from between two long rows of people towards Hitler at the vanishing point of the two rows, dead centre, brightly lit. The effect that he has on the masses is demonstrated by more travelling shots in the dark lit up by fires, flares and rising smoke. Plenty of songs are sung. These night scenes are becoming wilder, more tribal, more adventurous; fires and smoke seem to be everywhere. The people are whipped up into frenzy, into hysteria, there are fireworks, there is more military music, there are happy, smiling faces.

The next day, order is restored and the next speech is made, this time to the youth, 'the future' of Germany. The boys are in Hitler Youth uniform, they salute, there is a montage of young faces, of blond, bright-eyed, Aryan boys. The 'peace-loving nature of our people' is emphasised again. If we compare this to the excesses of the previous night we are not quite so convinced. 'You are the future, flesh of our flesh, blood of our blood'. This phrase has the ring of Hitler's 'blood and soil' dogma about it, although he would not yet attempt to add to German 'soil' by invading other countries, and people of other 'blood' were not officially eliminated as yet. He waited until 1938 for this.

The post-synchronised Hitler Youth song is sung to images of more cheering crowds. 'Uns're Fahne flattert uns voran. / In die Zukunft ziehen wir Mann für Mann, / Wir marschieren für Hitler / Durch Nacht und durch Not / Mit der Fahne der Jugend / Für Freiheit und Brot. / Uns're Fahne flattert uns voran, / Uns're Fahne ist die neue Zeit. / Und

die Fahne führt uns in die Ewigkeit! / Ja die Fahne ist mehr als der Tod.' ('Our flag flies before us. We march into the future man by man. We march for Hitler through night and through pain, with the flag of youth for freedom and bread. Our flag flies before us. Our flag is the new era. And the flag leads us to eternity! Yes, the flag is more than death.') With these words identification with National Socialism is complete. [7]

After having addressed the future generation of his Reich Hitler speaks to his present representatives, the troops, without which no NS Party Rally would be complete. Together they form his own private army: the SA (Sturmabteilung: Storm Troopers) and SS (Schutzstaffel: Protective Squadron), each in their distinctive uniform. In his speech Hitler speaks of a 'shadow', a 'rift', which refers to the recent events surrounding the SA, more specifically to the 'Night of the Long Knives', a series of (illegal, subsequently 'legalised') political executions authorised by Hitler. Members of the SA were executed, including their politically ambitious, independently-minded leader Ernst Röhm, who was a thorn in the flesh of both Hitler himself and Germany's official army, the conservative Reichswehr. Hitler shrewdly ordered the actions against the SA in order to get rid of a potential rival and at the same time to secure the support of both SS and Reichswehr. The 'Night of the Long Knives' was thus part of the unification of political and military forces under his regime. This was a crucial victory for Hitler and his address to the troops at Nuremberg is the verbal manifestation of this achievement. The new SA leader affirms his allegiance to Hitler, and the SA is thereby effectively absolved from the 'crimes' committed by their previous leader, Ernst Röhm. [8]

The Party Rally concludes with a final parade in front of the Nuremberg Frauenkirche. In his closing speech Hitler stresses once again the primacy of the Nazi Party in Germany and announces the 'Thousand Year Reich'. The Party anthem, the 'Horst Wessel Lied', is sung, accompanied by the compulsory 'Hitler Salute'. [9]

Filming such a huge event was quite clearly a very difficult undertaking, even though sets were designed for the Rally which allowed 'staging' of the proceedings, which in turn made filming easier. Post-production, too, proved to be arduous, particularly editing and post-synchronisation. This, Riefenstahl claims, had partly to do with her inexperience at making documentary films, but also with the totally new approach she had taken in filming and with her own spectacular vision. You get the impression that she was not a film-maker ever to make any compromises. She seems to have been a perfectionist and in complete control at all times. She made several enemies amongst the higher ranks of Party and Army because of her single- and bloody-mindedness and her perfectionism.

With specific regard to the editing she says in her memoirs: 'I had no model for creating the film, nothing to go by, so I had to experiment. Nor did I have any adviser or other assistants except for the women who spliced and sorted.' Despite these problems and limitations, she produced a coherent film whose varied editing rhythm is an integral part of her vision of grass roots solidarity with the regime. Through a combination of camerawork and editing she created a mythical atmosphere: day and night photography, telephoto lenses, moving cameras, close-ups, heroic poses, 'real sound', and no commentary.

What is the legacy of *Triumph des Willens*, and why is it still important today? *Triumph des Willens* still divides opinion: For the director and her fans it is a true historical document; for film analysts it is at best a document of a political vision, at worst a ritual of the mobilisation of all possible forces in the service of a dictatorial regime. More generally, Riefenstahl's work is admired and reviled in equal measure to this date. Disturbingly, her films and her websites are accessed by a worrying number of people with neo-fascist tendencies.

Riefenstahl was certainly exploited for her considerable talent by the National Socialists, and for her own part used the regime to her advantage. She therefore entered into a true Faustian pact with the Nazis. She may well have been in denial about her own motives, she may actually have believed her own protestations. As critics have pointed out, it might have been her 'lack of soul', the 'vacuum in her personality', her insensitivity towards any moral values that enabled her to keep her denial up until the end of her days.

There is no evidence that she was a committed Nazi, but nobody who sees her 'documentaries' can be in any doubt that she promoted National Socialism, that she gave the regime defining images that are still today regarded as just that. To this day, *Triumph des Willens* has not been shown in its entirety in Germany (and you may never want to watch it completely, either). None of its images were in fact available before 1977, when the first documentary about Hitler was made in Germany: *Hitler: eine Karriere* (*Hitler: a Career*) by the historian Joachim Fest. [10] It used scenes from *Triumph des Willens* in order to explain the phenomenon that was Hitler and how he fascinated 'the masses'. Anton Kaes, in his excellent book *From Hitler to Heimat*, says that despite the critical voice-over commentary in Fest's film these images were dangerous because 'Fest remains within the boundaries of the original images, as though Riefenstahl's manipulative and contrived shots imparted a true picture of NS reality'. These images are also still used in schools to demonstrate the power and allure of the National Socialist system for 1930s' Germany, and to show the faces of the most powerful men of that system. For what do we bring to our inner eye when we think of the Third Reich? Whether we have consciously seen *Triumph des Willens* or not, we are likely to have images from it in our memory bank of iconic representations as a result of the recycling of those images in other films.

Beyond recycling, but arguably showing the influence of *Triumph des Willens*, are some recent Hollywood productions, such as the *Star Wars* films (from 1977 onwards), *The Lion King* (1994), and *Gladiator* (2000).

On the subject of representing Hitler differently, with integrity and plenty of 'soul', Charlie Chaplin's *The Great Dictator* (1941) is a great antidote to Riefenstahl's film. A more recent German film is Dani Levy's *Mein Führer* (2005), a comedy that was a hit in some people's eyes and a miss for others. Another, and very different, treatment of the dictator can be found in *Hitler – ein Film aus Deutschland* (*Hitler - A Film from Germany*, 1977) by Hans-Jürgen Syberberg. There is further discussion of this film in our chapter on *Der Untergang*.

FOOTNOTES

[1] Bauhaus, an influential, leftwing school of modernist art and design, which started in Weimar in 1923, was later forced for political reasons to move to the more liberal town of Dessau and finally to Berlin. It was closed by the Nazis. Several of its most distinguished figures, such as Gropius, Kandinsky, and Schlemmer, emigrated.

[2] Bringing into line all parts of social, cultural and political life in Germany

[3] A process by which the victorious Allies sought to determine who had or had not been an active Nazi

[4] A very good review in the New York Times Book Review can be found online at www.nybooks.com/articles/20258.

[5] See, for example, Michael Moore's 'creative' documentaries, or Werner Herzog's 'truth-seeking' documentaries.

[6] In a different context, advertising bears all the marks of propaganda; it is less political, but still very insidious.

[7] This song is also used in the final scene of *Hitlerjunge Quex* mentioned above, the other major establishing film of the Third Reich over images depicting the heroic death of one Hitler Youth, who has been killed by a communist mob.

[8] Detailed background reading is easily obtained from the respective Wikipedia sites.

[9] To this day using the salute and singing the 'Horst Wessel Lied' is a criminal offence in Germany. If you read the lyrics – found on Wikipedia -- you will see why.

[10] Fest also collaborated on *Der Untergang*, see chapter 12

CHAPTER 4: SHADOWS OF WORLD WAR II: *DIE MÖRDER SIND UNTER UNS (THE MURDERERS ARE AMONG US, 1946)*

Die Mörder sind unter uns is Germany's first post-war film, made immediately after World War II, and is therefore a landmark in German film history. In this chapter we will explore the extraordinary circumstances of its inception at a time when Germany was in ruins and occupied by the military forces of the victorious powers, who had been the Allies in World War II against Germany. The film's director, Wolfgang Staudte, occupies a unique place in German film history, straddling very different political systems during his career: the years of National Socialism, as well as both sides of the divided Germany.

Staudte was born in 1906. He originally studied engineering and only then decided to become a stage actor. In 1933, because of his roles in plays that were critical towards fascism, he was virtually blacklisted by the Nazis and prevented from acting. In 1935 he first started making commercials which were so successful that he was later commissioned to make feature films. During his career within Nazi Germany, he always trod a fine line between working for the system – there was no other choice within the state-controlled industry if you wanted to be able to continue working – and at the same time trying to get away without compromising his own views and convictions too much. In this he was not alone. Indeed, there were many like him, the so-called 'silent opposition', working in the cultural industry during the Nazi period: It was well-known that he had leftist leanings, but he was considered so good at what he was doing and therefore 'useful' to the Nazis that they turned a blind eye and employed him anyway. In fact, his usefulness was such that he was exempt from being drafted into the military, even during the war, an astonishing fact, especially in the later stages of the war. As a convinced pacifist this was his most important aim: not having to carry a gun, never having to shoot anybody. But his special status was always a precarious one, and in one instance he had to compromise in a way that left a blemish on the whole of his subsequent life: He played a minor part in the notorious anti-Semitic film by Veit Harlan, *Jud Süß* (*Jew Süss*). According to his own assessment he did this under duress, because had he refused he would have had his special status of not having to serve in the army revoked.

We might ask ourselves, if his convictions were so strong, why did he not leave Germany, like so many other film and other artists, who emigrated around 1933, mainly to the United States, and many of whom returned to Germany some time after the war? In answer to this he would be the first to admit that his social and political conscience was not developed enough at that time; he was not able to foresee where the Nazi dictatorship could lead; he always believed it would be over soon, and sat it out, remaining as inconspicuous as possible. For him the most important thing at the time was to be able to keep working in his chosen field. Thus he was one of many artists stuck in the grey area of compromise during the years of Nazi rule.

Mörder marks the beginning of Staudte's preoccupation with German history. While hiding in Berlin in the last months of the war in order to escape the 'Volkssturm' in the final battle for Berlin, he wrote the screenplay for a film that began to address the issue of individual guilt and responsibility in a disastrous war which a ruthless dictatorship was able to inflict on the world. It was the first project that he felt committed to very strongly. He was also the first German film-maker to seek to make an anti-fascist film, the first of his films that he passionately believed in. The strength of his conviction, and his unassailable desire to work immediately after the war, is demonstrated by the tenacity with which he sought to realise his project. In order to appreciate the enormous difficulties he had to overcome, we need to take a detour and highlight the political, economic and social situation in Germany at the end of World War II.

The Potsdam Conference of 1945 decreed that Germany was to be demilitarised and that it had to pay war reparations to the Allies. In order to deal with Germany's immediate Nazi past and to prevent something similar from happening again, the victorious powers demanded 'de-nazification', punishment of the guilty, and fostered the process of democratisation through 're-education' of the German population. The Allied powers, America and Britain in particular, also believed that a new Germany had to play its part in Europe and in the world and should not be crippled by excessive war reparations and long-term political control by outside forces, but that a new German government should be put in place soon. They did not want another Weimar with an economically crippled Germany, open and vulnerable to political extremism. Economic strength would also be crucial for Germany to function within a wider community of states. For this reason the American-led European Recovery Programme, also known as the Marshall Plan, was set up in 1947.

'De-nazification' was a particularly thorny and difficult issue, since about 8.5 million Germans had been members of the NSDAP, the National Socialist Party. It did prove very difficult indeed to differentiate between various degrees of involvement of different people in the dictatorship, and therefore to determine the punishment that should be meted out to those most guilty. The insistence of absolute Allied control over these issues did not make things any easier. As soon as the war ended, anti-fascist committees – collective self-help groups – sprang up all over Germany, organised by Germans who felt very strongly that the Nazis had to be flushed out before they fled the country, and that Germans themselves were best placed to do this. However, these committees were banned by the Allies because they felt that Germans could not be trusted. You could say that by taking away any kind of power from Germans an opportunity for redemption was wasted.

The country was divided into four zones, each occupied by one of the allied forces. Berlin was equally divided into four sectors. The lack of harmonisation in the four zones and sectors with regard to de-nazification contributed to a lack of acceptance of the Allies' efforts among the German population. Each of the Allied powers had its own ideas about the appropriate measures. In the Soviet zone the changes were followed through most consistently, as part of a complete political and social restructuring, and very soon the pact between the USA and USSR that had been in operation during the war to defeat Hitler developed into animosity and the Cold War.

Cultural policy was also in the hands of the Allies, who grappled with the problem of the transition from immediate necessity to long-term change. In the short term cultural production was under the direct influence of the Allies, but in the long term Germans had to be given autonomy again over their own cultural affairs. The difficulties were felt particularly strongly in the Western zones. The British took a low-key approach to re-education, whereas the USA believed in the power of the media, especially film, and took the view that Germans should be exposed as much as possible to 'different' types of product. This American influence was perceived by many as 'cultural imperialism', especially since initiatives by German writers and artists were viewed with suspicion by the occupiers (similar reactions as to the anti-fascist committees set up by Germans). The mass media, namely newspapers and the radio, were tightly controlled by the Allies at first, and then, gradually, licences were given to German publishers and broadcasters. By now the Western zones were more or less in agreement about Germany's future: the overriding aim was pluralism and decentralisation, the consequences of which are still in place today in the organisation of Germany as a federal state. The Soviet zone went a different way, towards centralisation, which was one step towards another kind of dictatorship (see our chapters on *Spur der Steine* and *Das Leben der Anderen*).

Against this background and the physical consequences of the war (see below for more details) it is hardly surprising that there was no German film production in 1945. Film-making facilities had been destroyed or were dismantled by the Allies. Desperate German civilians looted any equipment that remained in order to be able to barter for bare necessities. Initially, after the end of the war, Germans were excluded from any form of entrepreneurial activity, including film production. As outlined above, the Allies considered it their job to repress any form of German initiative in any area because they felt Germans needed to be punished and because they did not trust any German ideas so soon after the end of the dictatorship.

Staudte's experience when seeking to get his film made illustrates very well the confusion that reigned in the four sectors of occupation in Berlin. At the time he lived in the British sector and therefore thought it appropriate to approach the British authorities for a licence to form his own production company, 'Wolfgang Staudte Film Production'. There were other private initiatives like his to gain licences, although quite often the applicants did not have any concrete project in mind. However, it would give them the necessary starting point. It cannot be stressed enough that the immediate post-war situation in Germany was chaotic, notwithstanding the declared overall aims of the Allies and their measures. There were loopholes and uncoordinated decisions. In this climate Staudte's application for a film production company was granted by the British, but they would not consider allowing him to actually make a film! He went to the Americans with his request.

The American cultural attaché was Peter van Eyck, [2] who told Staudte: 'The only films that will be made here in the next five years will be made by us!' This quote demonstrates two things: First, there was the sincere desire on the part of the Americans to lead the way in the democratisation of Germany. Part of this, they felt, was to expose its population to alternatives to the propaganda films that they had been watching for years. Second, there was the backlog of Hollywood films which could not be shown in Nazi Germany (see also chapter 3) and which the Americans now wanted to be distributed in Germany as soon as possible and in large numbers. This dual approach, democratisation together with commercial interests, characterised the American influence in post-war Germany. While a system of production and distribution licences developed slowly in the western sectors, productions from outside Germany filled the vacuum. However, some enlightened people realised quite early on that German audiences could be reached best by films made by their compatriots. Erich Pommer was one of those enlightened people. [3] However, at the time when Staudte applied for his production licence the arrogance of the western Allies was so prevalent that they refused to even consider the seeds of anti-fascism emanating from Germany itself.

In the Soviet sector the situation was different: The Soviet authorities granted Staudte's wish to make the first German anti-fascist film. This decision is consistent with the main preoccupations of the Soviet administration: the eradication of Nazism and consequently the re-education of the German people towards (socialist) democracy. The steps towards these aims taken in the Soviet zone were swifter and further-reaching than in all the other zones of occupation. Of course, very soon after the war the former 'Allies' became embroiled in Cold War activities and from then onwards film production in East and West Germany took very different directions, in line with political developments. (See also our chapter on *Spur der Steine*.)

At the same time as preparing for his first post-war feature film, Staudte got involved in the organisation of a 'Film-Aktiv' in the Soviet sector of Berlin. This association of several German film-makers paved the way for East German film production very early on after the end of World War II. (Please note: In this chapter, which occupies a transitional period of post-war German history, we have used the term 'East' Germany to denote the Soviet controlled part of Germany, before and after its formation as the state of 'East Germany' (the GDR)). As mentioned before, most of the infrastructure had been destroyed or was not accessible, such as the UFA studios at Babelsberg. However, it was discovered that the Tobis film studios at Berlin-Johannisthal (situated in the Soviet sector of Berlin) had not been bombed out and could be restored. The first Film-Aktiv project was a newsreel called *Der Augenzeuge* (*The Eye Witness*), which was in deliberate contrast to Nazi newsreels, i.e. it was sober and democratic in its reporting, avoiding any propaganda and 'noise', and with no flashy visuals. [4] The German population was hungry for visual information about current events, which this newsreel provided, and at the same time it was a cornerstone in the re-education of the population. Dealing with the Nazi past could ultimately only be done by Germans for Germans. In this, it seems that the Soviet occupation forces had more trust in German initiatives, at least in the early years, than their western counterparts.

The old Babelsberg film studios which had for three decades been the centre of film production in Germany, during the final years of the monarchy, in the Weimar Republic and during National Socialism (see also our chapters on *Metropolis* and *Triumph des Willens*) were gradually restored, and on 17 May, 1946, a new film production company was inaugurated by the Soviet administration. The mission of DEFA (Deutsche Film AG) was spelt out clearly in the inaugural speech: 'The film company DEFA has important issues to resolve. The most important one is fighting for the democratic reconstruction of Germany together with tackling the education of the German people, particularly youth, for real democracy and humanity' (inaugural speech by Major Tulpanow).

However, even before a functioning film production company was in place, Wolfgang Staudte's determination to make his film resulted, on 15 March, 1946, in a contract between his own 'Wolfgang Staudte Film Production' (which, as outlined earlier, had been licensed by the British) and the 'German Central Administration for Public Education' (which led to the setting up of DEFA). He did not waste any more time and began shooting the next day. So it happened that Wolfgang Staudte became the first post-war

German film-maker. For the next few years he would live in West Berlin and commute to the Soviet sector to make films in what was soon (in 1949) to become the newly formed GDR, an anomaly, to be sure, but not quite as unusual at the time as one might think: East Germany had not cut itself off completely in those days.

Apart from the extraordinary circumstances of its origins, *Mörder* is noteworthy for two central characteristics: the depiction of Berlin in ruins, and the exploration of 'German guilt', which is at the centre of the narrative. Both these issues are linked by the film's visual style, whose realism is infused with symbolism through the use of expressionist techniques as evident in German films of the early 1920s. [5]

Nothing is more real than real locations. Staudte filmed in a Berlin that had been ravaged by the war, in particular during the battle of Berlin (which is discussed in some detail in our chapter on *Der Untergang*) in the final days of World War II. All over Germany the situation was similar. More than half of the living space in German cities was destroyed. The infrastructure, such as roads, motorways, and bridges over rivers, had been bombed, many of them by the retreating German army. The Allied forces ruled over the smallest detail such as clearing the rubble from destroyed buildings, who should do it when, and how the population should be penalised if they did not comply. Resources were scarce and made even more so by the influx of refugees from the German eastern territories, which had been annexed by the Nazis and then lost in the war. To make matters worse, the winter of 1946-7 was the harshest in years, the effects of which were a complete breakdown of resources and infrastructure, affecting food and energy supplies in particular. Without material help from the occupying forces many Germans would not have survived that winter.

Germany had also lost large numbers of its population, above all men who had died as soldiers, others who were still prisoners of war (more than 8 million), and a great number of missing persons, more than 1.5 million. This situation left many widows and orphans who had to fend for themselves. In every German city women took a leading role in clearing the debris from destroyed buildings: 'Trümmerfrauen' (Rubble women), wearing scarves over their heads and carrying buckets, were a familiar sight everywhere, and can be seen in archive footage [6] and in the so-called 'rubble films', a genre of narrative film that developed in the post-war period, between 1946–1950, alongside 'rubble literature' which focused mainly on the disorientation of returning soldiers in a country faced with material, mental, and psychological breakdown. The main character of *Mörder* shares many similarities with post-war literary figures. (See also our chapter on *Die Blechtrommel*.)

Mörder depicts disorientation and deprivation very well, and it adds to these sentiments the depression and helplessness felt by many in those first months after the war. Again and again, the film's displaced characters are seen amongst the ruins of Berlin. Particularly in the early part of the film they seem to be in a state of shock and paralysis. We are then shown the attempts of survivors at creating new homes with very basic means. Here the film focuses on one block of flats and its inhabitants, in particular on two people with very different approaches to life after war, who are brought together by scarcity of accommodation: There is Dr. Mertens, who used to be a paediatrician before fighting on the Eastern front, who has returned from the war and has occupied a flat that he found empty on his return. Then there is a young woman, Susanne Wallner, who has been liberated from a concentration camp and who is returning to her flat – the

apartment that Dr. Mertens has occupied. The film opens with shocking images of crosses on makeshift graves in the middle of the city, above them ruined buildings. In the next scene we are witness to the confusion of Susanne's arrival on a train full of refugees and returning soldiers, a very familiar scene in Germany at the end of the war.

It becomes clear very early on that Susanne has a life-affirming approach; she embraces a new beginning and believes in the value of work to achieve this. Susanne is played by the newcomer Hildegard Knef, who brought simplicity and a fresh face to German film, in complete contrast to NS film divas. In her role she does indeed represent a 'Trümmerfrau' – pragmatic, energetic, and hard-working – even though her task in *Mörder* is primarily to support the leading man.

Dr. Mertens is a man locked in the trauma of his war experiences, full of moral outrage and pain. His inability to communicate and to work, his propensity for drinking, his drifting, his volatility and sentimentality, are the personality traits with which we are confronted over long stretches of the film. Together with Susanne Wallner we are initially left wondering what his traumatic experience was. Visually the film uses stark images of ruins and jagged contours of broken windows to depict the real post-war situation in general and his mental state in particular. Susanne's attempts at helping him are at first rebuffed, then, gradually, he begins to find access to his emotions. But still the shadows of the past are with him, signified by chiaroscuro cinematography - stark black and white, strong contrasts of light and shade, shafts of light penetrating the dark. Staudte uses and intensifies the authentic setting and invests it with strong symbolism to express the state of mind of the main character.

Disorientation and alienation are conveyed by oblique camera angles – low, high, and canted angles. Extreme camera positions and angles express extreme perspectives of extreme situations. The characters are seen mostly in shadow (with the exception of Susanne who is always clearly lit); grills, bars, broken windows and mirrors symbolise the destruction of war and the trapped status of the characters. These expressionist techniques are not only an important part of the narrative, but also a deliberate return to 1920s film-making (see also chapter 1 of this book), which, we may remind ourselves, has in common with *Mörder* the fact that it captured to a certain extent the disorientation of a previous war, World War I. Staudte's approach of mixing realism and symbolism effectively also marks a deliberate turning away from the lavish UFA productions of the Third Reich.

Another character serves as a contact point for both main characters, the watchmaker Mondschein who lives and works on the ground floor of the block of flats. He reflects and comments on the main characters' very different preoccupations, conveying to them his belief that really being alive means having a purpose in life. For him this purpose is to work tirelessly while he waits for the return of his son from the war. In contrast to Mondschein, profiteers who unscrupulously exploited the disorientation of survivors are represented by the 'psychic' Timm. He makes money by exploiting their need for certainty: turning to religion and the occult.

Christmas 1945 is drawing nearer and with it crisis point is reached. Gradually we find out that Mertens' repressed and unresolved trauma lies in events of three years ago, when, on Christmas Eve of 1942, his unit was stationed on the Eastern front, and when his commanding officer, Major Brückner, ordered the execution of a whole village of civilians, including women and children. Mertens is not just unable to forget the scene he witnessed or to forgive Brückner, who represents the 'murderers' of the film title, but also unable to forgive himself for his own cowardice in not trying harder to prevent it. Staudte raises here the issue of war crimes and the guilt not just of the perpetrators but of those complicit with them, the majority who were 'following orders'. And although Staudte himself never had to carry a gun during the war, he felt the need to exorcise his own demons which stemmed from his tacit acceptance of a dictatorial regime in order to survive.

For a large part of the story Mertens is convinced that Brückner died in action. However, Susanne finds out that he is still alive, in Berlin, and a successful businessman. She does not know of the traumatic events in which the two men were involved and sets up a meeting between them. The contrasts between the two male characters is worked out in their respective status, their character traits, and their demeanour: Mertens has not been able to get his life together, he is variously brooding, aggressive or self-pitying, Brückner has no awareness of his guilty past; because of his insensitivity he has no psychological damage, he is gregarious, the authoritarian head of a traditional family. He is already doing good business by turning steel helmets into saucepans, a fact that he cheerfully comments on: 'What does it matter whether you turn steel helmets into saucepans, or saucepans into steel helmets, the main thing is to make a living!'. His untroubled attitude is given shocking expression when he blithely consumes a sandwich wrapped in newspaper whose headline speaks of the millions of deaths in concentration camps. While Mertens is determined to confront guilt and to avenge the crimes committed by unscrupulous 'murderers', Brückner is unrepentant and unthinking: 'Who wants to be confronted with these ruins day-in day-out. We want to rebuild Germany and have fun.' [7] This opportunist attitude only increases Mertens' moral outrage. Many Germans at the time must have had such reactions. We are in no doubt whose side the film is on: Brückner's quickly-found 'normality' makes us shiver and sympathise with Mertens' outrage. A career such as Brückner's was, however, not unique in post-war Germany. In fact, Staudte had a good sense of things to come in the next few years, when many Nazi sympathisers or even ex-Party members rose to the top very quickly in West Germany.

The contrasts between Mertens and Brückner are presented very effectively by abrupt intercutting, e.g. between the life-saving operation that Mertens performs and Brückner's celebration of Christmas.

The two Christmases are linked by dissolving flashbacks. Thus Brückner is relentlessly linked to the deaths for which he is responsible.

Mertens' character development intensifies to such an extent that the only avenue that seems open to him in the end is to avenge the deaths and to overcome his own implication by killing Brückner. During his first attempt he is prevented from doing so by a desperate mother whose child is about to die from asphyxiation. He follows his duty as a doctor to save a life instead of taking one. On the second occasion he has cornered Brückner and confronts him with his crimes, casting a huge shadow on the wall behind the 'accused' in a scene whose fatal end could be the solution to his overshadowed past.

This time it is Susanne who intervenes and who convinces him that Brückner should be tried in a court of law. 'We must not be judges', she says, to which he replies: 'But it is our duty to accuse.' Staudte's original ending for the film entailed Mertens actually killing

Brückner. However, the Russian cultural officer intervened with the justification that nobody wanted to support vigilantism or personal revenge in the aftermath of World War II, and that the guilty should be tried by a judicial court.

Interestingly, at the same time as the release of *Die Mörder sind unter uns*, which accuses a German officer, the Nuremberg trials, in which officers of the NS regime were brought to justice, ended. In the Nuremberg trials, which started on 20 November, 1945, 24 individuals and six collectives termed 'criminal organisations' were prosecuted. The criminal organisations included the SS and the SA. The accused were tried for a range of crimes: conspiracy against peace, crimes against peace, war crimes, and crimes against humanity; or, in more concrete terms, murder, abuse, deportation, persecution and taking of human life. The main war crimes trial focused on the elite of the NS regime. *Mörder* and Nuremberg echo each other in their respective approach to the question of guilt: Just as *Mörder* emphasises individual responsibility, the Nuremberg trials consistently examined the contribution of each accused, and never made any general assumptions about collective guilt. The trials were also the beginning of informing and educating the public about the NS dictatorship, an issue that was very much on Staudte's mind.

In his film Staudte makes clear that the often cited 'Zero Hour' at the end of the Nazi dictatorship did not exist: Where others wanted to forget and start with a 'clean' slate, he spoke up for taking responsibility and against suppressing memories of the past. The film was a modest critical success, but not well received by contemporary German audiences. The bleakness, the lack of entertainment value made watching it too hard for most people. It is perhaps understandable that the German people wanted some relief from their difficult post-war existence and were not ready to confront issues relating to their recent past. Nowadays the film is seen as a small masterpiece, as a brave and very early attempt to raise awareness, an artistic contribution to social and political questions. Its limitations have also been pointed out: Compared to Italian neo-realism, which developed at the same time and whose settings were similar ruins to those of *Mörder,* it does not explore the wider social context, it stops short of a vision for the future. Its characters are trapped in their own mental states, whereas in neo-realist films they show us ways forward with a new sense of the present and with possibilities for the future. [8]

Another criticism involves the incredible loveliness of Susanne Wallner, who appears to have escaped her concentration camp without a scratch and who seems to be there only to support the man in a totally selfless fashion: the conventional female role that was not an accurate representation of women, who had to fend for themselves in post-war Germany. This somewhat unrealistic portrayal may be connected to Staudte's own family, or more precisely, his mother, who died when he was very young. Staudte was not an intellectual analyst of the roots of fascism, and he was not a communist, but he was a pacifist who spoke with his heart and tackled uncomfortable issues. But the role of women in contemporary society was not one of them. In the first few years after the war Staudte's natural professional home was in East Germany, at DEFA, which was the only place where he could raise the issues that preoccupied him, while West Germany's film culture developed towards entertainment and the often sentimental reassurances of the 'Heimat' film (for more on this see our chapter on *Heimat*). His next film, *Rotation* (1948), another anti-fascist film, was much more confident than *Mörder*, and despite its difficult subject of following a Germany family through the years of National Socialism it does not make any sweeping judgements about the involvement of ordinary Germans with National Socialism. It is a very good example of DEFA's early anti-fascist film production, at a time when Stalinist dogma and party loyalty were not yet paramount. However, gradually DEFA developed into a state-controlled film production company, leaning towards the dogma of 'socialist realism'. Staudte made one more film at the East German studios, *Der Untertan* (*Man of Straw*, 1951), then went on to work in West Germany, having been criticised for his lack of 'class consciousness' and his perceived 'formalism', which went against growing 'socialist-realist' tendencies at DEFA. *Der Untertan* was mostly ignored in the West at the time of its release, a fact that demonstrates Staudte's difficulty in establishing himself there. Staudte stubbornly believed in a culturally united Germany. He did not want to accept the actual division of his country which became obvious even before the two German states were formed. His career, like no other film-maker's, shows the early failure of any attempts at cooperation and common purpose across the border.

Despite criticisms of his early work, Staudte continued to be a thorn in the flesh of West German society with his films throughout the fifties and sixties. Within the Federal Republic, which was dominated by conservative and restorative forces and by economic prosperity in those decades, he did not give up the central theme of moral and historical responsibility that he felt. However, for a long time his oeuvre was perceived as somewhat ambivalent: Having lived in both Germanys he was a suspected communist in the West and a casualty of capitalism in the East. It was only much later, in fact not until his death in 1984, that he was appreciated for his attempts at historical continuity. Now his commitment to uncomfortable truths, his obsession with confronting and assessing personal experiences with regard to their moral implications, both for himself and others, is recognised. Staudte could have been a possible father figure to the later generation of film-makers of the New German Cinema, who shared his preoccupation with the recent past. Maybe his relatively obscure status at the time, compounded by the fact that he worked mainly for West German television in his later years, contributed to the lack of interest among young German film-makers. Quite possibly, also, they were so determined to break with their previous generation that they ignored him for that reason. (There is more on the issue of fathers and breaks with tradition in our chapters on *Aguirre, Angst essen Seele auf, Die Blechtrommel, Heimat,* and *Der Himmel über Berlin.*)

Finally in this chapter, let us pick up the thread of the early years of DEFA and contrast them with the later and final years. DEFA took over the former UFA studios in Potsdam-Babelsberg. The UFA was renamed, and it became the central and again centralised film production company of the GDR. Around 700 films were made there, including 150 children's films. And again, not all of them were propaganda films. However, soon state control and heavy censorship set in. Many films were made but then disappeared into the vaults, and could only be seen after the end of socialist rule in the GDR. You can read more about this in our chapter on *Spur der Steine*.

We have already mentioned that during the first few years DEFA worked with a variety of artists and craftspeople from a variety of backgrounds (East and West). *Die Mörder sind unter uns* is a good example of this. We already know that Staudte lived in the West and that Hildegard Knef, the female lead, was a West German actress. Her casting constituted a definite break with the past: She was virtually unknown and her young, fresh face was ideal for a film that wanted to break with Nazi film-making traditions as typified by UFA. Such were the pragmatic personnel decisions within DEFA in the first few years of its existence. Staudte himself assesses positively the freedom he experienced while working there: He did not face any censorship; he and his crew were trusted to make the right decisions. He also appreciated the fact that within DEFA people worked together. There were no competitive issues, everybody focused on the job to be done, on a new beginning. No personal vanities, no commercial pressures got in the way of vital work. The political aims of those early years chimed with his own: anti-fascism was high on the agenda and anti-fascist films were the kind of film he wanted to make. In fact, the one principle that governed DEFA at the time of its inception and throughout its existence was anti-fascism. Very soon after the breakdown of the Nazi regime, East Germans sought to address this issue, which was almost completely ignored in the West. They were determined to make a break with the recent past. DEFA artists were united in this. Later on in the history of the GDR, when ideology became more prevalent, and censorship sought to stamp out any critical reflection on the present, film makers turned again and again to the topic of anti-fascism. It was then a declared aim and at the same time a safe outlet for creative urges.

Because of its close alignment to politics, DEFA history is at the same time a history of East Germany under Soviet influence. From the moment of the initial division into zones of occupation in 1945, the Soviets exercised very tight control over the part of Germany that they occupied. This control manifested itself officially long before the division of Germany into two separate states, when, in 1946, a new political party was formed, the SED (the Socialist Unity Party), which came about as an amalgamation of the SPD (the original German Social Democratic Party) and the KPD (the German Communist Party). Very soon after the beginning, East German film production was centralised at DEFA, and was gradually brought under the leadership of directors loyal to the party and controlled by Soviet dogma. Unfortunately, at the end of the GDR this fact was used as the central argument for the assessment of DEFA films, namely that they all were propaganda and therefore not of high artistic quality. We now know that this was not the case and that many fine films were made at DEFA. During the lifetime of DEFA, the huge film production complex signified many things to the many people who were employed there: For some it was their home, even their family; for others it meant bureaucracy, betrayal, and selling off their individuality.

It is interesting to bookend *Mörder*, DEFA's first film, with *Die Architekten* (*The Architects*, Peter Kahane, 1990), DEFA's final film. A brief comparison between the two films allows us to contextualise the beginning and the end of an ideological experiment. Like *Mörder*, *Die Architekten* was made in a transitional period, like *Mörder* it dealt with a legacy – here the legacy of GDR ideology and reality. Like *Mörder* the film is a critical reflection of a dictatorial system. In contrast to the energetic new beginning surrounding the production of *Mörder* and its hopeful ending, however, *Die Architekten* shows the dead end to which this new beginning has led. It describes the fate of a group of architects whose efforts to create a good environment for people to live in are thwarted, for ideological and economic reasons. The film's characters, who once believed in socialism, are in despair about this development.

With the end of the GDR in 1990, DEFA was also dismantled and subsequently, after reunification, privatised. The whole Babelsberg complex now produces national and international films. Today it also houses the HFF (Academy of Film and Television) 'Konrad Wolf' – named after one of the most influential East German film-makers.

FOOTNOTES

[1] The 'Volkssturm' was the final, desperate attempt of the regime to enlist every male who was not fighting yet, the very young, the old, the sick, to throw themselves at the encroaching Russian army.

[2] A German actor who emigrated to the United States in the 1930s. The Americans brought with them many German émigrés in their effort to restructure and re-educate the German population. This seemed an obvious choice, given their usually strong opposition to Hitler and their ability to speak German.

[3] Erich Pommer, the former head of UFA in the 1920s, who was part of the American occupying force, admitted as much.

[4] This newsreel existed throughout the lifetime of the GDR, and during that time it changed from being pluralistic to being strictly censored, like so many things in the GDR.

[5] An American film style of the same period, film noir, shared certain characteristics with *Mörder*: disorientated protagonists, the fate of returning war veteran, visual style. See in particular *Crossfire* (Edvard Dmytryk, 1946) and *The Third Man* (Carol Reed, 1949), set in post-war Vienna.

[6] In Wim Wenders' *Der Himmel über Berlin*, for instance.

[7] In his opportunistic approach to life, Brückner could be compared to Grubitz, the unscrupulous Stasi officer in *Das Leben der Anderen*.

[8] See for example *Germania Anno Zero* (*Germany Year Zero*, Roberto Rossellini, 1946). In this context *Mörder* has been seen as a missed opportunity.

[9] See the illuminating book *Spur der Filme*, which contains interviews with former DEFA personnel.

[10] We are fully aware that we cannot do this fine film justice here, but recommend it highly to be watched on its own terms.

CHAPTER 5: REAL EXISTING SOCIALISM: *SPUR DER STEINE (TRACES OF STONES, 1965)*

This chapter's key film was made by the East German DEFA film studios, like the previous chapter's focus, *Die Mörder sind unter uns*. Together with *Das Leben der Anderen*, which is the subject of our final chapter, it very openly deals with and reflects political issues. Like *Das Leben der Anderen* it gives insight into the political situation in the former East Germany and its power over GDR citizens. Unlike *Das Leben der Anderen*, however, *Spur der Steine* was made during the lifetime of the GDR, more precisely in the decade following the building of the Berlin Wall and in a particularly repressive year within the GDR. Its specific interest lies in its vivid depiction of socialism as it really existed, and in the fact that this depiction was considered so dangerous by the censors that they banned the film completely. Thankfully it was not destroyed, but resurfaced after the reunification of Germany and is available to us now as an excellent film and a rare historical document.

Since the historical context of the film's production and subsequent ban is so significant, we will begin this chapter with a short overview of GDR history and that of its state-controlled film production company, the DEFA. For an outline of the beginnings of DEFA, please see our previous chapter on *Die Mörder sind unter uns*.

From 1949 onwards Germany was effectively divided into two states: West Germany became the Federal Republic of Germany (FRG) and East Germany became the German Democratic Republic (GDR). The FRG's status as a member of the Western democracies and the GDR being a member of the Eastern bloc constituted a clear division along political lines and meant a further step in the direction of the Cold War. For DEFA, which had produced films since 1946, the next major step was that it was brought under state control, which it was in 1952. Its official status was that of a 'Volkseigener Betrieb (VEB)', which is usually translated as 'People-Owned Enterprise', the name for all of the GDR's state-controlled businesses. It became the centre of film production of the GDR. However, we must remember that the borders were not yet sealed off completely, and West German film directors, actors, and other film personnel used the studios to make films, and East/West collaboration was still possible. Only after the Berlin Wall had been built in 1961 was isolation complete.

With the advent of the Cold War a decisive change happened in East Germany in the shape of tougher implementation of communist doctrine. Propaganda became prevalent. From 1952 onwards all film production at DEFA had to follow the doctrine of 'socialist realism'. This meant that all forces of film production had to conform to the projection of a positive attitude towards socialism, concentrating on the 'positive workers' (or farm labourers') hero' in its representation of reality, a hero not plagued by self-doubt or any other doubt! Stylistic artistry (e.g. unusual camera angles, rapid editing etc.) was not desired and even rejected as 'formalism'. [1] Reality had to be simple and straightforward. It cannot be stressed enough that from now on every political shift in the Soviet Union had a direct effect on the situation in the GDR in general and DEFA in particular. Thus the history of DEFA is also always a mirror of the political history of East Germany.

A very clear signal as to who was calling the shots in the GDR was given during the attempted workers' revolt of June, 1953, which began with strikes over the raising of productivity norms and soon spread to political demands for free speech and democratic elections, and which ended with forceful and bloody intervention by Soviet tanks. This successful show of force, and Stalin's death in the same year, resulted in a more liberal attitude in East Germany for a while, and by extension also at DEFA. Generally, more 'pure' entertainment was admissible in East German cinemas, such as Western European films, which were now shown for the first time. But, the line was drawn at the import of American films. In the five years following the uprising of 1953 and Stalin's death, DEFA films showed a new development: details of everyday reality of the GDR were represented; for example, there were a number of films portraying the lives of young people in Berlin. [2] New themes found their way into East German films which incorporated socialist principles but went beyond the narrow idea of 'socialist realism': solidarity and hope, innocence, authenticity, open-mindedness, life-affirming attitudes.

This changed in 1958 with a film conference of the SED (the Socialist Unity Party of the GDR). The perceived 'revisionism' of the films of recent years was harshly criticised.

From now on hard-line socialism was prescribed: 'Heroes of the fight of the working class and their party' and 'the active fight for communism' were on the agenda. Intervention through censorship measures undermined any representation of nuanced everyday reality. Strict propaganda became the norm.

During all these twists and turns of film production at DEFA one theme was always welcome: anti-fascism. A new generation of film-makers, among them Frank Beyer, who had studied at the Prague film academy, started their careers with anti-fascist films. Towards the end of the fifties, in another slight political shift, and within the prescribed themes, the young film-makers were able to reclaim some artistic freedom and a certain amount of individual stylistic expression.

Between 1949 and 1961 huge numbers of citizens, among them many artists, fled East Germany because of the oppressive nature of the political system of their country, and because of poor living standards when compared to those in West Germany. This exodus was a source of worry and embarrassment for the GDR regime. To stem the tide of 'defectors' the Berlin Wall (the 'anti-fascist security wall', as it was called in the East) was built in 1961, which closed off the very last border crossing towards the West. One of the startling facts of the reception of the Wall is that it was supported by most GDR artists who had remained in the East and who still believed in the ideal of socialism. Somehow there was the hope that this decisive enclosure would make the concentrated fight for a 'better socialism' possible and that this would result in greater artistic freedom. This hope was soon to be dashed. In fact, the sixties became the most repressive period for GDR film-making and the other arts, during a time when the GDR was in the process of establishing itself as a socialist state and did not tolerate any dissent. Even then, though, once in a while an interesting, even critical film slipped through the ever-tightening net of censorship. *Spur der Steine*, unfortunately, was one of those more nuanced films that did not escape the censors' interference.

Frank Beyer's whole career is a poignant example of the political and cultural developments in the GDR in the 1960s and beyond. As mentioned before, he, like other film-makers of his generation, started out making anti-fascist films, such as *Nackt unter Wölfen* (*Naked Among Wolves*, 1963), about resistance and solidarity at the Buchenwald concentration camp. His *Königskinder* (1962) was formally quite adventurous, unusual for a DEFA film at the time. His *Karbid und Sauerampfer* (*Carbide and Sorrel*, 1963) conformed to socialist principles in so far as it focused on a working class hero who procures much-needed raw materials for his employer. What makes the film interesting is that it is a free-spirited comedy with even an anarchic streak. Within the comic aspects of the film, Beyer managed to smuggle in the mocking of uniforms, both American and Soviet. Sadly, the relative artistic freedom and critical tenor evident in these early films of his were to be suppressed strongly not long afterwards.

In fact, almost the complete film production of 1965 suffered from one kind of censorship or another. Because the GDR was a satellite state of the Soviet Union there was strong dependence on events in the USSR, and every shift in ideology or change in leadership had consequences for the socialist states associated with the USSR. The decisive and disastrous move came from the 11th party plenary session of the Central Committee of the SED in December 1965, which forced through the most extreme censorship measures in the whole history of German film – including those taken during National Socialist times. The meeting was originally convened with an agenda on economic issues and reforms. This was the time of Khrushchev's death and the beginning of Brezhnev's rule in the USSR. It was also a time when it became clear that the totally centralised apparatus had become counterproductive for the economy and that changes had to happen. Khrushchev had started a process of cautious loosening of doctrine, but Brezhnev was against all reform.

During the 11th plenary session there were huge differences of opinion as to the direction the East German economy should take, even between individual members of the Central Committee. There are strong indications that because of these insurmountable differences surrounding economic issues the focus of the session turned to culture. A kind of war by proxy ensued, which was subsequently called 'a deliberate mud-slinging match' by affected artists. The meeting turned into a nightmare for the GDR's leading exponents of literature and film, who were attacked by party hardliners. Consequently, some writers had their books taken off the shelves, and this is also what happened to most films from that year. In the central party archive of the SED there is a quote from the then president of the GDR, Walter Ulbricht: 'Let us see who forces whom and who determines what in the German Democratic Republic.' Such a threatening statement shows clearly that the political powers elevated dogma over realism and were unable and unwilling to acknowledge real-life concerns. It also shows the rigidity and paranoia inherent in a totalitarian system.

Beyer's film *Spur der Steine* (1965) examined GDR socialist reality too closely and was therefore perceived as dangerous to the system. In the film the workers are triumphant, as required by socialist principles. However, their hero is a rebellious head of a team of joiners who leads his people into a strike against chaos and bureaucracy on the building site. Moreover, the Party is represented, albeit sympathetically, by the irreconcilable differences between two functionaries: as the contrast between progress and dogma. The censorship judgement on the film concludes: 'It shows a distorted picture of our socialist reality, which should be the struggle of the working class and their victorious Party.'

Considering this damning statement it is surprising that the film was actually completed and released, although generally at DEFA the various censorship measures could strike at any given time during the production process. Many other DEFA films never went beyond treatment, script, or the first days of shooting before they were banned. The fate of *Spur der Steine* was that it was taken out of distribution only a few days after its premiere, after so-called 'disturbances', which were in reality protests that had been organised by Party officials at a screening of the film. This provided the pretext for suppressing the film completely, even though it was an adaptation of a very successful and highly praised workers' novel and had been earmarked as the GDR's contribution to the Karlovy Vary film festival. The film can be seen as DEFA's last major attempt to view the country's political climate critically. In the infamous year of 1965 it was the film that drew most vitriolic contempt from the Central Committee of the Party and that proved to be the final nail in the coffin for Beyer himself and the directorate of DEFA, who were summarily dismissed and replaced by party loyalists. In this repressive climate the careers of several film-makers were destroyed for good; others were forced to work in other areas of cultural production.

Konrad Wolf, the most celebrated GDR film-maker and the then president of the country's Academy of Arts, noted at the time with particular reference to *Spur der Steine* that the greatest disaster in the history of the GDR's feature film production was being inflicted on its artists by sweeping censorship measures. Wolf went on more generally and critically to voice his misgivings about the current ideological climate in his country, if all topical films were deemed 'unsuitable' by the political elite.

One of the recurring debates conducted in GDR times was whether films should be 'close to the people' (i.e. stylistically conservative) or whether they should be allowed to tell their stories with more stylistic freedom. The latter was often attacked as 'formalism', i.e. the act of placing 'style over content'. This latter charge was not and could not be laid at Frank Beyer's door. In *Spur der Steine* the observing, neutral camera work never draws attention to itself. However, the film was criticised for not showing the struggle of the working classes in complete harmony with their Party's ideals. In actual fact Frank Beyer was a loyal member of the Party who believed in the socialist cause, but, like others, he perceived shortcomings in the way that socialist ideals were being put into practice in his home country.

The censorship measures that affected *Spur der Steine* also included Frank Beyer's ban from DEFA for years, which meant that he was in effect prohibited from making films, since DEFA was the only place in the GDR were you could make films for the cinema. He worked for the theatre for a number of years, then for television, and was only able to make his next cinema film in 1974 – *Jakob der Lügner* (*Jacob the Liar*), in which he returned to the topic of anti-fascism. But the hardliners within the system never forgave him completely, and he was never again able to find regular work at DEFA.

Now let us look at the bone of contention more closely to see how it could have caused such controversy. *Spur der Steine* is a literary adaptation with the focus on events on a building site of a power station. The protagonists are three people who work on the site. There is Werner Horrath, a representative of the Party who checks up on the implementation of the (political) orders from above and who keeps an eye on the employees at the site – a common feature of industrial relations in the GDR. Kati Klee is an engineer, and Hannes Balla is the leader of a team of joiners. Each of them believes in the importance of the work that they are doing for their country and their people. They are determined to solve the numerous problems on the site, each of them within their own brief and with their individual beliefs. After confrontations and conflicts which arise from their different status, from sexual tensions, and from directives from the Party, they realise that, despite their differences, they are effectively working towards the same aim. They come to respect each other.

Spur der Steine is an important historical document of conditions in the GDR during the 1960s, giving us valuable insight into the political and human difficulties of the time. That it is so persuasive is in no small measure due to the honesty and authenticity in the way in which it portrays its characters and follows them through an equally convincing story. All the characters, even minor ones, are well-drawn. Even the cameos are 'real' people, not one-dimensional, as we usually encounter them in other films. It may well have been precisely these multi-facetted characters – 'human' in their beliefs and fallacies, their strengths and weaknesses – that flew in the face of ideological dogma, which would have required party-loyal, clear-cut models.

Let us now 'trace' the film, all the while bearing in mind that it represents Beyer's own ideas of socialism, that it is a historical document and a well-told story. The narrative is not linear, but unfolds on different time levels, linked by a variety of flashbacks. There are two distinct official meetings at the building site: one involving the directorate of the enterprise and representatives of the Party who, in a kind of tribunal, sit in judgement on Horrath for 'political-ideological failure'. The other meeting is a workers' meeting, which must have taken place before the tribunal. At first we do not know why these meetings are taking place. Beyer uses the narrative device of gradually uncovering events in the following way: questions posed at the meetings lead to the depiction of past events that give answers to those questions. Gradually a whole network of events and interrelationships unfolds. This approach makes for a complex narrative structure. At the same time Beyer shows the importance of the 'group' (as signified by the meetings) as opposed to the 'individual' (whose actions are being discussed) and the way individuals were expected to accept responsibility for their actions, again through discussions within the group. During the meetings the various positions within the groups and their respective ideological backgrounds are successfully juxtaposed.

The events taking place on the building site before and after the meetings are told in an arrangement of flashbacks. The new Party representative Horrath and Kati Klee, the engineer, arrive more or less at the same time on the building site. Both of them are confronted with Hannes Balla, the larger-than-life joiner team leader who is admired and adored by his men and who is also recognised as the best worker on the site. Because of this he gets away with a lot of his outrageous behaviour: he takes all kinds of liberties, such as drinking and fighting; he shows off in front of his men by challenging and alienating the newcomers.

There is one extraordinary scene in which, after drinking heavily in the middle of the day, he leads his men to the village pond, and they undress and jump in the water. They ignore the policeman's cries of 'public nuisance'; Balla says: 'The village policeman has no authority to tell us anything, he is not from the water police.' They even start

singing, then round up the ducks, after which they pull the policeman into the water with them. It is easily understandable how such a scene could have provoked an outcry in Party circles – mocking authority was not a socialist virtue. (Ridiculing authority had been present in Beyer's *Karbid und Sauerampfer,* as mentioned before. Despite the serious issues that Beyer tackles, he does show a sense of humour.)

Balla displays sexist behaviour towards the new female engineer. In his work he also uses unorthodox methods to rectify the horrendous planning errors and to secure building materials for his team. In fact, Beyer cunningly sets Balla up as an obnoxious character, and at this point the viewer of the film might be forgiven for feeling antagonism towards him, wondering how he can possibly get away with such behaviour. This view changes gradually, when it emerges that he is really a very caring, if flawed, character, who has the best interests of his own men, his work, and later Kati and Horrath, at heart. However, in the first few scenes of the film Beyer focuses on the contrast between the three protagonists and their respective approaches to solving the problems on site.

In a planned economy such as the GDR was, orders come from above in minute detail. Everything is controlled centrally, down to the delivery of a single screw. The first criticism of these orders, which are followed to the letter on the site (and by extension in other areas of the economy), is voiced when Balla says with regard to the delivery of the wrong parts: 'What them up there mess up, us down here have to put right.' The 'putting right' consists of 'highway robbery' in that Balla and his gang hold up trucks destined for a different part of the building site and divert them to their own work area. Balla explains to Horrath that they are forced to do this in order to be able to accomplish their task. At first Horrath, as the Party representative, is not welcomed by the gang – Balla does not accept the Party, he never takes his hat off to anyone. Horrath has several discussions with Balla, trying to eradicate what he perceives as 'anarchism'. 'It's not anarchism,' Balla says, 'we organise and help ourselves.' Horrath reasons: 'There will always be shortages, but your methods are not acceptable.' However, gradually they come to respect each other, when Horrath realises that errors in projection have been made, that the wrong documents are being sent to the site – 'the plan is sacrosanct', says the cynical Balla. These scenes highlight the problems that a centrally planned economy with not the slightest flexibility can cause. All those responsible want the power plant to be built, they want to succeed in their efforts, but they are thwarted by mismanagement and the 'sacrosanct' plan.

We see state socialism at work in many scenes, such as the 'reward ceremony', which takes place regularly at the site. The directors declare the need to 'move forward for our socialist cause'; there are awards for the most productive workers. Balla is not honoured because of his lack of discipline, although he and his gang are the strongest performers. Horrath defends Balla. He realises the team leader's strength of commitment and tells the site directorate: 'We need people like Balla.' A weary director responds by doubting that putting trust in people improves them.

Kati Klee, the engineer, achieves continuation of the building work by reallocating materials. She is against resignation and obstinacy alike. But neither does she have definitive answers as to the problems caused by bureaucracy and mismanagement. Gradually Balla falls in love with Kati, just as she has fallen in love with Horrath. Behind the scenes Balla uses his influence with people in the village and manages very quickly to secure a private room for Kati – something that was unheard of in GDR socialist reality. It is referred to jokingly as 'Wohnraumlenkung Balla' - 'controlled allocation of habitation, Balla style'. The term 'Wohnraumlenkung' refers to the way in which living space was allocated in the GDR, centrally, like everything, ostensibly according to need. [3] Because there was an acute shortage of housing, however, people sometimes had to wait for years before they were able to get remotely the space that they needed.

The rivalry between Horrath and Balla continues, now for the affections of Kati. She starts a relationship with Horrath, a married man, and becomes pregnant. She insists on not telling anyone on site that Horrath is the father, in order not to risk his career. When the film had its brief outing in the cinemas and the screenings were interrupted by staged protests, one of the objections was that 'our party representatives don't sleep with strange women'. However, Horrath is shown as a human being in all his weakness. He does not have the courage to admit his relationship with Kati, but ultimately this is not out of selfishness, but out of misguided loyalty to the aims of socialism. The truth emerges, though, and Horrath is suspended.

By that time Balla has long accepted Horrath for what he tries to do: to use whatever is in his power to keep the building site going. Balla says: 'He's doing his best for the party, but they're only trampling on him and his principles.' Whether from inside the Party or outside it (Balla is not a member of the Party), and by different methods, Balla, Horrath and Kati ultimately have the same goals.

In his representation of ordinary workers Beyer is even-handed as well. They are not portrayed schematically as 'working class heroes'. It is true, they work hard, but when the introduction of a three-shift-day is discussed, they are adamant that they will not work three shifts, not even if it is necessary to complete the work on time. All the characters in this film have flaws; this is what makes them so interesting.

There is a brief conversation between Balla and one of the older generation engineers about possible ways for the individual to respond to the mounting problems within the system, specifically about the possibility of leaving the country to go west – as so many disillusioned compatriots had done and were still doing at the time. Balla reminds the engineer, who has lived through fascism and the war that he would be welcome in West Germany, considering all his decorations for services in the army. The engineer replies: 'That is exactly why I won't go.' This brief exchange can be seen as representative of the beliefs of many GDR citizens, and it offers us an explanation for their will to distance themselves from the past and from contemporary developments in the west.

Comparing the two states, Balla says: 'You cut up Germany in two clumps, a big one, and a little one. Over there? – Shit. Over here? – Where's the vodka?' What he seems to be saying here in his own flippant way is that leaving East Germany is out of the question, but that staying comes at the price of less than desirable living conditions which can only be endured by drinking.

By relating all the events that lead to Horrath's disciplinary hearing and his dismissal in great detail, and by making his characters nuanced and human, Beyer gives us a unique insight into the life of the GDR. Mistakes are made from above; the line has to be 'toed' regardless; the workers are upset because they are treated unfairly; they become undisciplined, get reprimanded; love between two people is interfered with; the state controls them all: engineers, party representatives, workers. One important motif of the film is to show the consequences of the arrogance of the SED and of government circles, the control exercised down to the last vestiges of the private lives of individuals, the scrutiny of every utterance, every breath, as to its party loyalty. Individuals become victims of this control. In an economic sense the disasters on the building site stand for disasters of and for a whole society. What is not apparent in *Spur der Steine* is whether there were any informants, Stasi or otherwise, in the workplace at that time. Every issue seems to be out in the open, discussed in all detail, with genuine attempts made to find solutions.

Spur der Steine in no way attacks the principle of socialism, even though it makes clear references to problem areas and points to possible ways of doing things differently. Beyer's positive stance towards socialism is exemplified in the words 'We need people like Balla on the site' – he might as well have said 'the country needs people like Balla' in order to survive. In fact, one of the workers says at one point: 'The Republic is not going to survive', based on his experience of doctrine and propaganda – an astute observation so early in the history of a state that did indeed collapse 25 years later. It is conceivable that the experiment of a socialist republic on German soil might have succeeded, if those with firm beliefs and commitment, and not the 'pencil sharpeners' within the Party, had been allowed to have their say. Beyer's film shows us that this would have been real socialism as opposed to state socialism. The film's message must have felt extremely threatening to the political powers in East Germany at the time.

After the 11th plenary session (see above), Konrad Wolf wrote a letter to the Central Party leadership, detailing his own stance towards the film and expressing his regrets about its ban: 'More than in the novel I see in the film the concrete expression of a progressive development in the fact that in it, albeit in dramatically heightened form, via the contradictory interaction between two characters (Horrath and Balla), one of the most important points of the revolutionary activity of our Party is played out. I am talking about the struggle for awareness of our people in the most important sphere of socialism, the sphere of work!' (author's translation). Later on in the letter he voices his concerns about the current deep crisis and the importance of future film production in his country.

Spur der Steine was one of the censored DEFA films that ended up in the vaults, the 'cellars', the 'freezers' – as they were called by witnesses from that period, and it did not resurface until 1990, the year of the dissolution of the GDR and with it DEFA. It needs reiterating that whatever film was banned at any given time was completely dependent on the predominant ideological signals from the Soviet Union. It was possible for a film to be made with the best of intentions and with the blessing of the Party, only to be shelved in reaction to ideological changes in the interim. Eye witnesses have compared this process to a valve being turned on and off at will.

The ideological sledgehammer tactics with regard to film censorship had undesired and certainly unexpected effects: East German audiences voted with their feet by turning away from the cinema. (Voting was compulsory, but, alas, going to the cinema was still a matter of choice!) To be fair, in line with similar developments in other countries, television played a certain part in keeping audiences away from the cinemas. Towards the end of the decade, surely as a reaction to censorship and dwindling audiences, many film-makers turned to documentary film-making, where they found a limited outlet for their creativity, since documentary film was not quite as strictly censored as feature film. Generally speaking, documentary films, together with children's films, were the most prestigious of the GDR film genres, worldwide, and are still recognised as forming an important part of the legacy of East German film production.

In the seventies, with the advent of a gradual 'defrosting' of East-West relations, the censorship grip loosened slightly. The best example of a truce between film-makers and ideologists was the feature *Paul und Paula* (Heiner Carow, 1973), a film, as the title

suggests, that focuses on the lives of its two
protagonists – not on political struggles. *Paul und
Paula* became the most successful DEFA film
ever in terms of audiences, a fact that clearly
demonstrated the need of GDR citizens for more
nuanced, more personal stories. There were
efforts to ban it, but it narrowly escaped.

As mentioned earlier, there had already been a trend to portray individual lives in the
late fifties, an attempt that was repressed shortly afterwards. Even in the seventies, some
films about individual, non-political, strong men or women, or films that were formally
too adventurous, were banned. And yet, by then, film-makers had learnt how to write
their critical messages into many interesting, intellectually and emotionally stimulating films,
amongst them literary adaptations and reinterpretations, costume dramas, and historical
films, in which subtexts of rebellion were created.

Let us now look at Beyer's career before and after *Spur der Steine*, which shows just how
passionate he was in his work. He was born in 1932, and, after completing a degree in
theatre studies, he started making films, adaptations of novels and anti-fascist films to
begin with. At the time when he was banned from film-making after *Spur der Steine* he
already had plans for his next film which was supposed to be *Jakob der Lügner* (*Jacob
the Liar*), an adaptation of the novel by Jurek Becker, for which he also had secured the
agreement of the author to write the screenplay. This project had to be shelved for
eight years before it could be realised. The film was released in 1974 and became the
first and only DEFA film to be nominated for an Oscar. Beyer was definitely much more
celebrated abroad than at home.

Not only *Spur der Steine*, but also some of his other films suffered from censorship in the
GDR, for various reasons. He seemed to have been caught between his own socialist
ideals, his constructive ideas of how to achieve socialism in practice, and the 'real existing
socialism' of the GDR. His plight is typical of many other cultural figures in the GDR
who were hit by the ever-varying, unpredictable ways in which censorship worked. And
although Beyer was eventually able to make films again, he continued to face problems
with hardliners in the GDR cultural 'apparatus'.

In an interview (many years after the 11th plenary session) he spoke about the
emotional effects that his dismissal from DEFA had on him: He fought very hard not
to let himself go, not to give in to his phases of depression, not to start drinking. He
talked about the various projects that he had in the pipeline at the time, some of them
'Gegenwartsfilme' (films dealing with contemporary issues as opposed to anti-fascist
films), all of which had to be abandoned.

Frank Beyer was one of many GDR artists to suffer personally and professionally as a
result of blacklisting. His fate was to be forced to work away from film-making, banned

from working in Berlin and Potsdam, for eight years. However, although his films found critical acclaim in the West, and particularly in West Germany (which was unusual for a GDR film-maker), he never considered leaving his country to work in the West.

The biography of Manfred Krug, who plays Balla in *Spur der Steine*, may stand for a different, but equally disrupted life, again one that he shared with many of his colleagues. He was a celebrated actor and singer in the GDR. To many people he was a cultural icon, the epitome of the direct, honest man with a strong sense of justice, which is the sort of character that he tends to play in his various roles in film and television. In a self-deprecating way he says that this is the only person he is *able* to play. His role in *Spur der Steine* certainly shows him as an unconventional, non-conformist, but committed and dedicated character. His strong popularity in East Germany was even state-sanctioned: He received numerous awards and a medal of honour for long-lasting cultural activity and benefit to society. With this high profile he was able to be more openly critical of certain events and trends in the GDR. Ten years after the *Spur der Steine* debacle he signed a (unsuccessful) petition against the 'Zwangsausbürgerung' ('forced expatriation') of a fellow-singer and poet, Wolf Biermann. 'Forced expatriation' was a way in which the East German state reacted against high-profile dissidents: they simply sent them off to live in West Germany. After Krug's campaign for Biermann he was half-suspended, which was another way of reprimanding dissidents, and which meant he was only able to find occasional work. In 1977, when he could not bear the situation any more, he applied for a 'Ausreisegenehmigung' ('permit to leave the state') for himself and his family. It was granted, and the family moved to West Berlin. He continued to work in the West, with film and television roles, and much later as a singer of jazz and sophisticated pop, for which he writes his own lyrics.

A similar fate befell the two lead actors in Beyer's 1978 film *Das Versteck* (*The Hiding Place*), both of whom left the country, for similar reasons as Manfred Krug and a large number of other cultural icons who emigrated in the seventies or were 'forcefully expatriated' in the same way as Wolf Biermann. What they all had in common was disillusionment with 'real existing socialism' in the GDR, which depended on the suppression of any critical views and which could not cope with nuanced discussion by cultural representatives such as writers or film-makers. Many GDR artists believed in the principle of socialism even though the concrete reality in their country was not what they wanted. They were unable to voice their opinions in a state that exercised all manner of overt or covert censorship, ranging from measures such as limiting the number of copies of a released film to tightly controlled reviews in selected papers, organised disturbances of screenings, or outright bans. A slow farewell from the classic utopian socialist ideas, which had been eroded, took place.

A brief look ahead to the 1980s shows us that in that decade only very few good films were made, especially in the area of feature films. A strong documentary strand developed at DEFA in the 1980s. In the second half of the decade, just like in any other sector of life in the GDR, discontent and criticism of the 'ancien regime' prevailed, especially among younger film-makers. Our chapter on *Das Leben der Anderen* takes you further into the GDR of the 1980s. It makes an interesting comparison with this chapter because it is set in the eighties and deals with censorship and surveillance of people involved in cultural production. For a look at the beginning of the DEFA film studios and a comparison with the end of the era turn to our chapter on *Die Mörder sind unter uns*.

FOOTNOTES

[1] Ironic: The first instance of 'formalism' in the history of cinema developed in the USSR – Russian Formalism.

[2] One of these youth films was *Die Halbstarken* (1956) with Horst Buchholz in one of his early roles.

[3] Ordinary citizens had to wait 5 years for a car!

CHAPTER SIX: INDEPENDENT MINDS: *AGUIRRE, DER ZORN GOTTES (AGUIRRE, WRATH OF GOD, 1972)*

We have decided to include this film in our selection of key German films for two main reasons. First of all, Werner Herzog is one of only a handful of German film-makers who started their career in the 1960s and who are still making films today. He is often considered the greatest living German film-maker. Both his feature films and his documentaries are consistently profound and often controversial. The controversies surrounding his film-making practices are grounded in his idiosyncratic 'philosophies' regarding film-making and the fact that he will go to any lengths (some would say regardless of casualties) to achieve his vision. He himself has also been quite vociferous in making his views known, a fact that has partly fuelled the discussion around his alleged megalomania. *Aguirre* was not his first film, but it was the defining film in his international career, and it is still being discovered and discussed by new audiences today – you only have to go to YouTube to obtain proof of this.

Herzog started his career in the late 1960s, when the cinematic revival in Germany that came to be known as New German Cinema was just on the point of taking off. He is generally placed within that group of German film-makers, even though he has maintained that he did not have much contact with the other members of the movement. (Rainer Werner Fassbinder, to whom we have dedicated the next chapter, had a similarly distant relationship with the group. Please see our chapter on *Angst essen Seele auf* for more details.) For Herzog the fact that his beginnings as a film-maker are from within the same time-frame is a mere coincidence.

However, if you consider New German Cinema as a broad category which operated within a certain time-frame and whose main characteristic was independence of film-making, the inclusion of Werner Herzog is justified. *Aguirre* is very much an independent film, one of the earliest examples of independent film-making in 1970s Germany, a decade that stands out in post-war German film history as bringing about many notable films by a number of young film-makers. Even if they were not a coherent group they shared certain characteristics which were unique to West Germany at the time. In order to understand the political and film historical significance of New German Cinema, any exploration of this phenomenon and its precursor, Young German Cinema, needs to consider the context in West Germany before and during this period of independent film-making.

In the 1950s the new Federal Republic of Germany (FRG), founded in 1949, was still occupied by the Western Allied forces (USA, Great Britain, France) and was governed by the right-wing CDU/CSU (Christian Democratic Union and its sister party, the Christian Social Union). The main political aims at the time were to establish the country in accordance with Western democratic principles, to make its new federal structure work, and to gradually reintegrate the country into the international community.

Economically, a so-called 'miracle' happened, made possible by generous help from the Allies and huge efforts on part of the Germans themselves. Rebuilding the country after the devastations of World War II was the result of much hard work, and to a point it is not surprising that West Germans concentrated on achieving this 'miracle'. However, a combination of these efforts and the strong political influence of the Western Allies on the fledgling democracy prevented conscious and critical reflection of the population with regard to their recent fascist past. A complete separation from the dictator-father Hitler in the minds of Germans (and many say in politics and society as a whole as well) did not happen. At the same time, Germany had become a 'fatherless' society in another way, with soldiers having been killed on the Eastern and Western fronts of World War II, leaving many children to grow up in single-parent families. The repression of the traumatic recent past manifested itself in excessive consumerism.

With regard to film production in post-war West Germany there was, to begin with, a gaping hole left by the collapse of the Nazi film industry. The West German market for films was quickly captured by the Americans, who filled the cinemas with their own products. As mentioned in our chapter on *Die Mörder sind unter uns*, the USA considered their own cinematic representations an important instrument of re-education. More generally, and as far as an emerging West German film industry was concerned, the occupying forces at first more or less dictated what was to be produced and what could be shown in cinemas. When German film production got underway again in the 1950s, supported by finance guarantees from the government, the number of films made in Germany increased in quantity, but not necessarily in quality. Indeed, at the Berlin Film Festival in 1961 the jury made the unprecedented decision not to award the prize for best German film at all because none of the submitted films deserved it. The 1950s in general were marked by an artistic low, with very few exceptions. Comedies, musicals, and so-called 'Heimat' films predominated. People seemed to want to forget rather than remember. (You will find more discussion on Heimat films in our chapter on *Heimat*.)

Very gradually, and at least partly under the influence of the French Nouvelle Vague of film making, which began in the late 1950s, a young generation of West German film-makers appeared, initially with short films because of financial constraints. These 'angry' young men had a new agenda. This agenda was given expression at the Oberhausen Short Film Festival of 1962, where 26 film-makers of shorts wrote and signed a manifesto in which they declared the death of 'the old cinema' and the birth of 'Young German Cinema'. Now, it is one thing to declare the end of 'daddy's' cinema, but quite another to actually create an alternative. The new artistic beginning was difficult: If you reject conventional commercial cinema, if there is a huge void left by the Nazis and World War II – the greatest talent had left Germany or had been decimated by the war – then where do you learn the trade? There were no film schools in Germany at the time; and the German film industry was more or less defunct commercially because of the failure of German films at the box office and artistically because of the break with traditions of the twenties during the years of National Socialism. The new film-makers had no choice but to start from scratch, to look for inspiration across the border towards France, and to start small by making short films.

Therefore it is not surprising that it took another few years for the Oberhausen declaration to bear fruit in feature films. *Nicht versöhnt* (*Not Reconciled*, 1965) by Jean-Marie Straub and Danièle Huillet is generally accepted as the first feature of Young German Cinema. After that, the years of 1966–67 were very productive years for young German film, with many young German directors releasing their first features, among them *Abschied von gestern* (*Yesterday's Girl*) by Alexander Kluge, *Der junge Törless* (*Young Törless*) by Volker Schlöndorff, and Edgar Reitz's *Mahlzeiten* (*Mealtimes*). In the long run only a handful of the original Oberhausen signatories stood the test of time and remained true to their principles, including Kluge, Schlöndorff and Reitz. Most of the others made only one or two films (some only for television), disappeared into other careers, or became mainstream film-makers. This is not at all surprising if you consider the difficulties they had to face. Their demands for a 'free' cinema – free from conventions, free from commercial interests, free from any kind of intervention – could only be fulfilled with the help of public funding and new film schools to foster talent.

The main protagonists of the first generation of young German film-makers were those mentioned above, who, true to the spirit of their manifesto, lobbied tirelessly for their aims to improve the conditions for non-commercial film-making. Gradually many of these aims were achieved: In 1965 the 'Kuratorium Junger Deutscher Film' (Young German Film Committee) was set up in order to provide loans for the production of non-commercial films. At the same time state funding was provided for two film academies in Berlin and Munich. The film-makers themselves collaborated in order to obtain funding, and they supported each other financially with regard to production and distribution. This was formalised in 1970 when 'Filmverlag der Autoren' (literally: Film Publishing Partnership of Authors), a film production and distribution company, was set up by thirteen young film-makers, including Alexander Kluge and Wim Wenders. It became the main distributor for independent German films. Its name demonstrates clearly the confidence of its partners –- they called themselves 'authors' or 'auteurs' in order to emphasise their individuality and the ownership of their films.

The year 1970 is generally regarded as the point when 'Young German Cinema' developed into 'New German Cinema'. It coincides with Rainer Werner Fassbinder, Werner Herzog and Wim Wenders all appearing on the scene – a second or even third generation of young film-makers. Even though Herzog and Fassbinder saw themselves only on the margins of this phenomenon it cannot be denied that they benefited from the generally more positive climate for independent cinema in Germany at the time; they were able to use the road that their predecessors had paved. On the other hand, they contributed greatly to the renaissance of German film-making in the 1970s, and are still today among the best-known German film-makers internationally. They did not strive to be commercially successful, and indeed never were during the 1970s. So in a sense their work was self-limiting. Artistically, though, they were celebrated internationally, mainly at film festivals, by critics, and in art house circles. Within Germany reception of their films was more muted. Unlike in France, where cinephile audiences appreciated art films and thus buoyed up domestic film production, in Germany cinema was often considered to be 'low culture' by art-lovers, who preferred to go to the theatre. Because of this tendency in Germany independent films were squeezed from two sides: The majority of cinema-goers watched mainstream Hollywood films and followers of 'high culture' largely ignored the cinema altogether. This means that indigenous German films attracted even fewer audiences than in other countries. Hence the relative failure at the box office of the new German films in the 1970s.

The New German Cinema was in itself not a coherent movement with declared stylistic or narrative characteristics. In fact, all of the above-mentioned film-makers were great individualists, each of whom has produced a coherent body of work, in true auteur fashion, but who cannot easily be compared to each other. Literary adaptations stood side by side with original treatments, black and white next to colour, experimental approaches against more conventional ones. However, the film-makers' declared aim of overcoming 'daddy's cinema' has yielded significant representations of German political and social realities, past and present: Topics such as Germany's Nazi past and West Germany's contemporary social issues were addressed, if in very different forms when tackled by different film-makers.

Even when films did not deal overtly with political or social issues, such as in the films of Wenders and Herzog, they still explored issues of identity and self-identity in what Silberman called 'a complex layering of national, familial and personal trajectories that helped to define a specifically German subject'. Thomas Elsaesser has coined the term 'cinema of experience' to bring together the individual approaches of the auteur-directors in New German Cinema with a specific set of circumstances in West Germany at the time, towards a notion of 'what it means' to be German. Elsaesser observes a strong 'investigative' streak in New German Cinema, manifested in strong social and political comments on both current and historical events, in both literary adaptations and original screenplays.

How does Werner Herzog fit into this? As mentioned above, his concerns were not (and still are not) political in the strict sense. He (like Wenders and Fassbinder) was not a signatory to the Oberhausen Manifesto. However, he is generally regarded as part of New German Cinema, making films within the specific set of circumstances in West Germany at the time as identified by Elsaesser. What distinguishes him from his contemporaries is that he is not specifically interested in 'reality' in a political sense of it, or in its direct impact on everyday people. What he perceives as 'narrow' political terms are not meaningful to him; he tends to separate aesthetics from politics. This does not mean, however, that his films are completely apolitical. Our discussion of *Aguirre* and its link with *Ten Thousand Years Older* (2003 – see later in this chapter) as well as his views expressed elsewhere [2] will indeed show that there are political undercurrents in his work, even though they might not always be clear and straightforward; and sometimes they are even problematic.

Let us now look a little more closely at how he approaches his film-making and his themes in general. We will then delve into *Aguirre* as a concrete example. His most important preoccupation is finding 'truth'. His 'truth' is not what he calls the 'accountant's' truth, but a deeper, more poetic form which he calls 'ecstatic' or 'essential' truth. This is not directly related to the truth as we commonly understand it when, for instance, we watch events related to us as they have supposedly occurred, most clearly in documentaries which, to the untrained eye, do exactly that – represent the truth. But whose truth is told, even in documentaries? Just think about *Triumph des Willens* for a moment!

In order to arrive at his below-the-surface truth and to communicate it, Herzog blurs the boundaries between fact and fiction, in both his documentaries and his fiction films. He has been criticised for 'staging' parts of his documentaries, e.g. when individuals in his documentaries recite lines that he has written for them, or when they re-enact earlier experiences or events. When you watch his documentaries, however, you sense that by doing this he has distilled the experiences of his 'characters' to an essence that results in a deeper kind of truth or reality. In order to do this convincingly, he must have an affinity with the individuals that he chooses as the focus of his documentaries. Indeed, he has an uncanny sense of the significance to him of a person, a subject, a theme. This is why his documentaries have such a profound impact on the viewer. In interviews he has said that 'only through invention and fabrication and staging can you reach a more intense level of truth that cannot otherwise be found'.

The same applies to Herzog's fiction films. Here fiction outweighs fact, but he tends to take as a starting point events that have actually taken place some time in history, or he focuses on a real historical person who he is intrigued by. When writing his screenplays he then proceeds to invest them with his own imagination. The locations for his fiction films are chosen with great care by Herzog personally. He says that landscapes or specific views are always the starting point of his visual imagination. He has often spoken of his aim to find unfamiliar and 'unused' landscapes. He contrasts these to the picture postcard views that are forced upon us, that indoctrinate us and shape the way we perceive the world. Instead he wants to connect us with visuals, with landscapes that are, as he says, already in us, that represent 'an inner state of mind'. This preoccupation of his corresponds to his specific vision of the truth: not representation of the real, the outside world, but a deeper world. His landscapes are often associated with exoticism and danger: he has filmed all over the world, on all continents, but most effectively in the jungle, where he finds his 'unused' images.

Once production proper begins, he tends to plunge himself and his crew into adventures that rival those of his protagonists. By really 'being there' in every sense, by subjecting himself, his crew and his actors to 'real' experiences on location, his films achieve an incredible physicality. The relative lack of dialogue contributes to this intensity. In post-production Herzog adds another layer of 'truth' by his choice of non-diegetic music on the soundtrack. We must remember once again, however, that he is not trying to use the real world in an anthropological, historical or political sense. This is key to understanding a Herzog film. He has often been criticised for 'distorting' reality and for exposing his crew to extreme dangers. This is all true (in a superficial way, Herzog would say!). However, the deeper meaning of his films can only be gleaned if we set these issues aside for the time being. Assessing Herzog's work is even further complicated by the fact that sometimes he does seem to express political affiliations, as we shall see in our analysis of *Aguirre*.

In a way his documentaries and his fiction films cannot be separated from one other; they comment on and complement each other. Each contains elements of the other in a unique combination that always shows Herzog's signature as an auteur-director.

Herzog's unique authorial approach may be understood further by relating it to his own background, his upbringing in a remote village in what seems timeless Bavaria around the end of World War II. He has often spoken of the isolation and austerity that characterised his childhood. Deprived of material wealth he developed a strong imagination and lived what he calls an 'essential childhood'. What he experienced and perceived were indeed 'unused' images: there was no cinema to go to; he saw his first film at the age of 11. Without doubt, such unusual circumstances have shaped his view of the world.

He is at odds with civilisation in so far as it has deprived us of seeing 'authentically', purely, of making discoveries for ourselves. What we tend to be offered is prefabricated by the media: 'worn-out images', as he calls them. He sees it as his duty as a film-maker to create a 'new grammar' of images. This is because, he says, we all have an 'essential childhood' buried inside us, and he wants to tap into that. There is in his films a hypnotic quality; he says the images he creates are there to be taken in directly, bypassing our conscious mind. Again and again in interviews he insists that his visions cannot and should not be analysed. Consequently, in a Herzog film we often feel as if we are in a dream, and this is exactly what he is trying to achieve: He speaks of accessing our 'collective unconscious' – the dreams that we all share, the 'essential childhood' we have buried inside us. Herzog appears to see himself as a kind of psychoanalyst trying to 'cure' us of civilisation!

Does he see himself as a German film-maker too? He would say that first and foremost he is a 'Bavarian' film-maker. He opposes this to 'Prussian', by which he means the north of Germany. Bavaria is a predominantly Catholic part of Germany, whereas 'Prussia' has a distinctly Protestant ethic. A 'Bavarian' film-maker, then, is a passionate one, one who relishes excess, in a Catholic sort of way: the baroque, the unfettered, as opposed to Protestant frugality. For Herzog, to be Bavarian means indulging in excesses and obsessions, such as those that have manifested themselves in the life of King Ludwig II, for instance, who had lavish castles such as Neuschwanstein built, or the composer Richard Wagner, who is famous for his grand operas. With everything we know about Herzog by now it is not surprising that he himself has staged several operas, and that his films sometimes feel operatic.

From a very early age Herzog knew he wanted to become a film-maker. However, film-making is an expensive matter. Therefore, in the early 1960s, in order to raise money for his first films, he worked in a steel factory and then, together with his brother, set up his own production company as early as 1963. This is a very important fact, since it shows clearly that he wanted to be completely independent, and it also demonstrates how serious and single-minded he was.

Among Herzog's recurring themes and cinematic devices are the solitary human figure in a foggy landscape; the limits of language, a correlative of the limits of socialisation; the re-creation of traumatic experiences, particularly in his documentaries; comparisons between the human and the animal worlds; the circling camera; and the long takes that slow his films down. His main characters are often larger than life, quite mad or at any rate unusual – in his documentaries he explores people who are traumatised by events in their past, or people who overcome a disability. In both documentaries and features he shows us people who challenge limits, who are undeterred by reality's boundaries, by reality's impenetrability. In a Herzog film the world is meant to bend and break in the face of a great will. As mentioned before, Herzog has a strong affinity with all his characters, whether this is because they reflect his own deep-seated ambitions or whether he feels a deep empathy with them for other reasons. Attachment and affinity have a darker side in Herzog: Of all his characters Herzog says he is most strongly attached to Aguirre and by extension to Klaus Kinski who plays him. Aguirre is a very disturbed character; Kinski was a similarly troubled man.

One of the primary inspirations for the character of Aguirre was a real-life person: an African revolutionary named John Okello. He was the leader of a revolution in Zanzibar in 1963, a self-proclaimed Field Marshall. Herzog listened to his radio broadcasts and describes his flamboyant, Old-Testament-like language as 'hysterical and atrocious fantasies'. This language provided the basis for Aguirre's way of speaking, which ties in with the manic behaviour of the self-proclaimed expedition leader in *Aguirre*.

The plot is basically very simple. It tells the story of an expedition in South America which, we are informed, took place in 1594, looking for El Dorado. In the prologue to the film we are told that El Dorado was an imaginary place, 'made up by desperate Peruvian Indians in order to get rid of marauding adventurers and ex-conquistadors'. However, the expedition is in ignorance of this fact as it sets off from Peru towards the Amazon basin in order to find the legendary city.

In the opening scene we see an almost unending expedition snaking down the mountain and into the Amazon basin. It takes us a while to realise where we are, though, and that we are witnessing an expedition. We have several conflicting sensations: This is impossible, incongruous, this is doomed to fail. At the same time the landscape takes our breath away, we can almost touch and feel it; it does have a strong 'corporeality'. It imposes itself on the audience as much as on the expedition. We are stunned: What are they doing here? The expedition dressed-up in their society's full regalia and their ignorance of the laws of nature shows arrogance on the part of the Spaniards. It has something almost blasphemous about it – as if they were invading a spiritual place.

The film music intensifies and heightens these images and our sensations, particularly the sense of spirituality. This is not entirely surprising if we look at the origins of the music. Florian Fricke, the composer, was the leader of a German avant-garde rock band called Popol Vuh, part of a movement called 'Kraut-Rock' which made extensive use of the synthesiser. In Popol Vuh, influences of early and ethnic music are quite strong. For *Aguirre* the model is the music of Carlo Gesualdo, a seventeenth century composer who wrote particularly for voices. Gesualdo's beautiful harmonies, though nearly 400 years old, sound surprisingly modern and, in their transformation by Fricke into electronically manipulated sounds, are perfectly suited to represent both the ancient qualities of the jungle and the eerie, uncanny sense of foreboding that hangs over the expedition. Together, the music and the images create an almost hypnotic effect.

The opening scene was filmed on the Eastern slopes of Machu Pichu in Peru, a mountain whose upper regions carry a strong tourist interest in that the Inca empire originated there. Herzog could have shown us the iconic, 'picture postcard' view of Machu Pichu in order to give us clear geographical coordinates, but he chose not to do this and instead zooms into the mountain itself, a device that serves to draw us into the scene and at the same time to disorientate us. Herzog wants us to experience nature in a way that extends beyond the cinematic frame, in a way that is boundless. Nature is so vast, it almost swallows up the figures in it. The expedition continues to zigzag down the mountain, struggling as it does so. They finally arrive at the Amazon basin and follow the Halluaga River, a tributary to the Amazon, into what is today Brazil. This is the geographical setting of the film, and, as outlined earlier, Herzog, his crew and his actors, were exclusively filming on location. At several points in the film we see drops of water on the camera lens – we are not used to seeing such reality in fiction films and this intrusion startles us. It seems clear that once you decide to film in such difficult circumstances, you throw yourself at the mercy of natural phenomena, which is exactly what happened in the course of filming *Aguirre*. Any set ideas of how and when to film exactly what needed to be modified according to nature's dictates, and consequently we get a strong sense of improvisation. *Aguirre* is therefore a fiction film with strong documentary elements. Incidentally, and in line with his 'realism', Herzog chose to employ native South American Indians to play the slaves. Altogether he creates sensations that cannot be otherwise fabricated, using real dangers, real armour from Spain, a real raft, authentic extras, and a genuine flute player. All these elements serve to blur the boundaries between narrative film and documentary.

However, nature in a Herzog film is always more than just a location. For Herzog it represents dreams, emotions and nightmares. In *Aguirre* specifically, it seems to signify on different levels; it sets both physical and metaphorical boundaries. The descent we have just witnessed is one example of this: At the most obvious level we have an expedition with a mission, although we feel uneasy about it from the beginning. On another level it can be read as a descent from civilisation to wilderness, which would correspond psychologically to the descent from conscious thought or order to our unconscious mind which is populated by dreams and repressed desires. As the expedition continues, this is exactly what will happen: the disintegration of 'civilised' reality.

Another example is the river itself. At first the waters are brisk, with rapids that are difficult to manoeuvre. Later it rises, the safe banks all but disappear, and the water literally and metaphorically keeps the people prisoners on their raft, trapped as it were in their unconscious. When it slows almost to a standstill their status as prisoners is intensified, and at the same time the eerie slowness reflects Aguirre's slow descent into madness. The experience of the 'indifferent' rainforest and the merciless river that keeps them trapped eventually drives everybody mad, makes them kill, or kills them. Herzog films the slow-moving river in long, almost hypnotic takes. He seems to tell us that whatever the mission of the expedition is, it is not going to go anywhere very fast. It is not by chance that less and less is said as the film progresses: the limits of language and by extension civilisation have been reached. Nature in a Herzog film has almost human qualities; it is a vital part of the characters' minds. But nature is also indifferent, 'dumb' (Herzog), a law unto itself, it resists human intervention, however much people are driven to overcome, to conquer, to transcend it, to go to 'the end of the world' – and this includes Herzog himself. There is no false reconciliation between man and nature; instead there is a tension between the dangers of nature and its beauty.

As for the historical context in *Aguirre*, it is important since the film reflects conditions within a colonial society and is largely accurate in that. However, the narrative of *Aguirre* is only very loosely based on historical fact. Lope de Aguirre did exist, as did the other named participants in the expedition. However, Herzog took great liberties in mixing events and those that were involved in them. The idea of El Dorado, a legendary Indian kingdom of fabulous wealth, originated in Hispanic America in the sixteenth century. It inspired dozens of expeditions by Spaniards. That much is true. The expedition and its make-up at the centre of *Aguirre* is an amalgam of two of those expeditions, one in 1540 and the other in 1560. Herzog himself says that his film is not based on fact. What attracted him to the story was the figure of Aguirre himself. The 'documentary' background to Herzog's film about Aguirre serves to highlight his approach towards fictional film-making in general: he plucks some individuals from history; he invents one of the members of the expedition altogether, the monk Carvajal and his diary; and he uses certain facts which he rearranges. Most important of all, though, is that he focuses on Aguirre himself, emphasising his revolt against the king of Spain, and giving his story a very different end to that of the real Aguirre. Once again, the 'superficial' truth of history is not as important as the 'deeper' truth of humans challenging nature and transgressing boundaries.

The expedition in *Aguirre* is made up of a cross-section of colonial society. Herzog makes very clear where he stands with regard to colonialism: The so-called 'civilised' members of this society behave in a very uncivilised way. This is where *Aguirre* has political relevance. After Aguirre's mutiny an 'emperor' is crowned who proves completely incompetent and has people killed just because they become a nuisance to him. Brother Carvajal is a representative of the Church which 'for the good of our God... was always on the side of the strong'. Here Herzog points to a strong interconnection between colonialism and the Church, which supported and enabled imperial greed. Once this microcosmic colonial society has boarded a raft in order to be able to make any progress at all, this raft – with cannon and horse – becomes a last bastion of 'civilisation'. As the expedition progresses their 'order' becomes disorder.

Gradually, each and every one of the members of the expedition is either killed or 'opts out' in some way of his/her societal role, although the division between the 'Emperor' and the rest is kept until his death: While he gorges himself on food his 'subjects' around him almost starve to death. It is as if they willingly conspire in their own destiny, which is death. They even precipitate it by throwing their horse, a possible source of food, overboard. This happens in addition to the fact that Aguirre kills his own men or has them killed. Their descent into the subconscious, the physical correlative of which is the Amazon basin, allows their repressed desires and savagery to be 'let loose' and to take over gradually.

The 'other' side of colonial society, the indigenous population, is represented either as individual members of the expedition or as 'primitive tribes' who live in the jungle adjacent to the river and by whom the expedition on the raft feels threatened. One of the two Peruvian slaves on the raft is ordered about by Aguirre and used as a musician

'to entertain the men'. The black slave is the ultimate commodity – he is defined solely through his 'blackness' and is used as a human scarecrow-cum-shield in the 'battle' against the 'primitives': It is believed that the 'primitives' who have never seen a black man will be frightened of him. When the expedition goes on land they send him ('Strip the negro') ahead, naked.

Herzog gives one Peruvian slave an opportunity to speak. He makes a speech which stands out from the other events, above all in its dignity: 'What the Spaniards have done

to us… I was a prince… Now I'm in chains like my people.' During this speech the slave looks directly at the camera, breaking down the traditional separation between the world of the film (the diegesis) and the audience: He is addressing us. (More on this presentational technique in our next chapter.)

The 'primitive tribes' remain on the shores of the river. Because they are unseen and attack from an impenetrable place and from a distance, the expedition is terrified of them: 'We cannot see our enemies.' They represent the expedition's greatest fears and nightmares. In addition, their savage acts and evidence of these are also a reflection or parallel to the events taking place on the raft. The skull which members of the expedition find on their foray away from the raft and onto land, is evidence of cannibalism amongst the 'primitives', but it is also a portentous sign of their own future fate.

The only direct encounter with the 'primitives' happens when a couple of Indians in a canoe approach the raft to greet the 'sons of the sun'. They are, ironically, looking for the sons of god 'because god left our civilisation uncompleted'. What happens is a complete inversion of 'civilised' and 'savage': the Indian man and woman are very polite, very calm, whereas the Spaniards are the aggressors. Carvajal tries to baptise them by telling them that the bible contains 'the word of God'. The Indian cannot 'hear' it – 'It doesn't speak' and, together with his wife, is subsequently baptised violently: 'These savages are hard to convert'. It seems the more threatened the remnants of colonial society feel the more they need confirmation of their superiority. This scene clearly states Herzog's criticism in this film of colonialism and the missionary zeal of the Christian church at the time. The 'primitive' Indians emerge from it as the dignified people; the Spaniards are the real savages, especially after Ursúa, a gentler alternative to savage colonialism, has been killed.

The strongest signs of the disintegration of this 'community' on the raft are when they all see the vision of a boat high up in a tree, or when poison arrows are shot at them from the river banks and they refuse to acknowledge their reality: 'These are not arrows,' they mumble. They are no longer a community but suffer from a sort of collective hallucination which is induced on one level by fever and near-starvation, on another by their inability to deal with the force with which nature imposes itself on them, and the more and more frequent confrontation with death. The 'others', the slaves and the 'primitives', are no longer in their service – the clear colonial order has been breached.

Herzog portrays the search for a 'new' New World – in the shape of El Dorado – as a figment of the imagination. He shows the effects of 'advanced' colonisation, burdened with redundant conquistadors, adventurers and vagabonds. Aguirre himself is a grotesque distortion of the search for gold, fame and power. He transgresses every possible taboo, everything that keeps a society together. However, he fails. The end is the complete

disintegration of his self. At the end, alone and raving mad, he cannot distinguish any more between the chattering monkeys who have joined him on his lonely raft and human beings. He raves about setting up his own kingdom and building a new society through incest with his daughter – being unable to differentiate between the living and the dead.

And yet, there is something in his fate that makes us feel sorry for him. His colonial society, which he served faithfully, has discarded him like a piece of junk. That Herzog, too, empathised with him, comes across clearly in a comment that he makes in the documentary film about his relationship with Klaus Kinski, *Mein liebster Feind* (*My Best Fiend*, 1999): When Aguirre/Kinski asks the members of the expedition: 'Who is with me (in rebellion)?', Herzog, in his commentary, says quietly: 'I was with him.' Here the two are conflated: Aguirre becomes Kinski, and Kinski becomes Aguirre. From the first thoughts of making this film Herzog could not conceive of anyone else but Kinski to play the lead. His unerring sense of choosing the right actors for his films is clearly proved by the extraordinary performance that Klaus Kinski achieved as Aguirre.

How Aguirre/Kinski's 'Wrath of God' speech was realised is an example of Herzog's and Kinski's working relationship, which can almost be described as sado-masochistic: Apparently, so Herzog explains, it was filmed after a vicious tantrum, provoked by the director, after which Kinski was exhausted, while still foaming at the mouth. This

is how Herzog was able to get the best performance out of him, because he knew exactly what his hysterical energy entailed, his so-called insanity, and how to evoke it. 'Sometimes I would even provoke him so he ended up shouting and screaming for a couple of hours, after which he would be so exhausted and in the right mood, very silent, quiet and dangerous.'

This is quite credible: When we see Kinski's ravings we get the impression that they are real, even if we do not know the background. Our fascination with these images stems from the physicality, and, in this case, the real violence. Other, rumoured, events surrounding the making of *Aguirre*, such as the exploitation and even the deaths of native Peruvians, have often been commented on, although they have turned out to be fabrications. For this and other films Herzog has been criticised. There have been wild rumours, specifically around *Aguirre* and the later *Fitzcarraldo* (1982, see below), both with Kinski in the lead. Herzog has often said that he does not appreciate such rumours, but he tends to fan the flames himself with his own accounts and sometimes contradictory statements.

Herzog had huge problems with the financing of this film because of expectations of difficulties, which were partly grounded in the proposed film itself with its assumed complications, but also in his own person – he had a reputation for being difficult to work with. It was eventually part-financed by German television. It is interesting to note that for *Aguirre* Herzog made a conscious effort to be just slightly more mainstream than in his earlier films in order to attract a wider audience. On the surface the film can almost be viewed as a genre film: There is a clear line between good and bad just like in a classic Western, and it has the content of an adventure film. At the same time, and despite its grand setting, it is a very personal film which, for Herzog, was a personal test of success or failure. His first ambition, to create a more commercial film, was not achieved, but artistically it was a triumph.

Of Herzog's numerous works some other films are worth mentioning, in particular those which resonate strongly with *Aguirre*: *Fitzcarraldo*, *Mein liebster Feind*, *Julianes Sturz in den Dschungel* (*Wings of Hope*, 2000), and *Ten Thousand Years Older*. If *Aguirre* has caught your imagination it is worth watching these additional films. They complement *Aguirre* in that they are all set in the Amazonian jungle and that they illuminate, contrast or take further issues from *Aguirre*, giving us valuable contextual information and thus building a more rounded picture of Herzog's work.

Mein liebster Feind is a documentary which Herzog made as a kind of homage to Klaus Kinski. The English title (*My Best Fiend*) expresses quite clearly what is at its centre, but it does not quite convey the strongly positive tone of the German title *Mein liebster Feind*, which has the word 'beloved ' in it. Herzog wants us to see that the film is neither about Kinski nor about himself, but that it is about the extraordinary love-hate relationship between the two.

In *Julianes Sturz in den Dschungel*, another documentary, Herzog takes the only survivor of a plane crash in the Amazon basin, Marianne Koepke, back to the jungle 25 years after the crash in order to retrace her steps through the jungle into safety. The trip turns out to be a kind of therapy for her, because she has not been able to face the jungle since the plane crash, and now she can. The most extraordinary fact is that Herzog himself was meant to be on exactly that plane on his way to filming *Aguirre*.

In *Fitzcarraldo* Herzog revisits not only the Amazonian jungle, but also the theme of transgressing boundaries, and he does it again with Kinski. Both *Aguirre* and *Fitzcarraldo* contain utopian dreams, founding cities or opera houses. There is in both films the irreconcilability of grand visions and the constraining world. Again, as in *Aguirre*, fact and fiction overlap. The journey taken through the jungle is real, including the famous hauling of a steamship over a mountain. Again, there were rumours of ill-treatment of native Peruvians. And again, Herzog refuses to compromise over reality. *Fitzcarraldo* has been compared to *Apocalypse Now* (1979), which was beset with similar location shooting problems but showed a similar lack of compromise. [3]

His short film *Ten Thousand Years Older*, which was his contribution to a compilation of short films called *Ten Minutes Older: The Trumpet*, gives us additional insight into his views on colonialism and post-colonialism. In this documentary he visits a Brazilian rainforest tribe that had been 'discovered' by the modern world in 1981, whose lifestyle and culture have, within the 20 years following their discovery by the modern world, been catapulted forward literally ten thousand years with huge repercussions such as illness, unemployment, and decimation among the older and younger members of the tribe. Again, Herzog's sympathies lie with the victims of such, in his words, 'barbaric' interference in the shape of modern civilisation. This exasperation with Western civilisation connects *Aguirre* with *Ten Thousand Years Older*. They both portray cultural conflict and a colonial world that respects no boundaries.

With *Aguirre* Herzog confirmed his status as the most independent of independent film-makers: The total budget for the film was a mere $370,000, of which a third was paid to Kinski. The crew consisted of less than 10 people and a very small amount of footage was shot, which meant that the actual footage used in the final film was of a much greater proportion than usual. This is in total contrast to Hollywood with its lavish production values and its huge amounts of footage ending up on the editing floor. Herzog's antipathy to Hollywood cinema is expressed in his interviews with Paul Cronin, where he speaks of 'scripts that press the right buttons at the right time, which is essentially film-making by numbers'. However, in 2007 he released a fictional remake of his documentary *Flucht aus Laos* (*Little Dieter Needs to Fly*, 1997), which is in a similar mode to *Juliane* in that it re-creates the trials of an individual, this time a man, who overcomes adversity in extraordinary circumstances and with great courage and tenacity. This film, *Rescue Dawn*, is Herzog's first Hollywood-produced project.

FOOTNOTES

[1] With reference to the terminology used by the French Nouvelle Vague

[2] As mentioned before, he has been very generous in discussing his views. See in particular his interviews with Paul Cronin, in 'Herzog on Herzog'.

[3] Francis Ford Coppola, the director of *Apocalypse Now*, is most likely to have been influenced by *Aguirre*

CHAPTER SEVEN: THE PERSONAL IS POLITICAL: *ANGST ESSEN SEELE AUF* (*FEAR EATS THE SOUL, 1974*)

The focus film of this chapter is an early contribution to the discussion around immigration in West Germany, at a time when the issue was not being addressed by politicians or society. Officially Germany was not regarded as a country of immigration, although clearly immigration was taking place, and the resulting issues were evident. *Angst essen Seele auf* is a courageous treatment of the fate of migrant workers and society's reactions to them, and is still today regarded as a significant contribution to the discussion. When the first complete retrospective of Fassbinder's *oeuvre* was held in the summer of 1992, the organisers decided to use *Angst* as their opening film because it was still so shockingly topical. It exposes mechanisms of human behaviour within society with specific reference to the issue of migrant workers, and at the same time it goes beyond the immediate issues and contains universal truths.

It is fair to say that in our selection of key German films none of our other film-makers' lives have been so inextricably bound up with their films as in the case of Rainer Werner Fassbinder. Moreover, no other German film-maker led such a fascinating, notorious and ultimately destructive life as he did. He was (and still is today) the most talked-about and prolific German film-maker who, in the space of just 13 years, made dozens of films.

While all film-makers bring with them a set of personal and political circumstances which find their way into their films – more or less explicitly depending on their artistic freedom, and according to conscious and subconscious choices – all of Fassbinder's films weave together personal and political circumstances in an unparalleled way, always carrying his own unique signature, even though that signature changed considerably in the course of his life and work. Above and beyond this, however, Fassbinder is regarded as the leading light of New German Cinema (for more details on New German Cinema see our chapter on *Aguirre*). This also implies that he was indeed bound up in cultural-political circumstances and therefore part of a more general break with cinematic traditions within Germany, not just a lone genius. His involvement in topical issues through film occasionally brought him close to other auteur-directors of New German Cinema, most notably in his contribution to the collaborative film *Deutschland im Herbst* (*Germany in Autumn*) in 1977. (See also our chapters on Reitz, Schlöndorff and Wenders.) Together with his contemporaries he was acutely aware of the division of Germany, the legacy of Germany's fascist past and West Germany's post-war development, topics that were taken up again and again in New German Cinema.

In order to assess his extraordinary creative output and to place *Angst essen Seele auf* in its context, it seems appropriate to provide a brief overview of his life and work. First of all, some staggering figures: Fassbinder was born on 31 May, 1945 in a small town in Bavaria and was found dead in his room in his Munich apartment on 10 June, 1982, at the age of 37. He had died of an overdose of drugs and alcohol. In his short life he made 43 films, most of which were feature-length. Since his first film was made in 1969, this means an average of one film per one hundred days over 13 years. He wrote, produced, directed, edited, and acted in most of his films.

His early life was characterised by constant change and loneliness: The only child of a distant father and a mother in ill health, he was often left to his own devices, especially after his parents' divorce when he was five. His early experiences and imagination were shaped by the comings and goings in his mother's guesthouse, his mother's lovers, and his experiences with destitute people, such as prostitutes, pimps and foreign workers. These encounters made a strong impression on him, which he later distilled in words and images. As a self-confessed 'cinema addict' he watched up to three films a day, five days a week.

On his way to becoming a film-maker, via the theatre, he sought to create a substitute family in the groups of people with whom he worked. This search for a family life he himself had never had can be traced throughout his life and work: The same people appear with him again and again, in varying constellations and in varying degrees of constancy. His most constant, yet always volatile, partners/lovers in both life and art were both women and men. Fassbinder also worked extensively with his mother, who appears in several of his films. His long-time collaborators included not just actors, but also composers, directorial assistants, and other film crew members. The same people would often appear as crew members and actors. The relationships among the people in Fassbinder's 'inner circle' were characterised by mutual dependency, huge admiration, devotion, but also manipulation. These personal attributes were complemented by tremendous creativity, discipline and professionalism. Fassbinder seemed to feed off the high drama surrounding and involving him. In fact, he often 'induced' it, lived it, and then worked it into his film characters.

For this reason, Fassbinder has been accused of using, even abusing people, to the point of sadism, of destruction. It is acknowledged, however, even by his critics, that he had an unfailing sense of how to harness the creative talents of his protégés, and, through

his unorthodox methods, brought out the best in his collaborators, many of whom have spoken and still speak highly and affectionately of him. Hanna Schygulla, for example, an early 'discovery' of his and the star in quite a few of his films, says that without Fassbinder she would not have a career. [1]

His first films originated from his work at the 'antitheater' in Munich, an avant-garde or fringe theatre, of which he was director. The influence of theatre on his film work is clearly visible in the mise-en-scène, the 'staging' of his films. Most clearly evident in his early films (1969-1971), the settings are either literally a theatre stage, or, if filmed on location, the characters and camera are often set up in a way that produces tableau-like frames – static shots with hardly any movement in them. The characters' strangely artificial acting, the almost emotionless delivery of stilted dialogue, in an accent that has not been heard outside a Fassbinder film, all these devices have a distancing effect on the audience. This was completely intentional (not bad acting!) and Fassbinder's trademark, reflecting his indebtedness to the radical theatre of the playwright, poet and theatre director Bertolt Brecht.

Since Brecht's Epic Theatre had such a strong influence on Fassbinder's work it deserves a closer look here. Briefly, Epic Theatre is the opposite of classical theatre which is based on realism, on actors that identify with their roles, act them out and consequently try to make the audience forget that they are in a play – basically creating an illusion. In contrast, Epic Theatre has a social-political focus, it is based on didacticism, i.e. the playwright wants to make a political point. This is achieved by a variety of means: the plot and the characterisation tend to be simple, the actors do not inhabit their roles, but rather present their lines to us. They often address the audience directly, i.e. they present, rather than represent their characters to us. Brecht used to instruct his actors to always be aware of the wider historical context of their roles, not to individualise them. There are other techniques that prevent our immersion in the play, shake us out of our complacency and make us think. These techniques working together to achieve a certain effect on the audience are called the 'Verfremdungseffekt', whereby something is made to appear unfamiliar or strange. It is often translated as 'alienation effect' and is deliberately employed to distance the audience from the story that is being presented to them, thereby encouraging reflection and opposition. The term 'dialectical theatre' is also used to emphasise the opposites of thesis and antithesis, as in Marx's theory of dialectics.

Fassbinder's second film *Katzelmacher* (1969) was a critical (if not a popular) success; and it earned him nearly a million deutschmarks in awards and state subsidies. He produced film after film, in often desperate financial circumstances, but his next five films did not enjoy much success. They were mainly his own adaptations of classical plays, which he transformed, up-ended, reinterpreted. He was at that time searching for and refining his own stylistic expression in order to be able to convince audiences as much as critics. Watching an early and a late Fassbinder film side by side you will notice just how much his style changed within a very short time. You could even be forgiven for not realising that they are by the same film-maker.

Angst essen Seele auf was his first international success, a story of the love between a young guest worker in Germany and an older woman. In the following year he directed his own adaptation of Theodor Fontane's novel *Effi Briest*. In his interpretation of the classic novel he foregrounds the pressures of society on the young woman. The best known of his works is surely his trilogy of films about the end of National Socialism and the first two decades of the Federal Republic of Germany (FRG or BRD in German), his *BRD Trilogie*, consisting of *Die Ehe der Maria Braun* (1978), *Lola* (1981) and *Die Sehnsucht der Veronika Voss* (1981). Together the three films constitute his personal interpretation of post-war West German history. Of the three films *Maria Braun* has been Fassbinder's commercially most successful work. As in most of his films the protagonist is female. He felt a particular empathy with women and their status in a male-dominated society in which, according to Fassbinder, they were regarded as inferior and were objectified for men's pleasure. Consequently, in film they were too often used merely to motivate men and were not given their own voice. In order to escape this objectification, Fassbinder maintains, they were forced to resort to less than noble means. His Braun is one of these women who have to fight in a man's world. [2] *Maria Braun* finally brought him the recognition that he craved so much: to be taken seriously in America. This was for him a yardstick against which he measured his success in storytelling. Although it is an explicitly historical film, whatever film Fassbinder made, the past and the present were always there in his work – even his films that are set in the past always resonate in the present. This is an interest he has in common with his contemporary auteur-director colleagues. In line with Brecht's influence on Fassbinder we, the audience, are supposed to question ourselves and our attitudes, such as small-mindedness, lack of love and compassion, and selfish materialism.

Angst essen Seele auf is a good example of Fassbinder's preferred subjects of outsiders and minorities in society, as well as his empathy with women. Again we have a (victimised, flawed) female protagonist, while issues of social angst, isolation and loneliness, and the mechanisms of stereotyping are at the very centre of *Angst*. In his second film, *Katzelmacher*, Fassbinder had already turned to the subject of immigrant workers in Germany: In the earlier film a Greek immigrant worker is taunted by the petit-bourgeois citizens of a small Bavarian town. Fassbinder was way ahead of his time in making this film. He is acknowledged as being the first to tackle a topic that nobody else was willing to touch. The main difference between *Katzelmacher* and *Angst* is one of style, his development towards more melodramatic techniques which allow the audience to identify with the characters. We will explore this difference later in the chapter.

In West German society at that time, in the sixties and seventies, foreign workers were perceived by many as a 'necessary evil'. They had been invited by Germany from 1955 onwards (from southern European countries such as Italy, Greece, Spain, etc.) by means of an agreement with those countries to bring 'guest workers' into West Germany, when it became apparent that in order to rebuild the country and to develop the economy the male workforce needed to be supplemented. The term immediately suggests transience. Commensurate with the idea that Germany was not to become a country of immigration, temporary residence was the aim. The migrants were expected to work in Germany for a limited time (usually a year), and then to return to their home countries. Many stayed, however, and quite often their families followed them to Germany. This caused significant demographic changes and subsequent discussion about positive and negative consequences of the influx, but still there was no political will to recognise more permanent residency. In fact, in 1973 active procurement of foreign workers was stopped, and 'consolidation', i.e. limitation, was now the aim. However, the authorities still did not deal with the issue, and because these people were never acknowledged as 'immigrants' there were never any serious attempts at integrating them into German society. No measures were taken to ensure any kind of equality between Germans and 'foreigners'. Very gradually the development of the European Community improved the status of migrants from member states. Nowadays it is mainly the large migrant population of Turkish origin (almost 2 million) that is suffering the results of this lack of integration policies and measures. However, it would be too short-sighted to simply say that they 'suffer'. In their midst a rich culture of 'metissage' has developed over the last twenty years [3] Our chapter on Fatih Akin's *Gegen die Wand* (*Head-On*, 2004) highlights both the issues and achievements of immigrants of Turkish origin in Germany.

The narrative of *Angst essen Seele auf* focuses on the relationship between a young Moroccan guest worker whom everybody calls Ali because they cannot remember his real name, and an older widow, Emmi. They find refuge in each other's company; they find love out of mutual acceptance.

Very quickly they decide to get married. The world around them does not accept their relationship and people react by rejecting both the 'dirty foreigner' and the older woman who should know better. The negative reactions of Emmi's colleagues, Ali's old friends and lovers, and most shockingly, Emmi's family, are explored. However, when, for opportunistic reasons, their environment changes, they are forced to confront their relationship more clearly. Fissures appear, cultural differences become more pronounced, and personal weaknesses rise to the surface. The end of the film leaves open whether their relationship can survive or not. In the press notes to the film Fassbinder assesses the possibility or impossibility of their situation by emphasising that it is the outside pressure that keeps Emmi and Ali together at first and that the conflicts between them begin to show when that pressure has subsided. This is where the film ends. A further exploration of their persistent problems, the inner structures of their relationship, is expressly not part of the film. Those issues would have to be dealt with in another film, says Fassbinder. *Angst essen Seele auf* therefore shows both reality and possibility, but no solution. The interplay between a repressive society, the resulting oppression of women and others on the lower rungs of the social ladder, together with personal weaknesses and fears lies at the centre of the story.

The film begins with Emmi entering a bar in order to shelter from the rain. In this very first scene, and throughout the film, doors and frames are used frequently by Fassbinder. Doors offer possibilities, as here when Emmi, uneasily, walks into a strange place where she will meet a man. Doors also close; people remain on their threshold, uncertain, undecided. A door may lead to freedom or it may imprison you. Frames enclose people, they restrict them, they display them as on a theatre stage. Emmi is as on a stage as soon as she is inside the bar. She is being watched silently by the other occupants of the place, foreigners, including Ali, and the barmaid. Wide-angle shots create an exaggerated distance between the group and Emmi. We are aware of Emmi's unease, of her feelings of inferiority. And yet, she is brave enough to stay in a bar full of strangers. Thus Ali and Emmi meet. There are very tender moments between them, played out quietly, with great sensitivity. She takes the initiative in asking him to come up to her flat with her and he ends up staying the night. Fassbinder deals with their first love scene very

sensitively through low-key lighting and by fading out to the next morning. In these early phases of their relationship there is no fear; there is only respect for each other and courage by both of them. In fact, when Emmi looks in the mirror the next morning, she is very aware of her situation, of having taken a significant step. She is able to face the challenges that this brings.

The language used throughout the film is that of the not very articulate. Ali speaks broken German, but despite this, his awareness of his own inferior status in society comes through: 'German master, Arab dog,' he says, making explicit his experiences as a guest worker. Emmi for the most part utters generalities: 'I learnt nothing in life', or 'my children live their own lives'. Such simple, almost banal and yet poignant phrases have a didactic purpose.

As a couple they do not just have to face xenophobia but also age-related discrimination, and this leads to a veritable gauntlet-running of the couple wherever they go. Emmi's tongue-wagging neighbours and colleagues make that very clear in their simple but deadly remarks which tend to stop when she is near. They then proceed to ignore her. There is a lunchtime scene on the staircase of the building where Emmi and her colleagues work as cleaners. Emmi is sitting on the stairs to the right, half covered by bars from the railings, while her colleagues sit only a couple of paces away from her, completely ignoring her. For all intents and purposes they could be in a entirely different location. Later, when they have decided that they need her as an ally against a newcomer from Yugoslavia, they sit in almost the same positions, except now the young woman from Yugoslavia is sitting by herself. Again on a staircase, but this time in Emmi's own block of flats, the neighbours say to each other: 'You need to clean more often with someone like that in the house.' Emmi becomes an outcast. By very simple means Fassbinder shows us the mechanisms of oppression.

In the bar, Ali's ex-lovers comment on Emmi as an 'old woman'. Emmi is becoming very worried about the age difference between them, whereas Ali is reassuring: 'You very good, big heart,' he says, to which she replies: 'But I am so full of fear.' His answer to this is the title of the film: 'Angst essen Seele auf' (literally: 'Fear eats the soul'). What he means by this is that people are dominated by fear, it keeps them from being able to act normally, it paralyses people. As with so many lines that Fassbinder's characters speak this is a simple but very profound statement indeed.

The causes and the purpose of stereotyping are made very clear in this film. Xenophobia and the common stereotypes that arise from it are used as an example of the stereotype as such. What is unknown makes us afraid because it threatens our fixed identity (which in any case may not be quite so strong, especially if we are victimised in the society in which we live). We are scared to face this potential change in us that meeting strangers might bring. Therefore we will do anything to exclude this potential threat. We do this by emphasising the differences between us and the 'other', expressed by phrases (from the film) such as: 'The dirty pigs, they never wash. They just want to take away our women and have sex with them...' However, stereotypes do not just arise out of fear. There is at the same time a fascination for, even attraction towards, the unknown. We perceive the 'other' as exotic, as desirable from a distance, which is another way of pointing at the 'other' as different from us. The simultaneous fear and attraction can result in envy towards those who have what we do not have. This tension, or ambivalence, is the defining characteristic of stereotypes.

Against this hostile background the relationship between Emmi and Ali holds up well. While they are threatened from outside they are not forced to deal with their own problems. This is a very realistic assessment of human behaviour that also translates well to societies and nations. Wars, for example, keep societies together; alliances are formed between states that have otherwise nothing in common, only the common enemy. (Just consider World War II, in which the USA and the Soviet Union, two incompatible political systems, were allies, with Germany as the common enemy.)

The turning point in the public's behaviour towards the couple occurs after they return from a holiday. Inexplicably, they find themselves confronted by changed behaviour from their neighbourhood and family. But this is not a dream come true: everybody has their own ulterior motives for being nice to the couple. The grocer needs Emmi's custom, the neighbours need her as an ally, her son wants her to baby-sit, and the colleagues have a new target and need her support. Emmi is relieved to be accepted into society once more, but as a result she changes. She becomes more 'German', she objectifies Ali, parades him in front of people, makes him feel very uncomfortable, and she ignores his cultural needs. For example, she refuses to cook for him the food he likes to eat. Fassbinder shows us that victims can also turn into perpetrators; they are not free from insensitivity.

Ali realises the change in her, and, in quiet desperation, he turns once again to a former lover for solace. The love scene between Barbara and Ali is shown in medium long shot, in a frame within the frame. Thus, again, we have the combination of strong emotions within a distancing mise-en-scène. Once again, Emmi faces herself in the mirror, realises her wrongdoing and goes in search of him. They make up, but there is a question mark over their future together.

At the end, quite unexpectedly, the narrative is lifted from the personal to the overtly political, when Ali breaks down with unbearable pain and the doctor tells Emmi that he is suffering from stomach ulcers. He calls these 'the guest workers' disease' and explains to her that they are due to the stresses that foreign workers are exposed to. The film ends with Ali in hospital and Emmi by his side. The story of Emmi and Ali is a simple one, in line with Fassbinder's belief that simple stories are more true than complex ones. They do not disguise basic facts and behaviours; instead they force us to confront them. We are asked to fill in our own details and to relate the story to other, similar issues, including those that impact on our own lives. We are also asked to fill in our own endings, find our own ways for change.

Angst essen Seele auf can be traced back to two other films: a story which is told by a chamber maid in Fassbinder's own *Der amerikanische Soldat* (*The American Soldier*, 1970), and Douglas Sirk's *All that Heaven Allows* (1956), produced in Hollywood, by Universal Studios. Fassbinder retained the confrontation between German petite bourgeoisie and immigrant, as well as the names Emmi and Ali from *Soldat*. *All that Heaven Allows* depicts the relationship between a middle-class widow and her younger gardener. It is set in small-town America in the 1950s and reveals a society that reacts viciously to the 'inappropriate' relationship. The film ends with the 'possibility' that Fassbinder mentions, but also with the confrontation with 'reality', and with potential 'impossibility'. In both films the final scene shows the men in their sick beds with the women looking after them, determined for them to get better, but at the same time confronted with a future in which they have to examine their relationship very carefully. The fact that a 1950s' film can be translated convincingly into a 1970s' film shows the insight of both Sirk and Fassbinder into societal mechanisms that do not change.

Arguably the most devastating scene in *All that Heaven Allows* occurs when the heroine's children, who have persuaded, manipulatedand and coerced her into abandoning the relationship with the young gardener, buy her a television set for Christmas, something which every lonely middle-aged woman needs, as a substitute for the personal fulfilment she has given up. In *Angst essen Seele auf* this key scene is transformed by Fassbinder into the equally important scene in which Emmi introduces her new husband Ali to her grown-up children and their spouses.

She has invited them to her home in order to tell them the important news, but they do not know yet what it entails. They are waiting in her living room, when she brings out her new husband and says: 'This is my husband.' Stony silence greets the announcement, and then reactions of horror and aggression ensue: 'This dishonour! You can forget that you have children.' Her daughter's abusive husband gets up and, in complete silence, commits an act of utter hatred and senseless destruction: He kicks in her television set. Without saying another word they all leave her flat. This scene is so effective because of the uncanny silence in which it is played out and the totally unexpected eruption of violence.

The film as a whole is testament to Fassbinder's enormous admiration of Douglas Sirk. Sirk (Detlev Sieck) was a Dane who made films in Germany but who left the country – like so many others – after the Nazis had come to power. He went to Hollywood, where he was initially not very successful, but became well-known in the 1950s for his 'sophisticated melodramas' in which he surreptitiously criticised the American Dream – without anybody at the time noticing that he was doing it. It took a number of years for European film critics to 'discover' the real messages, the subtext, of Sirk's films. This is when Fassbinder became aware of him. Sirk's influence on Fassbinder's films from 1971 onwards cannot be underestimated, and it has been acknowledged by Fassbinder himself on many occasions. In an interview in 1980 he said: 'After seeing Sirk's films it seems to me more and more that love is the best, the most surreptitious and effective instrument of social repression... Sirk knows how to handle actors, it's breathtaking... In a Sirk film women think. I've not noticed this with any other director. Usually, women react, do whatever it is that women do, and here they think. That has to be seen. It is good to see a woman think. That gives you hope. Really.'[4] This realisation quite clearly tied in with his own view of women as victims of patriarchal society and as strong human beings.

Fassbinder also acknowledges Sirk's influence on him with regard to the way Sirk manipulated narrative conventions within a Hollywood 'look', particularly with regard to the ambiguous endings of his films. The fact that it was possible to slip your own messages into a Hollywood film, to work on two levels, to criticise and entertain at the same time, was a revelation for him. Before meeting Sirk through his films, telling stories 'the Hollywood way' would have gone against his sensibilities as a European. Watching Sirk's films was a liberating experience.

However, *Angst essen Seele auf* does not just pay homage to Sirk, nor is it just a remake of *All that Heaven Allows* or a wholesale adoption of Hollywood style melodrama. It is situated in what could be termed Fassbinder's 'second phase' of film-making, which integrates his earlier, stark and minimalist films with a new, more melodramatic, style. Part of this style is to show emotions more directly, to court popular appeal more openly than his earlier films. The melodrama approach to film-making relies on the direct emotional involvement of the audience. Empathy and compassion are elicited through a combination of devices: the central figure tends to be a woman, the narrative revolves around personal relationships, music denotes and emphasises emotional turmoil, and there are many close-ups in order to allow the audience to identify with the protagonists. In the best melodramas, however, wider issues become apparent, such as the fallacy of the American Dream in Sirk's films, exemplified by the fissures in the nuclear family. In Fassbinder's approach to melodrama his principal concerns are still prevalent; his new, more melodramatic approach is modified, downplayed, and formed into a new whole. In true dialectic fashion one could speak of his earlier 'antitheater' work, influenced by

Brechtian Epic Theatre, as the thesis, Sirkian Hollywood melodrama as antithesis, and the minimalist melodramatic approach resulting from these as the synthesis. Thus Fassbinder manages to integrate disparate influences into his very own inimitable signature. The film-maker who was so desperate to become popular achieved what he set out to do. In the mid-seventies his mixture of traditional, popular, even trivial, melodramatic stories and his unconventional, minimalist style convinced critics and succeeded at the box office.

We have detailed above some of the devices that Fassbinder uses in order to put across his story of *Angst essen Seele auf*. In summary, we have found out that he employs a unique combination of melodrama and Brechtian didacticism. He uses these contrasting devices to great effect. Melodrama's big emotions are rendered in small gestures and words that are delivered almost without emotion, the only exception being the way aggressive behaviour is shown. Fassbinder achieves startling effects through the juxtaposition of silence and explosive aggression, whether it is physical (as in the television set scene) or verbal (as with the tongue-wagging colleagues). Silence is very important here to help us concentrate on the story without being distracted or manipulated by, for example, non-diegetic music. Yet we do identify with the victims of cruelty, even though (or maybe because) they are naive, not very complex characters. Their stories are reduced to simplified model situations that make the world transparent. They make us think and analyse our own situation and that of the world around us.

Fassbinder's visual style is similarly 'basic'; he employs mostly a static camera, with often medium to long shots in long takes to let the action take its course, to not manipulate us, often also to create discomfort. His mise-en-scène is minimalist; frames within the frame make visible the artificiality of the 'stage'. The frames also convey the fact that the characters are trapped in their situations and that they are often observed by third parties (including the audience). This makes us aware of our complicity – it both draws us in and distances us at the same time.

Angst essen Seele auf is an example of Fassbinder's 'middle period', before he developed his own brand of melodrama further in such films as his trilogy on the Federal Republic of Germany, or in his television adaptation of Alfred Döblin's *Berlin Alexanderplatz* (1982), which was one of his final works. Consistent with this qualitative change Fassbinder changed the 'personnel recruitment policy' for his films from *Angst* onwards. Up until then he had recruited exclusively from the radical 'antitheater' team, but now he enriched his team with actors from the 'old guard' of German film-making. (For a more detailed discussion of and distinction between the 'old' and the 'new' German cinema please see the introduction to this book, and the chapters on *Aguirre* and *Die Blechtrommel*). In *Angst*, for example, we find Brigitte Mira (as Emmi) and Barbara Valentin (as Barbara), both actors from an earlier period of German film-making. 'They are professionals and have a certain glamour which is important to me. They have always been good actors, they only acted in bad films,' Fassbinder said in 1979.

Angst essen Seele auf was the German submission to the Cannes Film Festival in 1974, and was awarded the International Jury Prize and the Christian Jury Award. Brigitte Mira was awarded the German Film Award in 1974 for best actress. She went on to become a staple in later Fassbinder films.

The critic Peter Buchka, who also conducted one of the rare interviews with Fassbinder, wrote on the day after his death in Süddeutsche Zeitung: 'Because he worked in such a self-destructive fashion, and because he turned his innermost self outside without any protection, all those rough edges, all those fissures have remained visible under the porous surface of his films, and they give us an insight into this disorderly, deeply sentimental and at the same time enormously professional life. It is almost impossible to describe the way in which imagination and reality have been mixed in this hurled-out oeuvre. Subconsciously Fassbinder testifies with every film to the restless search for his own identity.'

It is hard to imagine a more resounding testament to Fassbinder as an auteur-director, someone whose personal signature is the most prominent feature of his *oeuvre*. This view is generally held amongst most scholars and critics. However, given the fact that Fassbinder's death in 1982 became generally accepted as the end of New German Cinema we must not lose sight of his involvement with and contribution to it.

Fassbinder was a late-comer to New German Cinema. When he started making films at the end of the 1960s, the Oberhausen Manifesto was already seven years old, and its signatories and others had made their first films. Most importantly, however, there was an infrastructure in place which allowed Fassbinder and other late-comers to take advantage of a system of film schools and public film funding – a luxury that the pioneers had not had. While Fassbinder did not benefit from film schools (he applied but was rejected) he did receive public funding for his projects.

In an interview from 1977 Fassbinder describes his views on and his relationship with New German Cinema: He speaks of three generations of film-makers. In his view the first generation was occupied with working against the 'old' and with establishing something new. For that reason it took them a few years to actually make feature films. The 'in-between' generation pretended too quickly to be 'Hollywood' – they made one-off, expensive films, without having the necessary knowledge and skills. He saw himself, together with Wim Wenders and Werner Herzog, as part of a third generation, one that benefited from endeavours as well as mistakes made by earlier generations. In Fassbinder's words, 'We were lucky that we didn't have to fight. The generation before us made big films too quickly without knowing enough. We had the freedom. We started from scratch, even at the price of lacking professionalism to begin with. We are self-taught.' In his opinion it is only through learning by doing that you can really develop your own vision as a film-maker.

FOOTNOTES

[1] Hanna Schygulla was termed 'Europe's most exciting actress' by Time in 1985. She played the lead in Fassbinder's most successful film, *Die Ehe der Maria Braun* (*The Marriage of Maria Braun*, 1978). Schygulla also plays the mother in Fathi Akin's latest film, *Auf der anderen Seite* (*The Edge of Heaven*, see chapter 13.

[2] It would be quite interesting to compare and contrast Maria's character to the character of Susanne in *Die Mörder sind unter uns*.

[3] Metissage was originally a negative term meaning 'mixed blood', but it has been appropriated in a positive way, to mean merging cultural identities.

[4] In this chapter all translations are by the author, unless stated otherwise.

CHAPTER EIGHT: A POLITICAL FAIRY TALE: *DIE BLECHTROMMEL (THE TIN DRUM, 1979)*

Volker Schlöndorff's *Die Blechtrommel* completes our selection of key films of New German Cinema in the strictest sense, as the era of film-making in Germany between 1970 and 1982. Schlöndorff may not be quite such a renowned name as Fassbinder, Herzog, or Wenders, although he was and still is one of the key figures of cinema, both in Germany and in Europe. Across his work (and outside it) we find involvement with contemporary politics in general and a commitment to film politics in particular. The reasons for his relative unfamiliarity may be found in his flexibility with regard to different genres, including literary adaptations, resulting in a certain lack of recognisable authorship. However, his reputation for a certain 'blandness' is quite unjustified. By including him in this book we are attempting to rectify the situation in a small way. We have selected one of his literary adaptations, *Die Blechtrommel*, because it has been his most successful film in Germany and internationally, and also because it proves his adeptness at filming allegedly 'unfilmable' material. Our exploration will also provide an insight into the process of adaptation.

In general, films by new German film-makers of the late 1960s and 1970s were noted much more abroad than in Germany. Literary adaptations were the exception. They tended to be quite popular at the German box office, unlike many of the films from original screenplays. This is related to the continuing non-cinephile attitude of audiences in Germany – Germans, in particular those that might be the addressees for New German art films, prefer to go to the theatre instead, as we outlined in our introduction to New German Cinema in chapter 6. If they do go to the cinema it is because they have a propensity for literary adaptations.

Within the German film funding system as it operated at the time it was also easier to get literary adaptations financed and therefore made. This was mainly due to the fact that the film funding bodies based their decisions on submitted screenplays. It is arguably much easier to see 'value' in a literary adaptation than in an original screenplay: Those film-makers presenting original screenplays had greater difficulty demonstrating to the funding bodies what the finished film would look like, whereas those with literary sources had a 'pedigree' to point to. A not inconsiderable influence was and is exerted by television, which co-produced (and still co-produces) many films, according to the film-television-agreement (see more on this towards the end of this chapter).

There is indeed a long tradition of adapting literary works in German cinema. Several classic German (or rather German-language) authors' works were adapted for the screen from the days of silent cinema. Germany's most important author Johann Wolfgang von Goethe was one of them. The first Faust film was made in 1927 by F. W. Murnau, and of course *Der blaue Engel* was an adaptation of *Professor Unrat* by Heinrich Mann, to name but two. You may also remember that there were large numbers of literary adaptations in the GDR – if for different reasons. There, film-makers took recourse to them because they were deemed 'safe' in a climate of political repression. Since the books had already been published and 'approved', the hope was that screen adaptations would not encounter censorship interference. As we have seen in our chapter on *Spur der Steine*, this was not always guaranteed, though.

Some of Schlöndorff's best-known adaptations were his first feature film *Der junge Törless* (*Young Törless*, 1966), an adaptation of Robert Musil's novel *Die Verwirrungen des Zöglings Törless* (1906), and one of the very first productions of Young German Cinema of the 1960s. Then there was Heinrich Böll's *Die Verlorene Ehre der Katharina Blum*, made into a film with the same title in 1975, *Die Blechtrommel* (1950) by Günter Grass, our focus film in this chapter, and *Homo Faber* by Max Frisch, which he adapted for the screen in 1991. His *oeuvre* abounds with literary adaptations. When asked in interviews what makes him choose certain authors, who, on the surface, do not have much in common, he admits that there never is a plan, but that he conducts his own private dialogue with books – they tend to find him rather than him finding them, they tend to fit in with a particular phase in his life. His sources are indeed very different, with regard to genre, historical background and subject matter. He refuses to be tied down to any particular genre or political or moral message. (This does not mean, however, that he is apolitical, as we shall see later.) He likes to go his own way and observe without being involved in fashionable trends. However, and despite this eclectic approach, he always uses famous literary works, not light fiction: books by Musil, Kleist, Brecht, Böll, Grass, and Frisch, to name but a few. They are all authors that belong to the pantheon of German-language literature. Despite their differences they share a sense of history and flawed or struggling protagonists.

The work of one post-war German author in particular was adapted for film in preference to others: Heinrich Böll. Of all contemporary German writers Böll became the defining force in the literary representation of post-war Germany. In his short stories and novels he chronicled most authentically the times and transitions from immediate post-war events through the fifties with their consumerist boom in West Germany and further until his death in 1985. He was always associated with left-wing politics, was politically active in a high-profile manner, and therefore made quite a few political enemies. Already in the first half of the 1960s adaptations of his works were made for the cinema, e.g. *Das Brot der frühen Jahre* (*The Bread of Those Early Years*, 1962) by Herbert Vesely, *Nicht versöhnt* (*Not Reconciled*, 1965) by Jean-Marie Straub and Danièle Huillet. The aforementioned source novels are a clear indication of Böll's interest in recent German history. They deal with Germany's Nazi past (*Nicht Versöhnt*) and with the immediate post-war period (*Das Brot der frühen Jahre*).

Volker Schlöndorff was a great admirer of Böll's, and his first film well-received in Germany was an adaptation of a Böll novel, *Die verlorene Ehre der Katharina Blum* (*The Lost Honour of Katharina Blum*) which he made in collaboration with his then wife, Margarete von Trotta. [1] The screenplay to *Katharina Blum* was written by the author. Böll's simple story engaged with topical political realities. The subject was contemporary West Germany's obsession with left-wing terrorism of the 1970s, in particular the repressive tendencies in West Germany, where civil liberties were undermined and the right-wing press intruded in soul- (and sometimes life-) destroying manner into ordinary people's lives. The story fulfilled two of Schlöndorff's key beliefs: First of all, a work of art must have a valid social message, one that chimes with the audience. His second key term is decency, which he always privileges over any ideological content. For him a decent person is someone who is aware of and admits his/her contradictions and strives to resolve them. This applies to the characters in his films, but it also includes the film-maker. The most striking example is *Katharina Blum*, but the same preoccupation runs through Schlöndorff's entire *oeuvre*. The overwhelmingly positive reception of *Katharina Blum* in Germany came almost as a surprise to the director and the author.

Another German writer who caught Schlöndorff's imagination was Günter Grass. He was born in 1927, only ten years after Böll, and yet they are seen as belonging to quite different generations. Grass' writing could not have been more different from Böll's. Where Böll is known for his straight and simple style (he has been compared to Hemingway) and his short stories and short novels, Grass tends to write complex novels with convoluted plots in language that is equally complex, baroque, ironic, rude and sometimes even gross. Thus the two writers can be said to belong to two completely different schools of writing: the immediate post-war reaction to the overblown style of the National Socialists on the one hand, and a new style within German literature on the other, one which evolved from the publication of *Die Blechtrommel* onwards.

However, Grass shares Böll's political views and active involvement in politics. In his younger years he was a very angry young man indeed. He, like Böll, bemoaned the passivity, the apparent lack of coming to terms with Germany's recent past of the German people. [7] His most famous novel, *Die Blechtrommel,* was published in 1959. It caused quite a stir upon its publication because of its completely new literary approach. It was noted for its complexity in content and language and was both praised and criticised for its openly unromanticised sexual content. He was accused even of blasphemy.

Considering that the two above-mentioned authors are so wildly different in their approach, it is all the more astonishing that Schlöndorff managed to translate their most famous books equally successfully into films. *Die Blechtrommel* was Schlöndorff's international breakthrough. At the time it became the most successful German post-war film at the box office and has remained one of the most successful German films ever: In 1979, Schlöndorff received the Palme d'Or at the Cannes Film Festival for *Die Blechtrommel* – the first German director ever to win it. Also, in 1980, *Die Blechtrommel* won the best foreign-language film Oscar – the first German win since 1927! [3] You may remember that Emil Jannings won the first ever Oscar for Best Actor in 1927 (see also our chapter on *Der blaue Engel*).

The German film producer Franz Seitz had aquired the film rights to *Die Blechtrommel* and approached Schlöndorff to direct it, because he felt that Schlöndorff, with his pedigree in successful literary adaptations, was the right person for the job. Schlöndorff had reservations at first, not least because the famous source novel with its epic size and the complexity of its multi-perspective story meant a real challenge. [4] Detailed research into the original locations within Gdansk was necessary, even though it was the place where Günter Grass had grown up and therefore knew very well. The most difficult obstacle for Schlöndorff to overcome was the choice of actor for the unusual protagonist. It was not until he was completely satisfied that he had found the right male lead that he agreed to make the film.

Fortunately the producer had secured generous financing for the film, which was absolutely necessary in order to resolve all the above-mentioned problems at the pre-production stage alone. In order to achieve the right production design meticulous preparation was required, both researching the original locations in Gdansk and re-creating them as sets. Authenticity was of prime importance to Schlöndorff. Since much of the action takes place in the 'world' of the protagonist Oskar Mazerath, the family's living quarters behind his father's grocer's shop, these had to be given special priority. Schlöndorff and his creative team went to Gdansk in order to research the part of the city where Günter Grass was born. Grass' family home in Gdansk provided them with a wealth of original features from the days of his childhood which they were able to translate into their set of the family home. The place was rebuilt in the studio, larger and more labyrinthine than the original in order to represent little Oskar's complex universe. However, because of the extraordinary, fairy-tale character of the novel, 'authenticity' was not just a matter of staying true to original locations. In order to bring together the 'real and imaginary worlds' the whole set had to have a picture-book quality at the same time as being realistic, a combination that was hard to achieve.

Before we explore the film in more detail let us see just how extraordinary the story of little Oskar is, which will also explain why it was so difficult for Schlöndorff to find his lead actor. Oskar is a boy who lives in Gdansk with his parents in the twenties and thirties. At that time Gdansk, now in Poland, was called Danzig and was a 'free city', after having been part of Germany until the end of World War I (see also below). At the age of three Oskar decides that he does not want to grow up and become an adult like those around him. He literally achieves this by throwing himself down the cellar stairs, thereby injuring his spine, which stops him from growing. Consequently he develops into an adult trapped in a child's body. The book follows him until the end of World War II, by which time he has ended up in an asylum. From there he tells his own story. At the end of the war he decides to end his rebellion and makes the decision to finally grow into an adult. On a metaphorical level Oskar's refusal to become part of the adult world coincides with major historical events, and Oskar's world is also Grass' world. Such a multi-layered historical and fairy-tale narrative is very difficult to translate into film.

For the film, Schlöndorff decided to simplify the story and to abandon altogether the framing device of the adult Oskar telling his story. Thus the film begins in 1924, with Oskar's birth, and ends in 1945, and we are in Oskar's (child) world throughout the film. He is variously the first-person and third-person narrator; in a child-like and at the same time menacing voice he tells his own story, sparingly and effectively. Over long stretches of the film he does not speak at all – neither on-screen nor in voice-over; the visuals take over. Schlöndorff received Grass' approval for these major changes. In fact, the author contributed to the screenplay. Schlöndorff and Grass also worked together during the actual production process.

By now it has probably become obvious why Schlöndorff was so concerned about a suitable lead actor. It was a stroke of luck that he met David Bennent, the boy that plays little Oskar. David Bennent was the son of Heinz Bennent, who at the time was a well-known German actor of stage and screen. David was twelve years old when the film was made and was unusually small for an eleven-year-old. For Schlöndorff he had the right physical appearance, the right voice, and the right attitude for playing Oskar – he was perfect. In fact, Schlöndorff stated categorically that without David he would not have made the film. For him no other actor would have been able to represent Grass' protagonist and convey his extraordinary story better. He was convinced that this

'German fresco' – world history seen from below – with huge, spectacular images that are anchored by little Oskar with his dual characteristics of denial and protest, needed to be played by a child, not by an adult playing a child.

Since David appears in almost every single scene the filming made great demands on him, but Schlöndorff cherished him as he would his own child. More than that, he pampered him so that he would feel 'the greatest' during the filming process. This contributed to what Schlöndorff called 'a child's megalomania', the belief that he, David, had created the protagonist all by himself, a belief that he communicated to everybody who was prepared to listen, including Grass himself on his visits to the set.

From the beginning we are in Oskar's world. This is made clear by the voice-over narration, but also by the camera position and angle which consistently takes Oskar's point of view. Therefore, and logically, the first event we witness is his birth. In the book the description of it is very vivid, almost grotesque: The unborn Oskar has a clear sense of himself in his mother's womb and he begins his story from inside it. In order to convey the fantastic nature of this scene Schlöndorff filmed it in simple craftsman-like actions which he compares to the approach of Meliès, [5] with the real David representing the foetus, with handmade props that had to be built to the boy's size to make him appear smaller. We see David with a mask to hide his hair and with plastic eyelids to make him resemble a just-born baby. He is lurking in his mother's womb, represented by torn and flowing red rags, reluctant to leave it, and delaying his birth for as long as he can, but ultimately he can't avoid it. All the while he comments on it by telling us that he 'first saw the light of this world in the shape of two sixty-watt light bulbs'. This was filmed quite literally. His mother implores him to come out and promises him a tin drum at the age of three. He tells us: 'The expectation of a tin drum at the age of three prevented me from expressing my desire to return to my mother's womb more forcefully. Moreover, the midwife had severed the connection - there was nothing more to be done about it.' The child's voice-over, in an adult register, together with the deliberately grotesque birth process, captures the book's style very well. At the same time it makes us realise that this child has powers beyond the ordinary.

During the long sections of the film when Oskar does not speak at all, he listens intently to every adult utterance, and follows their every move with his piercing blue eyes and his reproachful stare, without saying a single word. He has long realised that his attractive, highly-strung mother is having an affair with his Uncle Jan, who is Polish, after having given up the idea of marrying him although she loves him. She marries Alfred Mazerath instead, in all likelihood because he is German. The three of them seem to live in a perfectly accepted ménage-à-trois. Oskar's Uncle Jan may even be his real father.

Oskar has not forgotten that he is owed a tin drum on his third birthday. On the day he is given his drum he immediately makes his decision to avoid becoming like the adults he observes. When his height is measured by Uncle Jan, who tells him how quickly he is growing and how soon he will be a grown-up, his mind is made up. This

is all shown through non-verbal behaviour, all through his stare – at the wall where his height is marked and at the adults. After having seen the trap door to the cellar left open by his father (whom he does not like, he prefers his Uncle Jan), he plans to fall through that door into the cellar in order to damage his spine, which will then arrest his growth. His plan works, of course, and there is even added value to this for Oskar, because his father is blamed for causing the 'accident'.

From then on, safe in the knowledge that he will get older and wiser in the shape of a child, he expresses his views via his drum, the beating of which also serves as a reminder to everybody of just how powerful he is. Soon he discovers his other, super-human, quality: He is able to make glass shatter by screaming. This can be achieved selectively,

wherever he directs his piercing scream. From then on he has an additional weapon against any unwelcome situation: 'No one dared take my drum away from me.' On his first day at school Frau Stollenhauer, the teacher, learns this to her dismay – he makes her glasses shatter when she tries to take his drum from him.

Through Oskar we experience the rise of the Nazis and their lure for the German population of Danzig. One day, when Oskar and his mother return home from one of her amorous outings, the street is full of Hitler's voice over the radio. We hear him say: 'The corridor was and is German.' 'The corridor' refers to the geopolitical situation of the 'free city' of Danzig: As a result of World War I, Poland was granted access to the Baltic via a so-called 'corridor', which cut off German territories to the east of it. The 'corridor' included Danzig at its northern end. This was a bone of contention throughout the 1920s and became one of the justifications for Hitler to invade Poland in order to 'retrieve' what was 'rightfully' German. In this historically important speech Hitler continues to insist: 'All those areas owe their cultural development only to the German people.' The film's characters do not pay much attention to the speech, including Oskar's mother who complains upon her return home to her husband: 'Everywhere the Führer is speaking, but not here in our house.' By this statement she is not expressing a comment on the speech but only the fact that they do not have a radio. This situation is rectified soon, and the picture of Beethoven which stands on the piano is replaced by a picture of Hitler. Again, this is done without any comment.

After a performance of a troupe of midgets at the circus, Oskar has the opportunity to meet them, naturally drawn to adults who are no taller than he himself is. The head of their troupe tries to convince him to come with them and perform in a circus, where he could use his screaming and drumming talents. He is only too aware of the political situation and prophesises: 'They will come. They will occupy the festival grounds, they will organise torch rallies, they will build stages, they will populate the stages and from there they will deliver sermons which will lead to our downfall.' In a beautiful juxtaposition of verbal prognosis and visuals, Schlöndorff shows us Hitler's photograph taking centre stage at the Mazerath home, and we see the stage being prepared for a political rally at Danzig's festival ground. In this montage the comparison is explicitly made between the Nazis and a circus.

The most circus-like scene of the film occurs during the Nazi rally. Most of Danzig, at least from within the German population, rushes to the festival ground to listen to the speeches and to watch the military pomp and circumstance of the Party display. A brass band is playing, uniformed men are marching, the youngsters are organised in their Hitler Youth and Girls' Association line-up respectively, and everybody gives the Nazi salute. Oskar approaches with his drum and hides under the wooden stage. He sits down and begins to play to his own tune; determined and disciplined he begins to play a waltz

rhythm. First of all, the marching boots get confused and lose their rhythm, and then very gradually the band falls in with the waltz and ends up playing 'The Blue Danube'. The outstretched arms start waving from left to right, and finally the boys and girls, previously separated, and the rest of the assembly form couples and start dancing.

However, history takes its course, Hitler cannot be stopped, not even by Oskar, and in 1939, after the German invasion of Poland, Oskar tells us in voice-over: 'The Hanse town of Danzig was able to celebrate the annexing of its Gothic brick architecture to the German Reich.' Hitler himself comes to visit Danzig. Schlöndorff decided to include only one shot of him in the film, but without showing him directly. Hitler is represented from his own perspective, showing only his hand, raised in a Nazi salute. The visual distortion that this shot creates is another example of how well the source book's message was conveyed in the film. It is also an instance of the 'unrepresentability' of Hitler in those days (see our chapter on *Der Untergang*).

Oskar's mother falls pregnant without knowing who the father is. She goes to confession and takes Oskar with her. While he is left waiting he discovers a statue of Maria and the boy Jesus, who seems to have his arm stretched out towards Oskar. He approaches the statue and looks at Jesus intently, perhaps waiting for him to say something. Feeling in

a generous mood, he climbs up, hangs his drum around Jesus' neck and places the drums sticks into his hands. 'Come on then', he says, 'play!' He is rudely jerked away by the priest and scolded for blasphemy. This was one of the passages in the book for which Grass was criticised heavily in Catholic Church circles. In the film it is perfectly conveyed through Oskar's usual determined intensity.

The sexual content of some scenes was also criticised, particularly with regard to the display of sexual desire of the 'child' protagonist. However, whatever sexual activity we are shown is never gratuitous – it is always used to further the story and highlight the state of mind of the protagonist, fully commensurate with the book. It is, after all, important to show that Oskar is gradually becoming an adult, if not 'growing up' in the physical sense. Oskar discovers sexual attraction at the age of 18, when, after the death of his mother, his father brings home a young woman, Maria, in order to keep house. He falls in love with her.

Representing sexual activity that involves a 12-year-old actor cannot be accomplished without great care. The most controversial scene is the 'changing room' scene, by the seaside, when Maria and Oskar get changed into their swimming costumes. It is Maria who taunts him by getting undressed and turning around to face him. As late as 1997 Schlöndorff encountered problems with this scene. In Oklahoma, a father happened to see it on a video which his daughter had brought home from school where they had discussed book and film in class. In his outrage the father tried to have the film banned on the grounds of 'child prostitution'. The case went to court, but was dismissed

because Schlöndorff was able to prove (by his own storyboard, which he had kept) that absolutely nothing untoward had happened and that David Bennent had been protected throughout the filming of this scene and the rest of the film. Nonetheless in Ontario, the film was censored, and this particular scene was edited out.

Throughout the film it is precisely the device of distancing Oskar from the world of the 'grown-ups' that conveys most effectively Grass'/Schlöndorff's message. Precisely because he develops mentally and sexually, but not physically, he is given the status of a jester, who has free rein to do whatever he wants, simply because he is 'only a child'. No matter what terrible deeds Oskar commits, he is constantly defended by the women who fall for his innocent child's appearance. And all the while, like a true jester, he says and does things that nobody else would; he is a trouble-maker, an oracle, a commentator on the state of the world – or rather the state of Germany. He does this consistently from the perspective of a child (literally, in the point-of-view shots), with a grotesquely distorted mixture of childlike behaviour and adult wisdom. He is the omniscient narrator who is able to see events from the inside (through what he experiences) and from outside: with the benefit of knowing about history (temporal knowledge) and about events taking place elsewhere (geographical knowledge). However, he is not a very reliable narrator. In the book his reporting begins when he is in a mental asylum, in the film when he is not even born. Also, his self-perceived omnipotence, by means of which he is convinced that he can influence world events as well as local ones, is not to be trusted completely.

The precocious Oskar of the film is more human and more emotional than the book's Oskar, no more so than in one key scene involving the Jewish toy shop owner, who appears to be the only character towards whom both the director and the protagonist have any real feelings of sympathy. When developing German nationalism takes on dangerous proportions, a three-tier society emerges with 'real' Germans at the top, Poles (as represented by Oskar's Uncle Jan) in the middle, and Jews at the very bottom. The toy shop owner who keeps Oskar's supply of tin drums replenished is Jewish. He is hopelessly in love with Oskar's mother and looks after Oskar when she goes to her trysts with Jan.

His role in the film is only small, but very important: as a representative in the story of all those Jews who were persecuted during the Nazi regime. Without being told explicitly what is going on we are witness to a terrible act of vandalism of his shop during the events surrounding 'Reichskristallnacht': 9 November, 1938, marked the abrupt change from largely administrative discrimination of the Jewish population to officially sanctioned violence in Germany. During that night synagogues were torched, Jews were openly abused, Jewish property was destroyed. While this is happening to Markus' shop we hear Oskar, the chronicler, in solemn voice-over: 'Once upon a time there was a toy shop

owner whose name was Markus', then: 'Once upon a time there was a drummer whose name was Oskar' and once again: 'Once upon a time there was a toy shop owner whose name was Markus. He took with him all the toys in the world.' This is the moment when Oskar, the boy, finds Markus in his shop – he has committed suicide. In a gesture of unusual compassion and grief, Oskar closes Markus' eyes.

Schlöndorff is clear about how he wanted to portray the Nazis. To begin with they are seen not as demons, but as stupid and laughable. However, when their power increases they become extremely dangerous and their actions have tragic consequences, as exemplified by the scene we just described. Schlöndorff emphasises this tragedy by casting the well-known actor and chansonier of the 1970s, Charles Aznavour, in the role of Markus. Although he only plays a small part, he is the most human character in the film, the only one who acts with dignity throughout. If Oskar had had a choice he would have wanted him as a father.

In *Die Blechtrommel* the theme of 'fathers' is central. There are real fathers, possible fathers, wanted and unwanted fathers, proper fathers, uncertain fathers, even, as Oskar suspects for himself, a choice of two fathers. The self-proclaimed 'father of the nation', Adolf Hitler, is shown as someone who has brought death and destruction, first to minorities within Germany, then to the countries he invades, and ultimately to all of Germany.

A strong link between the discussion of fathers in Grass and Schlöndorff's work and the 'absent fathers' of post-war Germany runs through the film. Within German cinema this links in with the lack of father figures or models for young film-makers after the war. Tracing Schlöndorff's long and distinguished career we observe that his work links the 1960s with present-day German cinema. Thus he could be seen as a kind of father figure within German cinema, even though we are not trying to say that he was the only one. Let us explore this link more closely.

As mentioned before, Schlöndorff's first feature film was *Der junge Törless*. For this film Schlöndorff returned to Germany from an extended stay in France. When he was seventeen years old he went to Paris as an exchange student, and ended up staying for eleven years altogether. During that time he worked as an assistant to some of the French New Wave directors of the late 1950s and early 1960s, such as Louis Malle, Jean-Luc Godard, and Jean-Pierre Melville. The thorough schooling by these modern masters of the cinema gave him a head-start in comparison with his German contemporaries, who did not have such opportunities. Schlöndorff was determined to make films in Germany because, as he said, there was 'no film industry' there, by which he meant the lack of contemporary, politically aware films. He has been very outspoken about his disappointment with the 1950s in Germany, not just in terms of film production, but more generally in terms of political conservatism, narrow-mindedness, and the lack of any set of ideals in West German society. If he had been in Germany at the time of the Oberhausen Manifesto (in 1962), he would surely have signed it.

Der junge Törless was a much-praised film, particularly for its visual style, which harks back to a time when German cinema was recognised as one of the best in the world, the 1920s. For Schlöndorff the influence of film-makers of the second half of the '1920s (such as Pabst and von Stroheim) is particularly relevant. Even though the original novel was written in 1906 and is set in the historical context of the Austro-Hungarian Empire, Schlöndorff injects it with recent German history – exposing the guilt of the fellow travellers, the silent majority who do not act in the face of injustice: passivity equals guilt. For more discussion of this see also our chapter on *Die Mörder sind unter uns*.

The visual style and narrative of his first film is thus commensurate with his declared aim of helping to turn around the desperately impoverished film cultural situation in the Federal Republic of Germany, which was to a large extent due to the lack of film-making traditions: The years of National Socialism had decimated creative film personnel; the break with the tradition of the 1920s was almost complete. Schlöndorff was lucky to have been able to learn his trade in France. He brought with him a professionalism that was rare in Germany at the time.

Schlöndorff has cemented his position as a 'father figure' by still continuing to make feature films today. He succeeded when others of his generation failed or succeeded only briefly or intermittently. In contrast to those in other countries and their 'new' films, West German auteur-directors did not tend to have common goals, except for their aspirations to become truly independent and to find new cinematic expression. It was obvious from their early films onwards that they had quite individualistic approaches to film-making. But their individualism was also in part due to the fact that they were required to compete with each other: The funding situation was difficult and protracted, which forced them into separation instead of cooperation. Many became conformist – more part of the establishment than rebels – or they worked exclusively for television. This was to a large extent due to the lack of models and traditions in German cinema. They were alone, quite literally 'fatherless'. Another factor was that Hollywood films dominated in Germany after World War II (and they still do today), which made distribution of German films difficult: even if films were made they were not necessarily shown on German cinema screens but only on television.

Film funding in Germany is a long, drawn-out process of decision-making by many different funding bodies and government committees. This is because Germany is a federal state, organised into so-called 'Länder'. These Länder have a great deal of autonomy in cultural and educational matters, and this includes film funding. Schlöndorff talks of his frustration with the 'heavy industry' of film funding, where decisions take forever to be made. He bemoans the resulting formulaic approach to new projects, the fact that every detail is analysed and assessed before any decisions are made. The concentration on screenplays as the basis for obtaining funding is problematic, since the finished product is not available, not visible. It is difficult, if not impossible, to understand a film at the screenplay stage. We mentioned the issues surrounding literary adaptations at the beginning of this chapter.

Schlöndorff, although never 'susceptible to ideologies' in the strictest sense, has nevertheless always been politically aware. Injustices committed by those in power have always provoked his outrage. His impulse has always been to be on the side of those who are victimised or vilified, or, in his own words, 'to support the rebels'. In the late 1960s and 1970s West Germany experienced its own brand of extreme rebel: leftwing terrorists, who called themselves the 'Red Army Faction' (RAF). Schlöndorff was interested in this phenomenon and its causes. At the time he even expressed certain sympathies with West Germany's leftwing terrorists, and criticised the disproportionate reaction of the West German state to the issue. He made two films that focused on this issue:

Katharina Blum (see above) and a contribution to the collaborative film *Deutschland im Herbst* (Germany in Autumn, 1977). He has always insisted that one needs to distinguish the person from the deed. Basic human rights need to apply to everybody, even to terrorists, which is why he supported the early release of two ex-terrorists in January 2007. He still does not hold back when it comes to political issues that interest him. In his latest film on the topic of terrorism, *Die Stille vor dem Schuss* (*The Legend of Rita*, 2001) he concentrates on a fictional member of the RAF, a young woman who has great enthusiasm for socialism and who, after killing a policeman, is 'rescued' by the East German authorities and given a new identity. Schlöndorff was criticised in some quarters for the positive characterisation of this 'naive cop killer', and also for the rather sympathetic portrayal of the Stasi (the East German secret police). In its much-praised realistic portrayal of daily life in East Germany the film makes for an interesting comparison with *Das Leben der Anderen*, the subject of our final chapter.

His political views provide us with a link to his 'fatherly' activities outside film- making. Back in the 1970s, Schlöndorff was active in film politics, representing the SPD parliamentary party on the Board of Directors of the 'Filmförderungsanstalt' (the federal film funding body), with the specific aim of improving the federal laws governing film promotion/funding. Other important roles in film politics and education are, from 1992 to 1997, as one of two chief executives of the Studio Babelsberg, which is based at the former UFA/DEFA film studios in Potsdam, and his current professorship at the time of writing at the European Graduate School in Switzerland. He is based in Berlin, where he also lectures at the German Academy for Film and Television. His detour into the business side of the film world – which found him involved in rebuilding the classic German UFA film studios from 1990-1997 and making no films during the period – seems a logical extension of the responsibility he feels towards developing infrastructures as well as the actual process of film-making.

Despite his varied roles in the film industry he has remained a film-maker: His commitment to German film was once again proved when, in 2002, Schlöndorff contributed to the international collaborative film project *Ten Minutes Older: The Cello* with a short film called *The Enlightenment*. He did this with the express intention to film in Germany while the other German contributors of the companion film *Ten Minutes Older: The Trumpet*, Herzog and Wenders, filmed on the Amazon and in the USA respectively.

He was once again internationally successful with the very German subject matter of *Der neunte Tag* (*The Ninth Day*, 2004), a film set in a Nazi concentration camp and another literary adaptation. This time the inspiration is the memoir of a Catholic priest who, together with other priests, was incarcerated in the so-called 'Pfarrerblock' (priest block) of Dachau and who, in the film, is forced to make a near impossible moral decision, pitted against a Nazi official's Mephistophelian temptation. The film is only loosely based on real-life events, which allows it to make very powerful observations of an often ignored group of concentration camp prisoners: those within the Catholic Church who resisted the Nazis.

To this day Schlöndorff does not shy away from difficult political subject matters, and his abiding preoccupation is still to uncover injustice and to side with the decent.

FOOTNOTES

[1] She went on to become a film-maker in her own right, directing politically motivated films such as *Die Bleierne Zeit* (*The German Sisters*, 1981), set in 1968, about the radicalisation of one of two sisters into terrorism, and *Das Versprechen* (*The Promise*, 1995), which chronicles the Berlin Wall in the story of two lovers who are separated by it.

[2] This is ironical if we consider that Grass only admitted in 2008 that he had been a member of the SS.

[3] An interesting coincidence: Schlöndorff's film shared the prize with Francis Ford Coppola's *Apocalypse Now*, a film that has been compared to Werner Herzog's *Aguirre, der Zorn Gottes*, which we have included here in our selection of important German films.

[4] *Die Blechtrommel* was the first part of Grass' 'Danzig Trilogy'. The second part, *Cat and Mouse*' – a much slimmer volume – had already been adapted for the screen in 1962 in black and white and in very simple images.

[5] Meliès was a pioneer film-maker who, around the turn of the nineteenth to the twentieth century, was the first to experiment with animated films, which he created by simple means in his studio.

CHAPTER NINE: MEMORY WORK: *HEIMAT* (1984)

The *Heimat* trilogy is the most ambitious and longest film project ever undertaken in Germany (even in the world?) and that alone would make it a candidate for inclusion in this book. *Heimat* 1 was made in 1984, Die zweite *Heimat* (The second *Heimat*) in 1992, and *Heimat* 3 in 2004. The three films together provide a chronicle of German history from 1919 to 2000, and they do this in a unique and very accessible way. Its creator, Edgar Reitz, spent 25 years of his film-making career dedicated to this project; it forms his life achievement – however, he has even hinted at the possibility of a *Heimat* 4. We will focus here on *Heimat* 1, which was the most successful of the three 'filmic novels', as Reitz terms his work.

Heimat 1 is a monumental film; it comprises 11 episodes (or 'chapters', to continue the novel analogy), which altogether provide 15 hours of viewing. It was first shown on West German public television in 1984, where 25 million West German viewers saw at least one of the episodes, and an average of 9 million watched every single episode – with a total population of around 55 million in West Germany these are staggering figures. The whole film was subsequently shown in cinemas in a 35mm print over two days in European and American cities and won prizes at numerous film festivals, the most prestigious of which was Venice, where it won the Golden Lion. It was also shown on American and British television, and again it was received enthusiastically and met with huge critical acclaim. The fact that no other German film has ever achieved such general approbation makes *Heimat* an even bigger success. (Around the same time as *Heimat* Wolfgang Petersen's *Das Boot*, 1981, was also hugely successful. It shares some characteristics with *Heimat* in its format of a television series and in its characterisation of 'ordinary' Germans during WW II. In other ways it represents almost the opposite of Reitz's approach – a handful of male characters are thrown together in an exceptional situation: the enclosed space of a submarine, fighting a war.)

There is an excellent BBC documentary (made in 2005 after the international release of *Heimat* 3) in which critics, film-makers, and Edgar Reitz himself have their say on the *Heimat* trilogy. To quote just some of the contributors: *Heimat* is praised as 'one of the most influential pieces in the German language ever conceived', 'one of the greatest films ever made', a 'unique piece of art', and 'a masterpiece'. None of them mention the more problematic aspects of the work, for which it has drawn criticism.

Edgar Reitz was one of the original signatories to the Oberhausen Manifesto of 1962. His own early contribution to changing the face of West German cinema was a number of experimental avant-garde short films which he made in the 1960s. He worked closely with Alexander Kluge; together they were and still are today the most 'German' of German film-makers. Unlike others of their generation they film exclusively in Germany and have dedicated their film-making to the 'German experience', thereby researching, exploring and commenting on German society and the underlying historical connections in a critical way. Where Kluge employs an intellectual approach with films that are often closer to the essay than to narrative film, Reitz has developed into the one German film-maker who, over the decades, has held a magnifying glass on the everyday lives of numerous 'German' characters. It is true, these characters are fictional, but together with their authentic setting in real locations they achieve a life-likeness which has prompted thousands of viewers to 'visit them'. More on this phenomenon later.

With *Heimat*, Reitz finally found his very own form of expression, even though the road towards it was not easy. His career as a feature film-maker started out well enough: His first feature, *Mahlzeiten* (*Mealtimes*), was released in 1967, one of the first of Young German Cinema releases (see also chapter 7). The film was nominated for the Golden Lion at the Venice Film Festival and won the Best First Work there. In 1976 he made *Stunde Null* (*Hour Zero*) in which for the first time he dealt explicitly with the topic of German history. The film contains all the seeds of *Heimat*, and we will look at this later on in the chapter. In 1979, *Der Schneider von Ulm* (*The Tailor of Ulm*), the true story of an early, obsessive and unsuccessful German flying pioneer, proved a bad omen for the obsessive film-maker: Reitz was bankrupt financially and his personal life was in ruins. As a 'fugitive' in a friend's holiday cottage over Christmas he took stock of his life and began, in a kind of self-therapy, to explore his early family life in the Hunsrück region of Germany, dipping into his childhood memories, which he wrote down in his 'Hunsrücker Geschichten'

(Hunsrück Stories). This period of self-reflection proved to be a turning point in his life and work.

1979 was also the year in which the American TV series *Holocaust* was shown on German television. It was a huge popular success, quite understandably, when we consider that its extremely difficult subject-matter had never been approached in epic fictional form: Germans followed for the first time a narrative that concentrated on a Jewish family through the history of the Third Reich's concentration camps. It proved a controversial piece of film-making because of its Hollywood-style representation of these traumatic events, which had previously been considered unfilmable for several reasons. It was thought that any filmic representation within a conventional narrative would trivialise the horrific images and experiences. A commercial undertaking with its identificatory and melodramatic approach was considered least able to convey the events with any kind of credibility. Its trivialisation of traumatic events, its blurring of fact and fiction was criticised: kitsch images would be perpetuated in the minds of viewers as 'reality'. For many in Germany, the Hollywood style was too uncomfortably close to the propagandist UFA style of the thirties – the target, as we know, of criticism from young German film-makers of the sixties and seventies. There were also voices who said that German history should not be written by Americans (Reitz was one of them). This is in itself a controversial statement, since Germans to a large extent had not managed to write their own history, or when they did, they were met with resistance or were all but ignored by German audiences – see our chapter on *Die Mörder sind unter uns*, and the discussion of *Hitler – der letzte Akt* (*The Final Act*), in our chapter on *Der Untergang*.

Edgar Reitz was one of the most vociferous in condemning *Holocaust*'s 'top-down' approach, which he contrasted with the 'bottom-up' approach of his own films and those of other New German film-makers. They were united in their will to start from their own experiences in order to deal with their country's troubled past. They wanted to present alternative images of Germany and to illuminate the connection of the past with the present. Reitz' friend and frequent collaborator, Alexander Kluge, for example, dealt explicitly with German history in his film *Die Patriotin* (*The Patriot*, 1978), in which a school teacher, Gabi Teichert, is literally digging up German soil in order to find pieces of German history that are worth teaching to her class. She also infiltrates party conferences to try and influence the present in order to build a better history that can be taught to young people in the future. In the same year Rainer Werner Fassbinder made *Die Ehe der Maria Braun* (*The Marriage of Maria Braun*), which focuses on a woman's life at the end of World War II. One year later, Volker Schlöndorff's *Die Blechtrommel* was released (see previous chapter).

This flurry of German films with German history at their heart, made around the same time, was not a coincidence. The 1960s in West Germany had, as in other Western cultures, seen political activism by the student movement which culminated in 1968. In Germany, some of the disillusioned student rebels subsequently went underground against what they saw as 'capitalist-imperialist forces' and began to commit terrorist deeds. They called themselves the 'Red Army Faction', a group that continued in various forms until the 1990s when they officially disbanded. They were in part a result of anger amongst young people against unfinished business within Germany regarding its fascist past, and frustration was vented in an upward spiral of acts of arson, kidnapping of key people in politics and business, and hijacking of planes, in order to achieve their aim of destabilising the West German state. They never had a large following, though. The reaction of the West German state was disproportionate, and for a time the whole population became suspect. There was almost indiscriminate surveillance as well as other repressive measures, and extended powers were given to and used by the police.

At the height of the terrorist acts and state repression, in the autumn of 1977, nine young German film-makers, including Fassbinder, Kluge, Reitz, and Schlöndorff, reacted with a collaborative film, *Deutschland im Herbst* (*Germany in Autumn*). This film consists of individual and very personal contributions: reflections on terrorism and its link with the repressed German past, and criticism of the renewed repressive measures by the state. For many intellectuals and ordinary thinking Germans (not just film-makers) the mass hysteria surrounding acts of terrorism, committed by relatively few perpetrators, was a symptom of unresolved past issues. This realisation prompted a certain sympathy with the disaffected young people who had become terrorists. Within German (film) history all this gave rise to a number of explorations of Germany's recent past. It was as if floodgates had been opened, as if the paralysis that had beset post-war Germany had been lifted.

Even though the individual film-makers' forms of expression were quite different, what they all had in common was the belief that there never had been, nor could have been, an 'Hour Zero' at the end of World War II, a clean slate, a 'changed' German society. One of Edgar Reitz' films may be entitled *Stunde Null* (1976), and it is a snapshot of one specific time and place at the end of the war, but the title does not refer to a new beginning; it is merely a moment of limbo for a handful of villagers in East Germany, suspended between the occupation by one Allied force, the Americans, and another, the Soviets. The meaning of *Stunde Null* is ambivalent in the tension between its possibility or impossibility in a similar way to that of *Heimat*. We will discuss the ambivalence of 'Heimat' later on in the chapter.

Stunde Null is an unjustly neglected film, a small masterpiece in its own right. At the same time it is relevant for this chapter in that it reads almost as a kind of preamble to the later *Heimat*, even though we established previously that the concrete idea for *Heimat* was born out of a desperate life situation. The link between the two works helps us trace Reitz's development as a true auteur-director with his own signature. On both scripts (and the other parts of the *Heimat* trilogy) he collaborated with Peter Steinbach (the setting of *Stunde Null* is near Steinbach's home town of Leipzig). The cinematographer in both films is the highly regarded Gernot Roll. Both films are filmed principally in black and white, *Stunde Null* completely so, and *Heimat* is shot through with moments of colour. We will look at this unusual device later on in the chapter. Both films use a cast of mostly non-professional actors, a choice that leads to great authenticity. Equally important is the consistent use of dialect, a device that was not common in German films of the time. What distinguishes *Stunde Null* from *Heimat* is its clear 'Momentaufnahme', a moment in history, a snapshot, carefully selected, and clearly focused and symbolic. As in *Heimat* the characters are ordinary people. Important historical moments are not perceived by them as such. In the case of *Stunde Null*, immediate questions of survival rather than a long-term chronicle are at the centre of the narrative. But similar to *Heimat*, the historical context is presented obliquely, through the eyes of the characters. This is what is meant by 'Alltagsgeschichte' – historiography of the everyday, from below.

'Heimat' is a quintessentially German term; it does not exist in other languages with anything like the same meaning, and therefore, when translated, does not have the same richness of connotations as in German. The translation 'homeland' or simply 'home' that you often find does not do it justice. Over the centuries German writers and philosophers have variously described it as the place where you were born and grew up, a refuge in which you feel you belong, where you feel safe, the place that you long for when you are away from it. In the nineteenth century, during the industrial revolution in Germany, the term was used as an antidote to the feelings of alienation felt by workers who had been forced to leave their villages in order to find work in the developing industrial cities. Such a deep-seated feeling can be misappropriated and abused for ideological purposes. This is what happened in Germany during Hitler's regime. In fascism the term became part of the 'blood and soil' ideology: 'Blood' came to denote not just family but 'German-ness', the 'Aryan race', which had to be kept 'pure' from outside, from 'racial pollution'; and 'soil' was used to bind Germans to their land patriotically and as a justification for Germany's territorial expansion. The ideology was very effective since it tapped into deep predispositions, which could then be brought out into consciousness and abused for political purposes. Our chapter on *Triumph des Willens* shows how this 'blood and soil' ideology was beginning to be put into practice.

After World War II, in a war-ravaged country, and everywhere amongst refugees and prisoners of war, the term 'Heimat' regained some of its pre-fascist meaning: longing for place and people that made you feel at home and safe. This is why, in contrast to 'Trümmerliteratur' and 'Trümmerfilme', a film genre sprang up in Germany which sought to express the longing for a better place and to combine this with the desire to escape the difficult material circumstances. Good early examples of this are *Schwarzwaldmädel* (*Black Forest Girl*, 1950) and *Grün ist die Heide* (*Green is the Moor*, 1951). The 'Heimatfilm' is a uniquely German film genre which developed in the restorative 1950s, the era of Adenauer, [2] in which a large number of films were set in an authoritarian and hierarchical world and therefore carry conservative, often even right-wing values. The films are always set in idyllic countryside, often in the Alps. They portray an unspoilt, pure Germany and are populated by mostly well-meaning, strong, healthy heroes and heroines – in short, a country that did not exist, that was only a dream. [3] The idyll is usually interrupted by outsiders who are expelled from the rural community or must prove themselves in order to be accepted. Folk music is a staple. The narrative is often melodramatic, with sprinklings of humour in it for light relief. Visually most of the 'Heimat' films link in with the lavish UFA film productions during the Third Reich, which were not necessarily overtly ideologically determined, but always contained the overarching 'Aryan' narrative, and served as entertainment and escapism for the German people. 'Heimat' films were often made by the same directors and used some of the same actors, and therefore demonstrate a problematic continuity with the past – another proof that there was no Hour Zero. Another genre, the war film, became popular in the 1950s. The emphasis had changed towards anti-war films, but the visual tradition and the directors remained the same. Thus, again, there was continuity with UFA film-making traditions.

The enormous popularity of 'Heimat' films shows that there was a genuine desire for people to reconnect with their country, or 'homeland' post-war. There was a need for the simplification of life after the horrific experiences of war. However, even at the peak of 'Heimat' film success there were critical voices: Wolfgang Staudte, for example, was aware of the trends of the film industry and the prevalence of certain genres in the 1950s: 'Perhaps the war film is the simplification of death, just as the Heimatfilm is the simplification of life.' He was referring to the unfortunate trend in West German cinema to produce (and, in the case of war films, to import) large numbers of such films. The young German film-makers of the 1960s reacted against this trend and the above-mentioned continuity. Some of them reworked, even subverted the Heimatfilm genre and created the 'New Heimatfilm', in which the reality of life in rural communities was shown in its often brutal circumstances and the small-mindedness of its people. [4] A slightly more differentiated view of the original 'Heimat' films shows that some of them had a certain progressive potential, for example the exploration of darker themes in *Rosen blühen auf dem Heidegrab* (*Roses Blossom on the Moorland Grave*, 1951), or more assertive role models for women in the later 'Heimat' films.

After the turbulent decade of the 1970s in which terrorism dominated domestic politics, the 1980s in Germany were marked by a turn to different topical issues, mainly the peace movement and the environment. The green movement gained in popularity, manifested by the rise of the Green Party which gained its first seats in the Bundestag, the West German parliament, in 1982. After the volatility and radical politics of the previous decade there was a shift towards more broad-based social issues. Protests against excessive consumerism, against property speculation, against the destruction of the environment and to protect the community led to a renewed interest in the community and regionalism in Germany. An important focus for both the green and the peace movement was nuclear power. The green movement raised awareness of the dangers of producing nuclear energy and waste. The peace movement was concerned with nuclear power in its most destructive form. The beginning of the 1980s was the time when NATO decided to station nuclear missiles on West German territory, and protests against this decision gained wide popular support. Therefore it is not surprising that within the peace and green movements the term 'Heimat' – now something that needed to be protected – experienced a renaissance. This is how Edgar Reitz was able to rehabilitate the term, after a long time of political sensitivity.

Reitz's own definition of the term takes its cue from the philosopher Ernst Bloch, for whom 'Heimat is a place where nobody has ever been'. Reitz interprets this as a very basic human experience: While growing up, children form intense relationships with internal images (and enjoy other, sensory sensual experiences). This is the source of all creative work, but also of personal expression, such as the way we bond with others, the way we love. In every form of love there is the memory of earlier experiences of feeling safe, of warmth, of family and home, etc. All those early experiences are present in the word 'Heimat'. We all know them. They are our own real experiences. As adults we strive to find these early experiences again, and we often assume that by going back to where we came from we will find them. However, Reitz is convinced that the closer we seem to get to this 'Heimat', the more it retreats. His films are an aesthetic attempt to 'conserve' time and to find 'Heimat' in memory. He came to this understanding in his time of intense personal crisis, which, as we mentioned before, caused him to do his own introspective work on memory. If we want to understand *Heimat* properly, we need to be aware of this premise: that, for Reitz, 'Heimat' exists only in memory, that memory is selective, and that it is ordered and reordered by the mind.

Reitz has compared film-making with the way memory works, in particular in the process of editing, which follows certain ordering principles and where the process of ordering is based on deliberate choices. Moreover, film is not reality, it only represents it. However, this does not mean that a narrative film cannot contain real experiences. For *Heimat*, Reitz, prompted by his own childhood memories, returned to the Hunsrück region in south west Germany where he grew up. For months he researched there by having numerous conversations with the locals about their own memories of living in Germany at different times in the twentieth century. From the beginning, Reitz' main interest was in 'time', more precisely 'lost time'. [5] *Heimat* represents his search for a time gone by, including his own, which he wants to preserve in stories. The epic series – or 'filmic novel', as he would prefer to call it – captures the story of four generations of a fictitious Hunsrück family, the Simons, who live in a fictitious village, Schabbach, which represents, however, an amalgam of three real Hunsrück villages. Their story, autobiography interwoven with memories of real people, is told through the passage of time, and brings memories to life in a certain order, so that they cannot easily be destroyed by the flow of time. Time is also essential in the way Reitz films his stories: He gives them time to unfold, the editing is slow, there are no dramatic visual effects, and the lighting is soft.

As mentioned before, *Heimat* I was a huge popular and critical success. The fact that it was a television production meant that for the first time millions of Germans were able to see a 'Heimat' film' that spoke of real people with real experiences through sixty years of German history, including the Nazi regime and the war. The film provoked strong identification with the characters and their lives. It also provoked a sense of release in that, quite suddenly, Germans felt they could talk about their own memories, including those relating to Germany's unfortunate past, in a more nuanced way. This effect cannot be overestimated: As detailed in our chapter on *Die Mörder sind unter uns*, there might have been a moment immediately after the end of the war and the Nazi regime in which there were strong currents in German society with a great desire to deal with the fascist past, but the country and with it the efforts at 're-education' were in Allied hands. Very quickly people wanted to forget, and later, during the 1950s, the emphasis was on rebuilding Germany and enjoying economic success. Psychoanalysts speak of the need to work through traumatic experiences, which include traumatic losses, which is exactly what Germany experienced when the absolute identification figure of Hitler had suddenly disappeared. The necessary 'Trauerarbeit' (literally 'mourning work') was not done, memories were repressed, and 'melancholia' (in psychoanalytic terms the result of repressed mourning) set in. We are not trying to suggest that Reitz' film alone healed a whole nation's melancholia, but it did open channels of communication that had hitherto been closed.

Because of its convincing characterisation and its strong sense of location *Heimat* also provoked more direct reactions, both from within Germany and abroad, some of which are quite amusing. A stream of tourists began to impose itself on the Hunsrück region where people started asking for the village of Schabbach. Some came on a pilgrimage to visit the characters' graves. One Hunsrück lady even tried to convince Reitz that she had recognised her own husband in the film. When Reitz informed her that the character had died quite a few years ago she responded that even films can get it wrong! Such confusion of reality and film was not what Reitz had in mind when making *Heimat*. In fact, he feels that there is a certain loss of the poetic value of his films through this successful reception.

Let us now look at how Reitz achieved such extraordinary responses. We will concentrate mainly on the first episode, or chapter, which sets the scene, introduces the main characters, and has all the stylistic ingredients that mark *Heimat* as a whole. Like all the other chapters this first one has a title: 'Fernweh' (Longing for Far-Away Places). This choice of title immediately introduces a tension into the whole story: Why 'Fernweh', if the film is supposed to be about 'Heimat'? The tension is deliberate, of course, just as 'Heimat' is explored in all its facets in the course of the film, positive and negative. And because Reitz has imbued the story with his own feelings and experiences, having left his home at the age of twenty, he knows exactly what 'Fernweh' is. By the way, 'Fernweh' does not only work in space, it can also be interpreted within and applied to time, therefore turning into 'longing for far-away times', which is the meaning of 'Heimat' according to Reitz. Interestingly, the opposite of 'Fernweh' in German is 'Heimweh' – 'longing for home'.

The first image we see is a milestone in the middle of a field with the words 'Made in Germany' on it. This can be interpreted as a slightly tongue-in-cheek reference to the high quality of the drama that we are about to see. It also serves to set the film apart from other productions, 'made outside Germany', and is a reference to

Reitz's strong views about what he perceives as American appropriations of German history: both literally, in that the country (West Germany) was occupied and influenced by America after World War II; and metaphorically, as 'cultural imperialism', exemplified by the above-mentioned television series *Holocaust*, but also more generally by the dominance of Hollywood films in West Germany since the war.

We are also told that *Heimat* is 'a chronicle in 11 parts' and that it begins on '9 May, 1919 - a Friday'. This situates the story precisely, and marks it immediately as experiential. A young man in uniform appears in the distance, walking across the field, towards the camera. Subtitles inform us that he is a soldier returning from the war and also that he has walked here from France. (The Hunsrück region, where the film is set, lies in the far west of West Germany, bordering on France. Therefore France represents the closest of the enemy countries of World War I.) The soldier, Paul, then stops and we follow his gaze towards a village in the distance. This point-of-view technique forms part of the camerawork throughout the film. It helps us to experience what the characters are experiencing. The village in the distance represents the distant 'Heimat' of the young man.

From the beginning the soundtrack is a combination of very strong winds blowing and forceful music with a strong, even rhythm and incorporating voices, situated somewhere between contemporary music and jazz. Strong emotions, tension and conflict are suggested through this. Both the wind and the music die down as Paul reaches the village. Music is used sparingly in the film and is therefore very effective: Often there are long stretches of silence into which the music breaks at decisive points. The music varies tremendously throughout the film, depending on the mood of any given scene. It variously suggests depth of feeling, gaiety, quiet reflection, turmoil, and it comes back time and again to a leitmotif that runs through the whole series. However, few instruments are used at any given time, and there is no melodramatic sweep. There is always an edge to the music composed by Nikos Mamangakis, a composer mainly of contemporary music that incorporates electronic sounds.

As Paul walks through the village, along the unpaved street, unaccompanied by music, he looks around him. We see what he sees, we hear what he hears: ambient sound, mainly animal noises. We also see various villagers looking through their windows, trying to place the stranger. This is how we are introduced to them, through his gaze that takes them all in, in passing. He is first recognised by Maria, who will later become his wife. His pace quickens as he hears the sound of his father's anvil from the smithy. The hot iron that his father strikes sends out sparks which are rendered in colour – the first instance of colour in the film. This must be an extension of Paul's intense emotion or memory at this sight. (Later on in the film colour scenes become more frequent and longer – particularly the extended images of beautiful countryside.) Not a word is spoken as Paul enters the smithy, takes off his rucksack and lends his father a hand, in movements so familiar to him that he applies them instinctively. Initially his father, Mathias, does not even acknowledge the momentous occasion of his son's return; he just wordlessly accepts his helping hand. He then tells him that the wheel on which they are working is for a villager whose son has been killed in the war. When the work is finished, the father looks at his son and simply says: 'Thank God'. His mother Katharina (or Kat) appears in the doorway, smiles broadly and says: 'Paul is back'. There are no great displays of emotion, just simple gestures. Before going to greet his mother, Paul walks over to the manure heap in the courtyard, and, with eyes closed, he urinates on it. These first scenes encapsulate what 'Heimat' means to Paul: familiar sights, sounds, smells – sensory experiences. The way in which they are rendered by the film is probably the most direct and convincing manifestation of 'cinema of experience' (Thomas Elsaesser's term, see also chapter 6). Reitz achieves this by the use of observing, direct, slow camera work, by lingering on people, objects, tiny details, glances, and by privileging facial expression over words.

To begin with, Paul's parents' living room-cum-kitchen is populated by the parents, his brother Eduard and his sister Pauline, but news of Paul's return spreads through the village and slowly a bewildering number of characters pile in to greet and ogle the returning soldier. They provide their own stories of the war and its consequences for Germany. These stories tend to be full of sweeping and prejudiced statements, reflecting the way in which a relatively remote community deals with world events. Throughout the film, this kitchen is the centre of social encounters, of important issues being discussed, of decisions being taken. Later on, when Paul has married Maria, she becomes an important member of this community. She will ultimately be the central character of the film, the mother figure, around whom people gather, whom they feel safe with, trust and ask for advice. Quietly she realises that Paul really loves another girl, Apollonia, who works for the local hotel and restaurant owner, but does not live in the village. She is identified as an outsider; many of the villagers regard her with suspicion. They call her a 'gypsy', and all kinds of stories circulate regarding her relationship with a Frenchman. The narrow-mindedness and limited horizons of the villagers is expressed by their prejudiced reactions to this outsider. Paul falls in love with her for the very reason that she is an outsider and is able to see village life from a different perspective. He himself is torn between love for his home and the inability to fit in after his experience of the war.

The tension within Paul, his 'longing for far-away places', is first signalled by another image in colour, the sticky fly-trap hanging from the ceiling above the large table in the kitchen. He looks at it from his chair, and gets up to free one of the flies that has been trapped but has not died yet. Again, Maria observes this tension in Paul and remarks

later: 'Now you've been here for three years but you're still not home.' Shortly after this, after failing to adapt to village life, obsessed by his hobby, the wireless radio, with which he catches the sounds of far-away places, he simply leaves the village one day, not to return until the end of World War II. He leaves behind a wife and two sons. And so village life goes on without him.

Eduard, in contrast to his brother, was exempt from military service because of a weakness of the lungs. He has remained in the parental home where his source of news about the outside world is the newspaper, which he reads avidly and from which he quotes aloud to everybody present in the kitchen, sometimes to comic

effect, when neither he nor his audience are able to differentiate between local, regional or national news. This parochial attitude is part of village life. Eduard is a drifter. Only years later, when he spends some time in Berlin for an operation on his lungs and meets Lucie, a brothel keeper and his future wife, is he coaxed by her into becoming an active member of the National Socialist Party and into securing the position of mayor in a small town near Schabbach, where they return. Lucie has ambitions in life. For her the Nazis are a godsend, and she realises quickly that Eduard can be manipulated, because of his combined traits of weakness and self-importance, into fulfilling her desire: to come up in the world, to converse with important people, and to put the Hunsrück on the National Socialist map, so to speak. Ironically, but completely in keeping with Eduard's character, he is present in Berlin on the historic night after Hitler has seized power on 31 January, 1933. But he does not realise the importance of the event, and only hears the rally at the Brandenburg Gate from his room. This is a quite realistic portrayal of ordinary people's perception of events around them. We have probably all been in situations whose significance has eluded us at the time. In fact, because Reitz follows this approach so stringently, he is only able to give us contextual information by inference, always depending on his way of representing 'selective memory' – a weakness in his approach for which he was criticised. This is particularly problematic when German history is chronicled and many important events are simply left out, such as the deep economic crisis of the early Weimar Republic or the depression of the late 1920s. The way in which Reitz treats aspects of the Nazi period has also been criticised for its selectivity.

One of the more lauded strands of the narrative concerns Eduard's career, through which Reitz traces the rise of National Socialism and people's perception of and collusion with it. By registering the smallest details of the characters' lives, and of every outside influence and inside contribution to wider issues of history, he lays bare the roots of fascism and its development in a rural microcosm of German society. Indeed, a large part of *Heimat* is devoted to the years of National Socialism and World War II. For the village, the first signs of change are that 'things are getting better'. These first changes happen in a chapter entitled 'A Christmas like never before'. The year is 1935. The dreaded inflation has subsided; there is a definite economic upturn. Infrastructural changes have been

made: Schabbach is now linked with the outside world by telephone, and later, in 1938, a prestigious highway, the 'Hunsrückhöhenstraße', is built nearby. We only find out later that this very highway is used to transport troops and materials to the western front in a war that was planned by the regime a long time before.

Pauline, Paul's sister, has married the watchmaker in Simmern, a nearby town, and she is pleased to tell her mother about the possibility of buying the flat above the shop. This flat is owned by a Jew who is being taunted by the local population, including Eduard, and will be forced to sell. 'The Jews don't have it so good any more, mother', Pauline confides. Turning a blind eye to the fate of Jews is one of the elements of sliding into fascism that is so effectively explored in *Heimat*. Pauline's reference to Jews and their fate in Nazi times is one of only a few, although in later chapters slightly more nuanced reactions towards the issue are voiced.

At one point we catch a glimpse of a concentration camp nearby when little Hans, a village boy, follows the telegraph wires on his bicycle. He chances upon the camp and is shown by a guard how to point a rifle at an inmate. Again, this happens almost by accident and is not elaborated upon. While Kat is visiting relatives in the Ruhr, one of her nephews is arrested and taken away by the police in the early hours of the morning. He is accused of being a communist and will end up in a concentration camp. It is completely realistic that the relatives play down the horrific incident by saying that he will simply be 're-educated' and then set free again. Such oblique references were made deliberately by Reitz. They are commensurate with his 'bottom-up' approach: He was interested in the characters and how they saw their situation, not in a historical analysis. However, we as the audience are able and almost compelled to think further. And this is one of Reitz' key concerns: For him the most intriguing things are those that are not directly stated, but those we infer. He considers the screen as the stage, while what goes on off-screen is just as important, if not more so. With regard to anti-Semitism Reitz wanted to explore it as an ideology, not necessarily in its concrete manifestation. However, we need to set these statements against the criticisms levied against *Heimat* (see above and below).

The most direct objections came mainly from the USA, against the fact that Reitz all but ignored the holocaust in his portrayal of Nazi Germany, although his film spends a long time dealing with that part of German history. You could argue that he restricted his knowledge to that of his characters, who probably did not know of the camps. As we mentioned earlier, this approach does have its dangers, not least because we get to know these people very well in the course of the film and empathise readily with them. On the other hand, and in Reitz's defence, there are a variety of voices within the film and we are encouraged to explore further the wider implications of the historical situation in which they find themselves – the 'off-screen' – even if they are not able to do this themselves. Thus, rather than 'closing the past' Reitz has opened (parts of) it up for us. Along with other New German film-makers he feels that there is a great danger in powerful images that are recycled time and again, such as the conventional portrayal of Nazis in uniforms, and images such as those used in the above-mentioned television series *Holocaust*. With regard to television in general, Reitz feels that viewers are presented with too many recycled images, often by means of (American) war films, and through German-produced relatively simple stories, such as those of many 'Heimat' films, films that do not encourage viewers to actively think.

'America' features mostly negatively in Reitz's work. In *Heimat*, the returning Paul at the end of World War II has become an American capitalist who proceeds to impose his ideas onto the country of his birth. This anti-Americanism has to be put in context. In film historical terms, the United States were able to impose Hollywood films on West Germany after World War II by virtue of the military power it exerted there. (Compare also Wolfgang Staudte's experience in our chapter on *Die Mörder sind unter uns*.) More generally, the United States, together with Britain, decided on West Germany's path to democracy, along with economic development based on capitalism and consumerism. Through NATO, which was again dominated by the United States, American forces (and those of other Western allies) were ever-present in large parts of the FRG. This resulted in frequent NATO military manoeuvres which contributed to the destruction of parts of the German countryside. The most controversial military action, though, was the stationing of Pershing and cruise missiles on German soil. In all of West Germany resentment against the United States grew throughout the 1980s, the final decade of the Cold War. No wonder, then, that America was seen as the antithesis to 'Heimat', the term that was re-appropriated in the same decade, this time by the left. The development towards the destruction of 'Heimat' by various forces (not all of them American!) is the preoccupation of the final chapters of *Heimat*.

To be fair to Reitz, he does portray 'Heimat' in all its contradictions: His *Heimat* trilogy writes 'Alltagsgeschichte', with the central experience of 'Heimat' with all its positive and negative connotations. Particularly in *Heimat* 1 these are: deep bonds of family and community which make those within feel safe, but come at the price of the exclusion of outsiders; and hard but meaningful labour of villagers set against self-importance and narrow-mindedness of other members of the community, with the negative attributes being shown as a breeding ground for fascist ideas. Thus, in his life's work, Reitz explores human behaviour in all its facets.

FOOTNOTES

[1] For a more detailed analysis see the introduction in: Anton Kaes, From Hitler to *Heimat*. The book also contains a chapter on *Heimat* 1.

[2] Konrad Adenauer, the first West German Chancellor or Prime Minister, from 1949-1963, leader of the right-wing CDU Party.

[3] In its myth-creation it shows similarities with the all-American genre of the Western.

[4] One example of 'New Heimatfilm' is Volker Schlöndorff's *Der plötzliche Reichtum der Leute von Kombach* (*The Sudden Wealth of the People of Kombach*, 1971).

[5] He re-read Proust's *A la recherche du temps perdu*', and the *Odyssey*, which for him is all about 'Heimat'.

CHAPTER TEN: BERLIN: SPIRITUAL UNIFICATION: *DER HIMMEL ÜBER BERLIN* (*WINGS OF DESIRE*, 1986)

Der Himmel über Berlin is one of the most acclaimed and best-known German films of all time, whose director is, together with Werner Herzog, the best-known contemporary German film-maker. The film has won countless prizes at major film festivals and is a highlight in the long career of Wim Wenders. These facts alone make it a key film in the German repertoire. Another reason for including it in our book is the portrayal of Berlin in this film: It offers a complex picture of the city – historical and contemporary, physical and metaphysical – just before the Berlin Wall came down. The film has now become a historical document of a city that since the film's release has changed beyond recognition.

Within Wim Wenders' *oeuvre Der Himmel über Berlin* occupies a special place: It marks his 'return to Germany' (as location and theme) after having spent eight years in the USA and making films which did not have German themes at their centre. But even in his 'foreign' films before *Himmel*, notably *Paris, Texas* (1984), he brings with him an 'Old World' (i.e. European) approach, a more intellectual one as opposed to the more sensual 'New World' film-making. His own ambivalent relationship with the USA and its different modes of filmic expression compared to Europe is also reflected in his 'foreign' films and in the statements he has made about the USA more generally. Since *Himmel* he has worked both in Germany and abroad, and has made both feature films and documentaries.

To put Wim Wenders in the wider context of German cinema we need to go back to his beginnings. He started out as part of the so-called 'third generation' of new German film-makers, at around the same time as Fassbinder. Unlike Fassbinder, though, who never went to film school, Wenders learnt his trade at the newly inaugurated 'Hochschule für Fernsehen und Film' in Munich (HFFM). You may remember that German film schools came about as a consequence of the tireless lobbying of the 'Angry Young Men of Oberhausen' (see also chapters on *Aguirre* and *Die Blechtrommel*). In this sense, Wenders was a beneficiary of the dedication of a previous generation of film-makers who wanted a new start for German film-making after the 'desert' left by the National Socialist dictatorship and World War II. However, Wenders also contributed immensely to the development of New German Cinema in the 1970s: He did not only make highly acclaimed films that helped put Germany back on the international cinematic map, but he also worked with lobbyists like Alexander Kluge in order to improve conditions for independent film-making in Germany. He was, for example, a co-founder of 'Filmverlag der Autoren', the independent production and distribution company for New German Cinema.

All of Wenders' early films, from *Summer in the City*, *Die Angst des Tormanns vorm Elfmeter* (*The Goalkeeper's Fear of the Penalty*, both 1971), *Alice in den Städten* (*Alice in the Cities*, 1974), *Falsche Bewegung* (*Wrong Movement*, 1975) to *Im Lauf der Zeit* (*Kings of the Road*, 1976), show male German protagonists on the move, lost and searching for identity, a sense of purpose – introspective drop-outs from society. Their status is encapsulated in the question: 'Why must there be such an enormous distance between me and the world?' which is asked by the protagonist of *Falsche Bewegung*. These protagonists are lost not least because of the absence of fathers, a theme that runs through New German Cinema. Germany within its historical context and in its present condition is always in the background. In his early road movies Wenders shows us 'loneliness in Germany', whether it is a trip down the Rhine Valley or along the German-German border. In his early films his characters' inability to communicate and to bond, to live life to the full instead of being on the outside, of observing rather than experiencing, gradually gives way to the possibility of friendship and love. This developing primacy of experience over observation becomes an important theme in Wenders' work. Male friendship, the vitality and openness of children, and, finally, the (potential) love between a man and a woman, are as central to *Der Himmel über Berlin* as the love of Germany. Another theme that can be traced through Wenders' films is the city as both an exciting place and a place of loneliness.

In *Himmel* Germany is a divided country whose status is condensed in an equally divided former capital city, Berlin. Wim Wenders is not a Berliner but he says he has always loved the city with its special status, divided between the two German states, with its western part cut off from the rest of West Germany, an island within East Germany. This strange creation was a legacy of World War II, which Germany lost and which led to the country's division. In the final days of the war the Soviet army invaded the eastern part of Germany and laid siege to Berlin (as explored in our chapter on *Der Untergang*). The three Western allies, USA, France, and Britain occupied the rest of the country. Henceforth the Western allies worked together, and Germany was effectively divided along the lines of East-West occupation. Even before the end of the war a decision was made to divide the city into four sectors, which corresponded to the four occupation powers. After the war the western sectors were soon merged into one, mirroring the status of the whole country. The lines thus drawn became the 'Iron Curtain', the physical marks of a global division into capitalism and communism, and East Germany was controlled by the Soviet Union. In 1961, at the height of the Cold War, when many East Germans fled or tried to flee the GDR, the Berlin Wall was built as, in GDR parlance, an 'anti-fascist shield' (see also chapters on *Die Mörder sind unter uns*, *Spure der Steine* and *Das Leben der Anderen*). Henceforth any attempts at crossing the border became virtually impossible. During the 28 years of the existence of the Berlin Wall political developments towards more freedom of movement did take place, but only limited change came about. In the course of the 1980s, due to certain political and economic changes towards more openness in the Soviet Union, the problems of the state-controlled East German economy, and pressure from the people of East Germany, the GDR weakened and finally the Wall came down. The Germany we know today is a reunified one; the Wall has become history.

Today it is very difficult to imagine a divided Germany and a Wall that cut through Berlin, but even as late as 1986, when *Der Himmel über Berlin* was made, most Germans believed their divided country would not be unified in their own lifetimes. This included Wim Wenders, who said he could never have imagined the fall of the Berlin Wall, which happened only three years later.

It is perhaps interesting to note that Wenders was one of the few West German film-makers to even show the Berlin Wall on film. During the whole lifetime of the Wall, not even films that were set in Berlin included it, neither as a topic nor as a backdrop. Watching those films, then, one could have assumed that there was no Wall.

It is possible that film-makers did not know how to deal with it, or that they deliberately ignored it. Whatever the reason for the omission, it does seem strange. In East Germany the topic of the Wall was even more taboo than in the West. There is a very illuminating story about how Wenders tried to obtain permission for filming certain location scenes in East Berlin. Wenders knew personally the then film minister of the GDR who had previously told him he would do anything within his power to assist Wenders in filming in the East. When asked about the topic of the film he explained that the main characters were angels, which meant that they were not bound by physical laws, and that the film was to be shot from their point of view. 'So this means that they can pass through walls and THE Wall?' Wenders did not get permission to shoot in East Berlin. To reiterate: this was only three years before the end of the Wall.

Der Himmel über Berlin did not go through a long gestation period. On the contrary, the project came about almost as an emergency measure to save Wenders' Berlin-based production company Roadmovies GmbH which had been idling for a while and was in danger of going bankrupt. What started out under considerable financial pressure turned out to be Wenders' most poetic film with not a hint of the problems behind it visible. Very quickly Wenders had to come up with a treatment for the film. He was certain that it should be a story set in Berlin, this 'no-man's land' city whose heart had been ripped out, and that he wanted something contrasting against the reality of this stunted place. One of his ideas was to have children as protagonists, and although he soon moved away from that, children still occupy a central role in the film, and some of the characteristics of children are preserved in the protagonists that he finally settled on: guardian angels that roam the city and whose viewpoint is one of the guiding principles of the narrative. They provide all the links that Wenders was looking for: On account of their ubiquitous presence and their omniscience they are able to link space and time. Of course, film is particularly suited to communicate these links through editing, which is precisely a means of linking space and time, and the narrative of *Der Himmel über Berlin* is communicated with bravura editing. This means that the topography of the city can be covered easily and for the very fact that the protagonists are angels, who are accepted to have been around for a very long time, they also link the present with the past. There are plenty of links between past and present in the film, which we will see later in more detail.

Angels as protagonists lift the story out of a merely 'worldly' setting onto a metaphysical or allegorical level. Interestingly, though, it is not religion that Wenders is interested in; it is the connection of his protagonists with human beings that is at the centre of the film. This manifests itself in the fact that the meeting place of all of Berlin's angels is not a church but a library full of people reading and thinking. The angels are able not just to move amongst people without being seen, but also to listen in to their thoughts, and so for us these thoughts become audible. But still the angels are removed from human experience, they are observers. The strongest link between this observational state of being and human experience evolves when one of the angels, Damiel, falls in love with a human and decides to give up his eternal existence in order to become human himself, in full knowledge of the fact that he will then also be mortal.

It is appropriate now to examine the two titles by which the film is known a little more closely. The original German title, *Der Himmel über Berlin*, translated literally, means 'The

Sky (or Heaven) above Berlin'. This emphasises the real Berlin with its real places such as Potsdamer Platz and the Wall, a city divided between East and West. At the same time the 'sky' above Berlin is undivided, and so are the angels' movements. The history of Berlin and with it of Germany is also visible. There are plenty of references to history in the course of the film, including clips from archive footage which, interwoven with the fictional story, serve to make history relevant for the present time. The real Berlin also includes the inhabitants of the city, with their daily lives, their joys and sorrows, their loneliness, their special-ness and their ordinariness. All this makes up a poetic portrait of the city. The English title, *Wings of Desire*, on the other hand, focuses on the yearning of the angels to partake in humanity, first and foremost by listening to people's thoughts and by trying to comfort them. Desire is also evident in Damiel's love story: the desire for a woman and the resulting desire to become human. Both titles have a wealth of meaning and connotations in their respective language, but stress very different, yet equally important aspects of the film. Ultimately the film is a portrait of and a declaration of love to Berlin and to humanity. That Wenders manages to bring these aspects together so convincingly is his and his collaborators' great achievement.

We mentioned before that there was much pressure on Wenders to make a film using his Berlin-based production company. He knew that he wanted to film in Berlin; he had vague ideas of setting and characters, but not of narrative development, let alone a screenplay. For this he contacted Peter Handke, an Austrian author and poet with whom he had collaborated several times before. Wenders is a great admirer of Handke, in particular of his pure and sophisticated language, which is the kind of language that the angels were supposed to speak. Instead of speaking everyday language Wenders' angels preserve a kind of archaic, poetic, beautiful language which is set apart from the simplified everyday language of human beings. For Wenders only Handke could write such language. The author agreed to write some of the screenplay, ten scenes to be exact, including the opening poem 'About Childhood'. However, they were in frequent contact during the production, and Wenders admitted later that Handke's scenes were like a beacon for him, like a backbone to the story, in the quite frightening experience of making a film without a screenplay. He himself wrote the remainder, from day to day, improvising as he went along.

Wenders' proposal of a film with angels as protagonists was so extraordinary that he encountered scepticism amongst many of the people he approached with the idea. Fortunately, the key people, the cinematographer Henri Alekan and the actors Bruno Ganz, Otto Sander – the two principal angels Damiel and Cassiel – as

well as Peter Falk, reacted very positively. Alekan was Wenders' number one choice of cameraman because he felt that only the veteran French cinematographer would be able to convey the sweeping, flowing movements of the angels. In the finished film Alekan's black and white cinematography is reminiscent of Expressionist film-making in 1920s' Germany. By employing such an accomplished director of photography and by choosing a location with so much historical resonance Wenders has managed to build a kind of bridge between the present and the past of German cinema.

To provide a bridge between angels and human beings Wenders needed an 'ex-angel', one that had 'converted' to being human before, and who would be in Berlin at the time of the main character's decision-making and transformation process. It was clear to Wenders that this ex-angel had to be an actor of high recognition value and at the same time he needed to have the gravitas and the kind face to be convincing as an angel. We probably all know Peter Falk as Inspector Columbo, the classic television detective series in which he combines authority with a unique kind of humanity. Wenders' instincts proved correct: Peter Falk accepted immediately when he was told that he was to play 'the film star' an ex-guardian angel in a film which had, as yet, no script. Moreover, Wenders remarks that after Falk's arrival in Berlin, whenever he walked around Berlin he was recognised and greeted like a friend by people. There is one short scene in *Himmel* where the ex-angel Falk wanders around a wasteland near the Wall. Several youths walk

by and say to each other: 'Isn't this Columbo?' 'Nah, he wouldn't be walking around Berlin like this, in such an old coat.' Wenders' great admiration for Peter Falk is evident in all the scenes involving him, and whoever thinks Wenders does not have a sense of humour can only be directed to these scenes.

For Wenders, Henri Alekan's and Peter Falk's collaboration, together with Peter Handke's willingness to engage with the production, if in a limited way, provided the cornerstones for his project. The improvisatory nature of the production had its advantages: Everybody on the team, crew and actors, worked much more closely together than they normally would. There was the uncertainty of what would happen next, both in the film and for the members of the crew, and that kept everybody on the set much more involved in the process. Unusual in feature film-making, but commensurate with the improvisatory character, *Himmel* was shot chronologically, quickly and spontaneously. That, too, added to the final product's sense of clarity and unity. Wenders is convinced that without a script it is possible to catch the truth of a scene better and more immediately. All of the actors provided in part their own lines. This, too, was a result of working with an unfinished screenplay. On the down side there were many sleepless nights spent by Wenders, who was burdened with the responsibility for the crew, the cast, the film, and often was unable to answer questions from his collaborators as to 'what would happen next'.

We mentioned before the involvement of Bruno Ganz as the angel Damiel. He had worked with Wenders before as the lead in *Der amerikanische Freund* (*The American Friend*, 1977). According to the director, Ganz had exactly the right 'ingredients' in his personality to be able to play an angel convincingly. These 'angelic' features manifest themselves above all in his face, which is here capable of showing childlike emotions, compassion and kindness. (If you compare these qualities in his acting with his performance as Adolf Hitler in *Der Untergang* you will realise just what an astonishing actor he is.) Otto Sander, who plays the angel Cassiel, is above all a stage actor, similar to Bruno Ganz. However, we have seen him in a small role in *Die Blechtrommel*. He also acted in *Das Boot* and has been associated, again like Ganz, with New German Cinema. As Cassiel he is sceptical of Damiel's wish to become human and questions his convictions. However, his own story, including his own becoming human, are picked up in Wenders' next feature film *Bis ans Ende der Welt* (*Until the End of the World*, 1990-91), which also has the same female protagonist as *Himmel*. She is played by Wenders' then girlfriend, Solveig Dommartin, whose first film role this is. While preparing for the

part as a trapeze artiste in a circus, Marion, she insisted on doing all the scenes herself, including the trapeze acts, and did not use a stunt double at all. By the end of her thorough preparation, during which she was trained by one of the best artistes and trainers in Germany, she was actually offered jobs as a trapeze artiste in the circus!

As in Wenders' previous films there are characters in *Himmel* who are lost, either in an emotional or a physical sense. We see them roaming the streets of Berlin (or the skies above it), looking for relief from their loneliness. Marion is one such character; 'Homer', played by the veteran German stage actor Curt Bois, is another. Wenders does not underplay the significance of isolation of people in the city, alone in apartments, in the underground, the music club. However, *Himmel* is above all a film about approach and arrival. In fact, there are two distinct 'modes' of arrival, both introduced in the exposition to the film. The first mode could be called the 'heavenly approach', which is presented to us in the first few shots. It is signalled by a view of the sky, then a super-imposed eye, then a panoramic view of the city of Berlin from above. The relationship between above and below is established visually by the angel Damiel's view from West Berlin's 'Gedächtniskirche' and by children looking up from below and pointing out to each other that there is an angel up there. Adults around them take no notice. The Gedächtniskirche is highly significant historically: Most of this famous church was destroyed by bombs in World War II. It was decided not to rebuild the church but to preserve its damaged spire as a memorial to the war, and instead to add a modern church building. At the time of the division of Germany the 'Memorial Church' was West Berlin's definitive icon of the destruction and subsequent division of Berlin. The church is situated at the beginning of

the Kurfürstendamm, the most famous shopping street in the West of a then divided Berlin, a street which was held up to the East as a triumph of capitalism.

The strong black and white cinematography is accompanied by soft ethereal music with cello and harp being the most distinctive instruments. In the space between diegesis and non-diegesis we hear a cacophony of voices that turn out to be people's thoughts. They become louder as we, together with the angel, get closer to them. The camera follows one young father with a baby, and then swoops up towards blocks of flats. For the first time we experience how angels pass through walls of buildings and individual rooms. Within these rooms we see many quite lonely people (or at least people on their own). The thoughts we hear are the ordinary, yet totally unique and therefore not ordinary, thoughts of people.

The second mode of arrival could be termed the 'worldly' or 'technological approach'. Peter Falk is sitting in a plane as it approaches Berlin. We only know the destination because, again, the angel Damiel is present and is listening to Falk's thoughts. Those thoughts are, quite logically, in English. Falk improvised this scene completely: He thinks about the fact that he knows very little about the part he is about to play, which in the

film narrative is meant to be a film set in Nazi Germany, but of course his thoughts also refer to his part in *Himmel*, since he did not possess a script. In Falk's involvement in a historical film we have again a connection between past and present. The shooting of this film within a film will be taken up later on in this chapter.

The opening of *Der Himmel über Berlin* is multi-layered and multi-dimensional. Immediately from the opening we are struck by the serenity, the calmness, the loving, which is conveyed through the angels' presence, both in the sky and on earth. They are at the same time distant from the action and close to it by virtue of their interest in people's lives. This could result in a voyeuristic experience: Spying on the thoughts (and lives) of others. [2] However, if anything, it is the opposite of voyeurism: The audience is directly involved by taking the angels' viewpoint, whereby the camera and the microphone are the angels' eyes and ears. By the way, soulless voyeurism is one of Wenders' criticisms of contemporary society. This criticism is implied, for example, in the many — often flickering and showing nothing or very little — television screens that are in evidence in his films. It forms the core of his later film *The End of Violence* (1997), which would make an excellent counter piece to *Der Himmel über Berlin*. [3]

As we watch *Der Himmel über Berlin* we soon notice that it is mostly shot in black and white. We also notice that the black and white vision is related to the way the angels perceive the world. Whenever the film cuts to a scene in which no angel is present, it is filmed in colour. Wenders chose to distinguish the two worlds like this because for him the angels live an ancient and essential existence, for which black and white seemed especially appropriate. Human beings populate a colourful world, they live short lives, they are fully immersed in life, whereas angels stand by. You could also say that black and white here signifies a somewhat barren existence, without involvement in the sensual, more colourful, messier, but also richer world of human beings. [4] The world of the angels is further differentiated from that of human beings by means of the poetic language they speak. As mentioned before, all the dialogue spoken by the angels was written by Peter Handke, whereas Wenders supplied the more 'ordinary' human dialogue.

We have also mentioned that the place for angels to congregate is not a church but a library. It is in fact the architecturally stunning State Library, the 'Staatsbibliothek' of Berlin. It is a very inviting place, where people like to linger and read. In the film we see a cross-section of people sitting at the tables, reading. Their reading inspires their thoughts, and we hear those 'thought-voices' because we share them with the many attending angels who lean over them, laying a hand on someone's shoulder, listening, smiling, and acknowledging each other. As we move with the camera from person to person their thoughts become audible. This happens so quickly, with one voice dissolving into another, that the layers of murmuring cannot always be distinguished from each other, making it

virtually impossible to subtitle everything. The sounds keep swelling and layering until they sound like music, a choir of voices in a secularised cathedral – language transformed into music. Wenders calls it the 'music of human knowledge'. This scene is perhaps his strongest declaration of love to the people of Berlin, and to humankind in general.

There are several scenes that, by lingering with individuals as they are watched over by the angels, achieve a different kind of poetry and compassion. The angel Cassiel is witness to an accident which results in a man dying in the street. The man thinks many thoughts about his life in an inner monologue entitled 'The Poem of the Dying Man'. As soon as Cassiel holds him an almost imperceptible change comes over him, and he dies in peace. Inside an ambulance racing through the night a pregnant woman lies, extremely agitated. Cassiel is with her, holding her. And again, she visibly relaxes. Much later in the film Cassiel is on the roof of the 'Europa-Centre', a hubbub of commercial activity in West Berlin (it is the building with the Mercedes star on top), again not far from the Wall, where a man is about to commit suicide. Cassiel cannot prevent the suicide. We do get the impression that the angels are really quite powerless in trying to change an outcome; all they can do is relieve a situation.

Marion is the main example of an individual who is searching for real meaning in her life. Damiel is her guardian angel, and is very impressed with her: A girl who can fly! The most evocative of Marion's scenes are those in her trailer, when she is quite alone, and Damiel hears her thought-voice (in her native French). The trailer scenes are also examples of Henri Alekan's meticulous photography: Alekan himself set up incredibly complex lighting, which is not evident to us but whose effect is the most intricate, deep and glowing black and white photography. In the second trailer scene in particular the photography works miracles by placing us, with the angel, behind Marion's mirror, the solid surface of which dissolves so that we can see through it and look at her face directly. When we cut to Damiel, a complex mix of empathy and longing, for life, for Marion, is written on his face. We will also learn that as an angel he is not truly effective; he has to become a human being first.

The film's evocation of German history as linked with the present is most direct in the story of an old man called 'Homer', played by Curt Bois in his eighties, who is first seen in a scene at the library where he looks at photographic portraits of well-known faces of old Berlin. From there we cut to documentary footage of the days immediately following World War II, where we see victims of the war laid out for identification. Then we see Homer wandering on his own around a wasteland that used to be Potsdamer Platz, which he knew in the 20s and 30s, all the while searching for signs of the once lively central square of his Berlin of the past, the space of his memory, but in vain. Again we cut to archive footage, this time in colour, shot by the Americans immediately after entering Berlin in 1945. By describing what the area looked like Homer is recounting the history of it, of Germany: He speaks, or rather thinks, about flags that suddenly appeared in Berlin, about the fact that people were not as kind as they had been before. He is thinking about rising National Socialism, of course. His inner monologue was also not scripted. Curt Bois only needed prompting from Wenders, whereupon he improvised most of this account. When *Der Himmel über Berlin* was shot, Potsdamer Platz was indeed a wasteland next to the Wall; dispossessed people camped there, they dumped old furniture there. The armchair, for example, that is shown in the film was used as found. [5]

Peter Falk, in his role as an actor taking part in a historical film set in Nazi Germany, is mostly confined to the ruins of an air-raid shelter, where he sits and wonders what will happen next. He takes the opportunity to observe his fellow actors, mostly extras, we assume. Apart from the fact that it is set in an air-raid shelter, we are never told what exactly the film is about. [6] During a couple of rehearsals for this unnamed film, Wenders cuts back to archive footage, in colour, of endless amounts of rubble – again we are right at the end of World War II, when Berlin and many other German cities had been destroyed by Allied bombing. Again, a little later, the improvisatory nature of filming *Himmel* is demonstrated by a scene in which Falk tries on a whole array of hats until finally settling on one. This was inspired by his real search for a hat. When we see him draw his fellow actors we see his own drawings, which Wenders included spontaneously after being impressed with his skill. While Falk draws, the camera remains on his face which expresses quiet joy at the facial expressions of his models. This moment testifies to Wenders' insistence that he does not choose his actors to 'act' a part, but to 'reveal' themselves in the role without holding back. The lines spoken in voice-over are Falk's own.

During the film there are two scenes which take place at two different but identical-looking fast food trailers. Both of them are run by down-to-earth Berliners who sell their 'currywurst' (a Berlin speciality consisting of cut-up sausage with tomato ketchup and curry powder), a food item that is as ordinary as it is revered by many. Such places seem unlikely spots for significant encounters, but Wenders makes them so. They turn out to be a refuge and meeting point for lost souls. Both encounters involve Peter Falk. In the first one, the 'companero scene', he reveals himself to the approaching Damiel who, we must remember, cannot be seen by mortals. 'I can't see you but I know you're there', he says

to Damiel, looking in his general direction, while the vendor looks at Falk as if he was mad. Falk then proceeds to explain to the angel the joys of human life and ends the (one-sided) conversation by shaking his (invisible) hand. This encounter helps Damiel to make up his mind about becoming human. It is a very touching and at the same time funny scene.

The other encounter happens later on in the film, at night, when Marion, alone, joins Falk at another fast food trailer. She is looking for Damiel without knowing it yet. Falk, however, knows it and he encourages her in her quest. It has become clear now that the two fast food stall scenes are indeed significant, and both the audience and the ex-angel Peter Falk now know what his part in the film is: it is the actual and quite pivotal role of being the catalyst between Damiel and Marion, of finally bringing them together.

It is during Damiel's transformation scene when the Wall is most prominent. The two angels, Damiel and Cassiel, are walking inside the 'no-man's-land', the strip between two sets of Wall. [7] The Wall is visibly quite heavily guarded. As angels, they do not leave any footprints in the soil. Damiel is talking about his first steps into human life and he tells

Cassiel exactly what he will do on his first day. Cassiel is still sceptical. But Damiel has taken his decision, and suddenly his footprints appear in the soil: he has become human. Cassiel realises how dangerous this is, picks him up and carries him over the Wall on the western side. We cut to Damiel, now in colour and himself seeing colour for the first time. His angel's armour plating comes flying through the air and lands on his head. He looks up and sees a helicopter hovering. He also has the extraordinary experience of seeing and tasting his own blood for the first time. 'Now I begin to understand', he says, smiling mischievously. From now on he will begin his search for Marion.

In the cellar of the old Esplanade Hotel (which, again, no longer exists), where rock bands play and where Damiel, while still an angel, has seen Marion before, they finally meet at a concert by Nick Cave and the Bad Seeds, a band that Wenders very much admires. Marion is wearing a red dress, the strongest colour possible, as a symbol for her life-force. In a monologue written by Handke she explains to Damiel the difference between 'being alone' and 'loneliness'. It is clear to both of them that they have arrived at their destination; from now on they are not going to be lonely any more. This is the final triumph of the film: two human beings have found each other in love. A fairy tale on a grand scale has come to its conclusion.

It will have become clear in this chapter that *Der Himmel über Berlin* is more than a fairy tale, though. It manages to combine the fairy-tale strand with unforgettable, totally original and courageous, images, present and past, resulting in a love declaration to Wenders' favourite city and its inhabitants. The film literally knows no boundaries and is tinged with a sadness that has been called 'German melancholy'. It highlights the historical significance of Berlin's empty spaces as well as the special characteristics of Berliners. As an urban film 'it insists that human joys and sorrows are the city' (Tony Rayns).

> 'It is only in Berlin that I could recognise what it means to be German...for history is both physically and emotionally present... No other city is to such an extent a symbol, a place of survival. It is a site, more than a city' (Wim Wenders).

Other films have been made about Berlin, before and since *Der Himmel über Berlin*. The earliest example that is still available is Walter Ruttmann's *Berlin, Symphonie der Grossstadt* (*Berlin, Symphony of a City*, 1927), a completely novel, breathtaking, abstract film in which the city was presented as rhythm, speed, patterns of movement. In 1929, a much less audacious but equally experimental film was made by a group of friends,[8] *Menschen am Sonntag* (*People on Sunday*), whose title suggests that it has people at its centre rather than the city itself. It was an early example of using non-professional actors in a semi-documentary approach. Those two films and perhaps Fassbinder's *Berlin, Alexanderplatz* (1980), together with *Himmel über Berlin*, would make a worthwhile collection of Berlin films. To these could be added a documentary made after the fall of the Wall, *Berlin Babylon* (1995). This film, whose cinematography is most definitely indebted to *Der Himmel über Berlin*, takes a critical look at Berlin's architectural development in the 1990s – which seemed to aim at filling all those holes and empty spaces that were so prominent in Wenders' film.

In 1980s' German cinema *Der Himmel über Berlin* was something of an exception, both with regard to its serious subject matter and its recognition as an outstanding film. The

1980s was not the finest decade in German film-making. Lifestyle comedies and romantic comedies dominated. After *Himmel* it took more than ten years for another German production to receive international acclaim: *Lola rennt* (*Run Lola Run*), the subject of our next chapter, and another urban film.

FOOTNOTES

[1] Curt Bois' career is another one of those 'German' biographies: Born in 1901 in Berlin, he worked in theatre and film, was well-known in the Weimar years, went into exile to the USA in 1933, in danger because of his political views. In 1950 he returned to Germany, to the East in fact, which he left, disillusioned, however, in 1954. He managed to work more or less continuously in theatre, film and television, and died in 1991. He was very much an actor's actor.

[2] There is a certain parallel between *Himmel* and *Das Leben der Anderen*, see our final chapter, in the trope of spying and listening: Wiesler's involvement gradually turns from cold spying to compassion.

[3] *Metropolis* was the first German feature film to deal with surveillance cameras as used by Joh Fredersen to control his subjects.

[4] In this context, consider the Powell and Pressburger film *A Matter of Life and Death*, which uses the same distinction between black and white and colour.

[5] The location for the circus, by the way, was in Kreuzberg, near the Wall. The space that was representative of so many other vacant lots in Berlin in those days is no longer there. It now houses a supermarket and a block of apartments.

[6] It is reminiscent of Wenders' film *Der Stand der Dinge* (*The State of Things*, 1982), in which a film director spends his time at a film set, waiting for further developments.

[7] Also called the 'death-strip', because the East German border guards had the order to shoot anybody who tried to cross the space.

[8] Billy Wilder, Edgar Ulmer, Robert Siodmak, who, after emigrating, all went on to have major careers in Hollywood.

CHAPTER ELEVEN: BERLIN: NEW ENERGIES: *LOLA RENNT (RUN LOLA RUN,* 1998)

The focus film of this chapter is again set in Berlin. It is acknowledged as the first real international success of German cinema after many years of stagnation, in effect since *Der Himmel über Berlin.* There are interesting similarities, but also significant differences between *Lola rennt* and *Der Himmel über Berlin.* Both the parallels and departures could be traced within the contexts of significant political, economic and social changes in Germany, and of 'old master' Wim Wenders – versus 'new blood' –Tom Tykwer – both of whom share an affinity with this unique city, although neither of them is originally from Berlin. The city changed considerably between the *Himmel* of 1986 and the *Lola* of 1998, and yet, as we will see, it still occupies a unique place, owing to its turbulent history.

We must remember that in 1986 Berlin was a divided city, the front line between the Western and Eastern bloc, the place where two opposing political systems met. This proximity, together with the contested status of the city as an island within the GDR, resulted in displays of political and economic power – political in the East, economic in the West. Whereas East Berlin was the capital of the GDR, West Berlin was an isolated outpost of the FRG. [1] This isolation led to an off-centre mix of population. The marginalised position of West Berlin was most clearly visible near the Wall – as we saw in *Der Himmel über Berlin*. Only three years after shooting *Himmel*, the groundswell of public unrest in East Germany, with demands for reforms and for the Wall to be abolished that had been gaining strength throughout the 1980s, together with political and economic reforms in the Soviet Union, achieved the seemingly impossible: The Berlin Wall began to crumble on 9 November, 1989. What had started as a desire among East Germans to simply be able to cross over into the West to 'see what it was like', led, within less than a year, to the reunification of the whole of Germany. The Wall was gradually (with the generous help of souvenir hunters) dismantled, and after only a few years there was hardly a trace of it left. Today you would be hard put to track its former course through Berlin except for very few remains that have been left intact for commemorative purposes, and for the lines in the ground immediately to the east of the Reichstag that remind us of its existence. The gaping holes and empty spaces that form an important part of the visual narrative of *Der Himmel über Berlin* have all but disappeared as well. Berlin is no longer isolated, indeed it has become the capital of Germany once again, but it still has not become what could be called a city with a 'mainstream' identity.

Throughout the 1990s Berlin was turned into one huge building site in order to bring it up to the standard of an international city. It had to be prepared for its renewed function as the capital city of Germany with its associated need for government accommodation, of which the restoration of the Reichstag as the seat of the new parliament is the most prominent example. Dwellings had to be redeveloped, particularly in the east of the city where the emphasis during GDR times had been on building new prefabricated blocks of flats instead of renovating old stock. Many of the measures for Berlin's renewal have been controversial. There is an excellent film, *Berlin Babylon*, made during the 1990s, which documents the years when cranes dominated Berlin's skyline. It takes a critical look at decisions taken by architects and representatives of government, and their financial implications. At the time of writing Berlin is 'unfinished', and the best film-makers will continue to make use of this quality.

In our chapter on *Der Himmel über Berlin* we mentioned another film that captures the mood in Berlin in the 1990s. Its German title, *Das Leben ist eine Baustelle*, literally translated as 'Life is a Building Site', released internationally as *Life is All You Get*, speaks for itself. It is a feature film that originates from the same stable as *Lola rennt*, and was shot just one year before, in 1997. The stable consists of a team of film-makers who formed the production company 'X-Filme creative pool'. Tom Tykwer wrote the screenplay, Wolfgang Becker directed. [2] The film shows realistically a suffering Berlin in the aftermath of the fall of the Wall and in the middle of political change. In this film the building site that is Berlin becomes a metaphor for the lives of various characters. History or politics are not central, although we see a political demonstration being broken up with force by police, and there are critical comments by one character who bemoans the fact that East Berlin is overrun by capitalists trying to make a fortune.

In *Lola rennt* politics is even further removed from the agenda. The Berlin we see here is important, but more as a 'set' than as a focal point. It could almost be argued that the film could have been set in any city – Tom Tykwer himself has alluded to this – and yet: the specific 'unfinished' urban environment of Berlin provided him with a backdrop that fits perfectly with the story he is telling. There is in *Lola*'s Berlin a sense of artificiality, particularly evident in the empty streets, some remaining building sites, and the two buildings relevant in the film whose facades are either imposing (such as the casino) or somewhat neglected (for instance, the bank). This is emphasised by the lettering on the bank, which is almost sloppily applied, as if the film-makers were not particularly interested in authenticity. This impression is confirmed when Tykwer says that he was above all concerned with the authenticity of interiors. He was also very clear that both the bank and the casino needed to have a 'museum-like' quality, with old-fashioned interiors, ornamental doors, large spaces and high ceilings. Since Berlin does not possess such a casino or any bank that would be suitable, the film-makers rented buildings not made for the purpose and fitted them out as needed. However, Berlin's empty streets are real enough; the Friedrichstraße in particular can be made out clearly, an iconic Berlin street which, in the divided city, used to be synonymous with an important border crossing between East and West Berlin. As mentioned above, though, political issues are not directly part of this film.

How do you start an urban film? How do you approach the 'city' narratively? There are certain conventions which tend to be used to do this. A well-known trope is 'arrival' – as seen in Peter Falk's plane journey in *Der Himmel über Berlin*, for example. A further possibility is an establishing shot of the city, or of a famous square or building, which then leads to the introduction of individual characters that will become part of the narrative. We have a variation on this in *Himmel* as well, when the city's expanse is introduced to us from an angel's point of view. *Lola rennt* takes a different approach. After the prologue (which we will discuss later on) we experience a fast-forward animated opening, in which the camera briefly focuses on an aerial shot of Berlin and then races as in a roller-coaster ride down towards the city and homes in on a typical Berlin block of flats, and the back part of the building set around a courtyard. It is recognisable as a nicely refurbished middle-class dwelling. The camera does not stop; it races through a window, into one of the flats, down the hall and into Lola's room. Breathtakingly quickly and effectively the first urban location is established. The second location, a phone booth which marks the connection between Lola and her boyfriend Manni, is approached by the camera with a similar urgency. This is a city environment and time is clearly of the essence.

We are now witness to a frantic telephone conversation in which Manni panics because he has forgotten a plastic bag containing 100,000 Deutschmarks on an underground train, money he was supposed to deliver to his gangster boss in twenty minutes. He is in a terrible state, and only Lola can help him. We get the impression that she is usually the one who comes up with the right ideas at the right time, and that she is the one with an overwhelmingly strong sense that 'love conquers all'. She promises him that she will find a solution and starts to run across the city towards her father's bank. She has no means of transport because her moped was stolen, which is why she could not meet Manni in time to save him in the first place. This is the simple premise of the plot. However, she is unsuccessful in her attempt at securing the money and gets another chance, and then another one. Three wishes: a fairy tale. The difference between a traditional fairy tale and this modern one, though, is that Lola makes her three chances happen all by herself; she is the driving force, no good fairy is needed. Lola emerges as a superhuman heroine.

The prologue to the film introduces us to another layer of meaning leading to philosophical questions. Two quotes appear on the screen. One is from T. S. Eliot and addresses the human quest for knowledge, which always brings us back to where we started; the second one comes from the most famous football trainer the German national team has ever had, Sepp Herberger: 'After the game is before the game.' High culture and low culture meet in these quotes. Putting the two together achieves an ironic effect. The second quote also introduces the idea of 'the game', an idea that is carried on in the subsequent animated sequence. On that level Lola's superhuman qualities and her three attempts could be interpreted as forming a video or computer game. The idea of time is introduced by a ticking clock and the image of a swinging pendulum – swinging between deep meaning and banality? Above the face of the clock we see a kind of gargoyle which proceeds to swallow the camera (and us). At the same time, music starts on the soundtrack, an insistent techno-pop rhythm with keyboard and slight hints of classical music, an interesting fusion which became a danceable record – probably a first in film music. The music was composed by Tom Tykwer, Johnny Klimek and Reinhold Heil, long-time collaborators. From now on the music will be with us nearly continuously throughout the film, again emphasising speed and urgency.

After the gargoyle has gobbled us all up it spits us out among large numbers of people who are milling and rushing at great speed, an effect achieved by fast-forward camera work. Some individuals are picked out by the camera, the frame-per-minute count decreases, they look at the camera and give the impression that they might be the protagonists of the film we are about to see. We do indeed meet them later, but not as protagonists. In voice-over, we hear a soothing male voice telling us what a strange species human beings are, always in search of answers to fundamental questions such as 'Who are we?' or 'Why are we here?' All of a sudden we are lifted into the realm of philosophical musings which seem to be slightly out of place or hyperbolic compared to the previous playful images. However, for German audiences the voice asking these questions is immediately recognisable as that of a well-known fairy-tale raconteur, a fact that once again mixes irony into the message.

One of the people in the crowd is Schuster (as we find out later), the security guard at Lola's father's bank. Holding a football he looks straight at the camera and tells us that the ball is round and the game lasts 90 minutes, and the rest is theory. Again we have the juxtaposition of the exalted and the profane. He then kicks the ball high in the air,

the camera pulls up with the ball and from high above (60 metres in fact) we see people forming on the ground into the name Lola. Here the many (300 real people in order to form each letter) get together to compose the one whom we have not met yet. But at least now we know who the main character in the story is.

The story proper begins with above-mentioned telephone conversation, which continues in the same dazzling vein as the prologue and titles, both visually and aurally. The cutting is rapid, Manni talks quickly, there are split screens to indicate Manni's and Lola's closeness (and presumably to 'save the time' which cross-cutting would

have taken). There are black and white flashbacks to visualise the background story of how the money was lost and how Lola's moped was stolen. There are even stills (in the shape of picture postcards) showing exotic holiday locations when Manni remembers that a tramp must have found the plastic bag and will surely by now have booked his holiday. In short flashes filmed on video with handheld camera we are privy to the tramp finding the bag, hardly believing his luck and running away with it. The figure of the tramp is another ironic insert in the film: He is played by Joachim Król, one of Germany's finest actors, who is all but unrecognisable here, playing a character whose surname is 'von Au', the 'von' denoting aristocratic descent. Later on, while running, Lola has fleeting encounters with the people from the prologue, and their own future lives are presented to us in montages of stills, snapshot style.

These are the principles of Tykwer's switching of formats: whenever Lola is present in a scene it is filmed in 35 mm, when she is not, on video; flashbacks are in black and white, flashforwards in a rapid montage of stills. You may remember Wim Wenders switching between black and white and colour [3] to indicate the presence or absence of angels in *Der Himmel über Berlin* – it does not seem too far-fetched to suggest that Tykwer admired that film and utilised some of its techniques. However, the dazzling array of cinematic tricks are all his, and he has admitted that he wanted to make a film about the 'possibilities of life' which needed to encompass the 'possibilities of cinema'. It is indeed a declaration of love for the cinema when Lola's omnipotence is expressed in 35 mm film stock – anything is possible in the cinema! Tykwer was praised by critics and colleagues for his skill at integrating the various themes of his film with this virtuoso cinematic display and making the whole film look effortlessly playful. This must also be one of the reasons why *Lola rennt* has become something of a film-makers' film. Tykwer's frequent references to or quotes from other films show off his knowledge of cinema history and provide another level of playfulness.

However, Lola has one more cinematic trick up her sleeve: As soon as she starts her first run we seem to be entering a computer game, for our heroine turns into an animated character for as long as it takes her to run downstairs and to navigate her way round the vicious-looking boy with his ferocious, teeth-baring dog, both of whom seem to be intent on tripping Lola up. Here our super-heroine is shown as even transcending reality in order to fulfil her mission. As she leaves the house she has turned into a human once more.

The twenty minutes in which Lola must complete her task are filmed in real time. With three runs altogether this means that these speed-dominated sequences last sixty minutes. Tykwer has interspersed them with two 'red scenes' which we will discuss later. Lola's constant movement in the running scenes was challenging to film. Tykwer explains that the crew experimented with all kinds of vehicles, such as jeeps, cranes, three-wheelers, and even a wheel-barrow in order to be able to keep up with Lola as she runs. The almost deserted streets of Berlin must certainly have helped, too. These streets also provide a metaphor for Lola's mission: She is alone against the rest of the world.

Arguably the most important theme of the film emerges in the course of the narrative with its three variations (see below): the interplay and consequences of chance, accident, coincidence and fate, including the 'what if' question, which moves the film into the realm of the conditional. Coincidence in this film is an urban phenomenon. It would have been impossible for this narrative to unfold in a rural environment. The causality principle is introduced by the images we see on Lola's television screen: a massive (and possibly the world's longest) game of dominoes which is set in motion and causes a chain-reaction. If we cast back our minds to the cause of Manni's problem, it was the fact that Lola's moped was stolen from outside a shop, a freak incident with life-and-death consequences.

The variations in the space-time continuum of the three runs are minimal, but they have very different outcomes. Each time she goes on her run, her encounter with the dog on the stairs is very slightly different. This either slows her down or speeds her up by only a couple of seconds, but again it has enormous consequences. There is also a generous sprinkling of free will and determination thrown into the theme mix: When the chips are well and truly down, Lola's will controls the situation and gets Manni out of trouble. For this is her ultimate aim: to secure his and her survival and that of their relationship. The first time we are witness to Lola's power is in the initial telephone scene, which she ends with a loud scream that shatters glass (reminiscent of Oskar Mazerath in *Die Blechtrommel*, who was also able to control his world). We will hear this scream again when she plays roulette at the casino in order to win the much-needed money: With her ear-splitting scream she literally wills the spinning ball to land on the right number.

For most of the film, speed and split-second reactions are essential. However, there are several instances where 'waiting' becomes important and is set against the dominant tempo. Towards the end of Lola's final run both Manni and Lola experience an intervention: In Manni's case it is a blind woman at the phone booth who has been listening to his desperate telephone conversations. By 'blind chance'[4] she is decisive in the help she gives him: She tells him to 'wait' while she listens, and then she points to the tramp pedalling by on his newly-acquired bicycle. Is she a good fairy? For Lola everything seems lost after she has missed her father on her third and final run, and she closes her eyes in 'blind faith' and utters a kind of prayer for help, all the while keeping running. A lorry very nearly runs her over, she is stopped in her tracks, and at this moment she sees the casino in front of her. Blindness is shown here as a way to enable 'inner' perception, it highlights the importance of 'stop and think (or feel)' as an antidote to 'seeing' and 'acting' all the time. This need to involve all the senses, together with the poles of chance and fate, also in the guise of accidents, and a strong will, is a recurring motif in other Tykwer films, too. (See for example *Winterschläfer* [*Wintersleepers*, 1997], *Der Krieger und die Kaiserin* [*The Princess and the Warrior*, 2000], but also *Heaven* [2003], scripted by Kieslowski.)

In the short and very still 'red scenes', which are often overlooked in discussions about the film but described by Tykwer as the central scenes, we see Lola and Manni bathed in red light, on the bed, in a suspended state between life and death – literally, for both these scenes occur immediately after one of them has been killed, Lola by a gunshot and Manni by an ambulance. They discuss their relationship and what they mean to each other. This is so important that Lola decides that it is not time to die yet. She frees herself to begin another run which may rescue them. There is something truly utopian about these scenes. The utopian tenor is picked up elsewhere in the words of Tykwer's song called 'Wish'. Franka Potente, the actress who plays Lola, sings (or rather speaks) the words: 'I wish I was a person with unlimited breath, I wish I was a heartbeat that never comes to rest...' These very slow scenes balance out the otherwise frantic pace of the film.

In contrast to these utopian ideas there is reality outside Lola's influence: there are the very real scenes between her father and his lover Jutta, who is also a business partner in his bank. Three times Lola comes to see him at the bank, in each case at a slightly different time. Once she misses him. The other times the reactions she gets from him vary according to how much her father and Jutta have progressed in their conversation regarding their future together. Jutta is trying to tell him that she is expecting a baby, but that it is not his. It is only in the second episode that she manages to convey this fact, and Lola's father reacts very badly. His hurtful behaviour towards Lola triggers her idea of taking him hostage in order to extract the money from the bank. In any case, it is obvious how estranged father and daughter are, and in all likelihood mother as well, who sits at home, drinking. Tykwer is making comments on the complications of modern families, including generational conflicts, a topic explored in his previous film, *Winterschläfer*.

The fact that Lola's family is not where she wants to belong makes her resolve to save Manni, her love, even stronger. This desire eclipses every other issue, including the relevance of the city itself. It is clear that *Lola rennt* would not have been possible in a rural setting, and also that Berlin serves a certain function, such as heightening the strangeness and artificiality of the setting; but Lola, although obviously familiar with the city, is not aware of the surroundings through which she runs other than as means to an end. This sense of non-connectedness is also evident in the fact that the spaces that she covers are in the real Berlin not linked to each other. In other words, the film-makers took great liberty with the individual locations. They took this approach partly because of the accessibility and/or emptiness of certain (east) Berlin streets, which obviously made filming easier. However, this non-connectedness in Berlin also makes a statement: At the time (and to a certain extent even now) Berlin was a unified city in a political sense, but the differences between east and west were still clearly visible, and they also existed in the minds of Berliners. Tykwer might have wanted to comment on that symbolically. Lola's power to control and rearrange her own environment may also be reflected in the disconnected spaces that she conquers.

If we compare this to the Berlin of *Der Himmel über Berlin*, which Tom Tykwer must have seen and must have been impressed by, we find that Lola, similar to the angels in the earlier film, is not bound by 'physical realities': she sprints through Berlin in a way that would not have been possible for ordinary human beings. However, whereas she is unconnected to most of her fellow-citizens unless they are 'useful' to her, the angels show compassion and, accordingly, the city is 'unified'. Would it be too much to read into these differences that perspectives have changed? That in some way the social-historical-political context of *Der Himmel über Berlin* with its longing for unity has developed into an instrumentalised, consumerist view of the world? (See also below.) Some perspectives do not seem to have changed, though: In *Lola* and in *Himmel* one of the central themes is the importance of love and personal relationships. In *Lola* the in-between scenes in bed do contain some sort of existential message, even though the protagonists are groping for words rather than speaking in poetic prose. In *Himmel* Damiel leaves his angelic existence for love of a human being. In both films the desire for a close personal relationship is the driving force that enables the protagonists to overcome obstacles.

During the final run, Lola, in one of her split-second decisions, hitches a lift with the passing ambulance. Inside she finds Schuster, the security guard, who has had a heart attack and is being looked after by a desperate medic. She simply sits next to the sick man and holds his hand. Immediately his pulse steadies. This scene definitely recalls

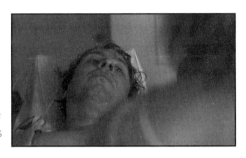

the ambulance scene in *Der Himmel über Berlin*, where the angel Cassiel calms down the fretting pregnant woman, even though you might argue that Lola is simply making amends for her earlier behaviour which caused Schuster's heart attack in the first place.

In several places in this chapter we have alluded to parallels between *Der Himmel über Berlin* and *Lola rennt*. They include the circumstances of their production. You may remember that Wenders was almost forced to make a film in order to keep his production company afloat. Tykwer found himself in a very similar position with X-Filme creative pool. Both films were made on a small budget and produced within a very short time. In this sense they were both 'survival' films in the self-reliance of the auteur tradition. They were both partly financed through the German system of state funding. *Lola*'s state funding was particularly complex, a reflection of new laws governing public film funding in the Federal Republic of Germany. The emphasis is now on 'federal': German films receive funding through the individual 'Bundesländer' (federal states) if they fulfil certain criteria, such as filming in certain locations. In the case of *Lola*, the film received funding from the federal states of North Rhine-Westphalia and Berlin-Brandenburg. In addition to this there was funding from the (central, not federal) Ministry of the Interior. Like many recent cinema films *Lola* was co-produced by one of the federal public television stations, WDR (Westdeutscher Rundfunk), based in Cologne, North Rhine-Westphalia), and by the joint French-German TV channel ARTE.

The differences between the two films are equally significant, not just for a direct comparison between them but in a wider context of differences between New German

Cinema and film-making in contemporary Germany. To name but a few: the introspective, slow, sweeping style of Wenders' film has given way to speed, in all respects, including the editing of *Lola*. Wenders embraces all humanity, Tykwer concentrates on individual, very carefully chosen characters. The angels watch over and care about every human being, Lola runs past people in the streets whose future lives are shown to us, but she does not care. She has a very specific goal that necessitates the instrumentalisation of the city and its inhabitants, including her own family. Without over-interpreting these differences it could be said that Germany has changed, within the context of changes in the world economy, of course. *Himmel* is a romantic-philosophical meditation; *Lola* is a romantic-philosophical rollercoaster. Where *Himmel* defies all genre conventions, *Lola* plays with genre conventions. Tom Tykwer has called his film 'a romantic-philosophical-action-thriller', a critic called it 'a techno-romantic-post-nouvelle-vague-Berlin-crime story'. As we have seen, stylistically Tykwer incorporates every cinematic trick in the book. This postmodern approach to genre and style not only shows off Tykwer's own self-confidence but points to a new self-confidence in German film as such. If you remember, in *Der Himmel über Berlin* Wenders created poetic images never seen before and used an equally poetic style of prose. Tykwer on the other hand gives us a thunderstorm of images that manipulate the space-time-continuum – again as never seen before. It is only in the 'slow' scenes that he gives his characters space to catch their breath.

Wenders, the old master, and Tykwer, the new kid on the block, had a significant encounter at the award ceremony for the German Film Prize of 1998, where Wenders received the award for best director – for *The End of Violence* (1997) – which he passed on to Tom Tykwer (who had also been nominated, for *Lola rennt*) for him to keep until he received an award himself. This testifies to Wenders' admiration for Tykwer and his conviction that the younger man had what it took to become a distinguished film director himself. This act could also symbolise the passing of the baton from the older to the younger generation.

You may remember from our discussions of New German Cinema of the 1970s that the young film-makers (such as Fassbinder, Herzog, Reitz, and Wenders) were above all concerned with the independence of their films, i.e. the freedom from political and commercial pressures. Their task was nothing less than the renewal of German cinema through a complete break with past film practices, working against the dominance of Hollywood, and finding their own film language. They worked in a climate of political radicalisation. They were not interested in commercial success, but more in self-expression and in redefining what it meant to be German at that time. However, it cannot be stressed enough that they did not form a coherent 'movement', which would have been too strong a term for the rather loose group of German film-makers of the time.

Lola rennt is a good example of another renewal within German cinema, which began around the middle of the 1990s.[5] A new generation of film-makers wanted to reach beyond the soul-searching, commercially unsuccessful films of New German Cinema. They felt – and still feel today – that it should be possible for German films to be both artistically sophisticated and successful at the box office, both in Germany and internationally. Film-makers such as Tom Tykwer, Wolfgang Becker, and Fatih Akin (as the best-known example of German-Turkish film-making, see also below and our chapter on *Gegen die Wand*) have actively sought to combine artistic quality and commercial success, and they have achieved this, if not with their first features, then with their second or third. Tom Tykwer talks of this renewal as 'Young New German Film', an obvious reference to the earlier New German Cinema but a rather awkward term. It might be more appropriate to call it a 'New Wave' of German film-making just before and into the new millennium – although we need to be aware that it may not be so helpful to try to group together film-makers that do not have all that much in common. And then again, it must be more than coincidence that there has been new life in German film-making in the last ten years or so. What the two 'movements' discussed here have in common is that what came before them were indeed periods of stagnation and lethargy, both in German politics and society, and in the film industry. This time the stagnation lasted throughout the eighties and into the nineties.

This new 'awakening' in German film-making is even less of a coherent movement than New German Cinema. It did not have a deliberate starting point such as a manifesto but gained momentum gradually. There was no clear break with a previous generation. As Tykwer says, his generation is characterised by complicated family relationships, a clear break with the previous generation is not possible, and there is nothing concrete to fight against.[6] This view is reflected in his early films, including *Lola rennt*. Looking at the wider context, we might add to this that the geopolitical map of the world is quite different now than it was in the 1970s. Globalisation has transformed our lives, and in domestic terms, in 1998, Germany's political direction changed when a new coalition of the Social Democratic Party (SPD) and The Green Party (Die Grünen) was elected to run the country after 16 years of government by the Conservatives (CDU/CSU). A reunited Germany is slowly finding its own identity – the legacy of its troubled history is being dealt with more decisively and with more clarity.

When *Lola rennt* burst onto the cinema screens in 1998 it did not take off everywhere immediately but caught the imagination and admiration of critics and at festivals gradually – they might not have known quite what to make of this whirlwind of a film to begin with. It won many awards, including eight German film awards and a prestigious Sundance Film Festival award, which helped the film to break into the US market. It was praised by American critics as a 'cinematic miracle', and it broke box office records for German films even though it was shown with subtitles. Its international reception was unprecedented, and even the German film-going public appreciated it. This is remarkable given that much more established and renowned German film-makers find it hard to make inroads at the German box office, a fact that has partly to do with the dominance of Hollywood cinema on German cinema screens. The real mark of its enduring success, though, must be that it has become influential amongst film-makers who actually quote it in their own films. The phrase 'running like Lola' or similar has been heard many times.

Very significantly, the film managed to convince both critics and audiences to rethink their preconceived notion that German films were too inward-looking in their subject-matter, too provincial, possibly stern, humourless and plodding, inaccessible or uninteresting for audiences, a notion which may have had some justification at some point, but which is definitely outdated now. It also needs to be mentioned that the lack of German film marketing abroad is partly responsible for the poor record of success of German films before *Lola rennt*. The dominance of Hollywood cinema (this includes distribution) that we mentioned before has also been a hindrance in bringing German films to the attention of larger audiences. The distribution arm of companies such as X-Filme creative pool has as one of its declared aims to distribute German films more widely.

In *Lola*'s wake, many more German films have achieved international distinction and distribution. And while it is perhaps an exaggeration to say that it was Tom Tykwer who single-handedly put German film back on the international map, he has done a great service to the German film industry and his film-making colleagues by proving that entertainment and artistry are not mutually exclusive, and that German films can carry universal messages. Since *Lola*, certain subject-matters and visual styles 'made in Germany' have proved universally interesting, such as multi-cultural and intercultural films from Germany, particularly those of Fatih Akin, whose *Gegen die Wand* (2004) we will discuss in chapter 13, historical films such as *Nirgendwo in Afrika* (*Nowhere in Africa*, 2002), *Der Untergang* (2005), our focus film in chapter 12, and *Sophie Scholl* (2006), or films about the GDR, such as *Good Bye Lenin!* (2003) and *Das Leben der Anderen* (2006), which we will discuss in our final chapter. While we are not suggesting that all these films have achieved international recognition through Tom Tykwer's pioneering alone, it is true that he at least paved the way for smaller productions to be taken note of.

For the final paragraphs of this chapter it is interesting to see where Tom Tykwer is now and what other, lesser known film-makers who emerged at the same time have been doing. His distinctive and flamboyant visual style, particularly his kinetic, fast-paced and flashy editing is most clearly evident in *Lola rennt*, but also in his earlier *Winterschläfer* and in the films following *Lola*. In his next film; *Der Krieger und die Kaiserin*; the fairy-tale element is present once again, so is a strong female lead, again played by his then partner Franka Potente. He went on to make *Heaven* (2003), from a screenplay by the Polish director Krzysztof Kieslowski, a film-maker who must have had a considerable influence on Tykwer, although Tykwer has not made specific reference to this. Just like Kieslowski's protagonists, Tykwer's live and act between the poles of coincidence and fate, with women as the driving force. With *Heaven* Tykwer began to move away from Germany; from then on he also started working with international crews and actors. His next film, *Perfume* (2006), was a literary adaptation of the best-selling novel by Patrick Süsskind, a contemporary German author. It was adapted for the screen by Bernd Eichinger (see also our chapter on *Der Untergang*). Tykwer continues to work internationally.

Among all the international and commercial successes it would be wrong to forget the 'smaller' German films made since reunification. There have been many extremely interesting films that have sadly not achieved wider distribution. The 1990s brought about films dealing with reunification, mostly from an eastern perspective, often by former DEFA film directors. A surprising number of them contained 'verloren' (lost) or 'Nacht' (night) in the title, such as *Verlorene Landschaft* (*Lost Landscape*, 1992), *Wege in die Nacht* (*Paths in the Night*, 1998), both by Andreas Klein, or *Nachtgestalten* (*Nightshapes*, 1999) by Andreas Dresen. Other young film-makers turned to subject-matter such as social issues in contemporary German society, often focusing on family breakdown and young people on the margins. Hans-Christian Schmid is one such film-maker who has consistently turned out thought-provoking films on such issues. Christian Petzold's interest lies in what he calls 'ghosts' – the ghosts of the protagonists' personal or political past, which are at the same time ghosts haunting Germany. *Yella* (2007) is the first of his films to achieve international distribution, a long overdue recognition of his importance. Andreas Dresen, a former DEFA film-maker, has been called 'the German Ken Loach' because of his honest, authentic portrayals of people at the lower end of society's spectrum. His *Nachtgestalten* is set in Berlin, like *Lola*, but is pervaded by a strong social conscience. It would make an interesting companion piece to *Lola*.

FOOTNOTES

[1] Bonn was the capital of West Germany, from 1949 to 1990, and until 1999 the seat of government for the united Germany, before its move to Berlin.

[2] Becker is probably best known for his subsequent *Good Bye Lenin!* (2003).

[3] Although he was not the first to switch film stock to denote contrasts: see for example *The Wizard of Oz* (1939) or *A Matter of Life and Death* (1946), to name but two.

[4] Might Tykwer have paid indirect homage here to Krystzof Kieslowski's film *Blind Chance* (1986) which is constructed in a similar way to *Lola*, with three different outcomes depending on chance?

[5] We are not trying to imply, though, that all contemporary German films are in the style of *Lola rennt*, nor that they should be! There are some excellent recent German productions that do not resort to visual flamboyance. See also the end of this chapter.

[6] Hans Weingartner's film *Die fetten Jahre sind vorbei* (*The Edukators*, 2004) gives some insight into these changes by juxtaposing 'old' and 'young' radicals.

CHAPTER TWELVE: REPRESENTING A DICTATOR: *DER UNTERGANG* (*DOWNFALL*, 2004)

No account of key German feature films would be complete without this one. It not only tackles the most sensitive topic of twentieth century German history and has therefore been received with strong emotions, but it has also been enormously successful internationally. It was nominated for an Oscar in 2005 and received 14 other international awards.

Der Untergang is the story of the last days of Adolf Hitler and his entourage, hidden away in the 'Führerbunker', where extraordinarily deluded decisions were taken and where unbelievable events took place, just a few days before the end of World War II. It was only the second time that a German team with German actors made a feature film that represented Hitler with any kind of 'realism'. As this is a film depicting highly emotionally charged historical events, careful decisions had to be taken in respect of the authenticity of the material and of its portrayal on screen. This 'realistic' approach is in strong contrast to one of our other key films, *Die Blechtrommel*, which also depicts recent German history but chooses to do this in a totally different, fairy-tale-like way.

Der Untergang's subject matter and its representation make it such an important film in the cinematic repertoire of Germany that, more than for any other film in our selection, we need to pose questions about its provenance and its legitimacy. We will also examine other German cinematic representations of Hitler's final days and compare them to *Der Untergang*. Inevitably, given the difficulty of assessing any recent film, and in particular one that deals with such a 'loaded' subject matter, this chapter also contains more question marks than our other chapters – many questions are thrown up which cannot be conclusively answered. [2]

Let us take a look at the historical basis for *Der Untergang* first. Within historical studies there are in principle two main approaches: first, the 'scientific' approach which examines data and analyses structures in society. This approach is the more abstract of the two; it is able to establish useful historical trends, but is not interested in the actual experience of individuals. It is therefore not really a promising basis for a feature film. Another, quite different, approach is historiography, which describes events and puts them into context. This has the advantage of analysing individual events and drawing conclusions accordingly, but runs the risk of being at worst anecdotal and at best 'subjective' in its interpretations. Joachim Fest, the German historian on whose research and publications the film is based, applies the detailed, descriptive approach of historiography to his subject: the final moments of World War II, concentrating on the battle for Berlin on the outside and the confinement of select Nazi personnel, including Hitler himself, in the 'Führerbunker'. Although not unanimously praised for his work, Fest's historical account nevertheless achieved a huge readership and sparked intense discussion.

Fest describes his main argument in the foreword to '*Der Untergang*', the book that accompanies the film: Hitler had always insisted from the beginning of the war that he would never surrender. In 1945 he admitted that the regime could fall, but that it would take with it a whole civilisation. This insistence was borne out by his 'Nero' or 'scorched earth' orders of spring 1945[3]: every single premise for civilisation in Germany, such as utilities, roads and bridges, was to be destroyed in order to create a 'desert'. What the Germans themselves did not destroy, the enemy would. Hitler was not concerned who carried out his wishes, just as long as they were fulfilled. (More on this later on in the chapter.) Fest is convinced that Hitler's nihilism can be traced through the whole of the Third Reich, and that what happened in the last few months of his regime was just an intensified, amplified version of this fundamental attitude. What seems to be clear from accounts of eye witnesses is that even in the last weeks of life in his bunker his authority remained absolute.

There are many question marks over what really happened in these last few days and weeks, as so few people had been shut away with Hitler, and most of these eye witnesses could not be approached at the end of the war for various reasons. The first historian to attempt to shed some light on the events was British: Hugh R. Trevor-Roper provided valuable information as early as 1947. However, many basic facts remained (and still remain) unclear, partly because most of the research was done after important personnel had disappeared – they were either no longer alive, had hidden themselves away, or they were Soviet prisoners of war for up to ten years. Even after some of them had returned and were available again, there were no serious attempts at interviewing them in connection with the events of those final days. One important reason for this was that in the 1950s the end of World War II was regarded as a 'disaster', which precluded in many people's eyes the responsibility of individuals for what happened in the final days. In addition to such less than noble reasons, Fest argues that in the fifties and sixties there was, within historical research, a shift towards the above-mentioned analysis of trends, of structures, and away from the description of individual events. Invaluable eye witness statements were therefore lost.

One more piece in the jigsaw puzzle of eye-witness accounts was provided in 2002 by Traudl Junge, Hitler's private secretary, when her memoirs were published. [4] This publication was the trigger for film producer Bernd Eichinger to start working on a film about the specifics of the end of Hitler's regime, details of which had interested him for a long time. And not just him: the bizarre end of the dictator and his entourage has fascinated hundreds of thousands of people for a long time.

Eichinger wrote a screenplay based on Joachim Fest's and Traudl Junge's accounts of those days. He felt very strongly that it was time for this topic to finally be tackled by Germans themselves. There had been depictions of Hitler in the Anglo-Saxon world of film-making and on television. But why had Germans not tackled it before? One reason was the above-mentioned lack of reliable information about the specific events surrounding the end of the Third Reich. More generally, though, as we have learned in previous chapters of this book, in post-war Germany the recent past was not confronted properly. Initially, the occupying Allied forces decided what was permissible and what was not within Germany (see also our chapter on *Die Mörder sind unter uns*), and when West Germany gradually developed towards political, educational and cultural independence, the West German population (with few exceptions) had all but shut themselves off from any confrontation with their Nazi past. (See also our chapter on *Heimat*.)

Eichinger combined personal interest in the subject matter with extensive experience as a film producer. He sought Joachim Fest's and Traudl Junge's expertise and support for his film. His instincts told him that the time was right to make this film because German audiences were ready for it. This was a brave attempt that was bound to be controversial: Questions were asked as to why it was necessary to make this film, after nearly 50 years. What exactly were German audiences ready for? How was it going to be done and what were audiences supposed to learn from it? With every historical film decisions have to be made as to the exact representation of the material. However, in this case, the speculative and sometimes contradictory nature of the way in which some important details were remembered and reported made it even harder to decide what to include, which of the conflicting versions to follow. We are all aware that once events have been cast into cinematic narrative, especially if that narrative aims at realism, they become somehow 'fixed' in our minds as the truth. Even a documentary film is only based on choices by the film-makers; its truth is relative. In this book alone, we have seen this relativity in our discussion of *Triumph des Willens* and also in Werner Herzog's approach to documentary film-making. In a feature film the film-makers generally take more artistic freedom to express themselves, even though in a historical film the options are more limited. However, even a historical film contains only a selection of the 'truth', and the more 'realistic' the portrayal of events is supposed to be, the more 'fixing' occurs, right down to manipulation of the audiences by creating (necessary?) identification figures.

In addition to this, in any (particularly German) representation of Hitler the stakes are even higher. This vexed issue has plagued generations of film-makers. Serious early debates concluded that Hitler could not be represented directly and realistically, only through grotesque or farce. This is what the film-maker Hans-Jürgen Syberberg did with his seven-hour-long *Hitler – ein Film aus Deutschland* (*Hitler – A Film From Germany*, 1977). In this film, which is an ambitious exploration of the historical and cultural conditions in which Hitler could thrive, Hitler himself is never shown as a 'human being', but is variously reported on by narrators in the third person, as a puppet, as a phenomenon born from Richard Wagner's grave, and so on. Even now, over sixty years later, many Germans feel that he should not be given a human face at all. This is why they find Eichinger's 'realistic' approach hard to stomach even today. The post-war discussion about Hitler's representability is apparently still not over. [5] David Thomson wrote in the British newspaper *The Independent* that a Hitler who is just an immense and inhuman incarnation of evil is somehow easier to cope with than someone who 'was a regular human being – subject to illness, mood swings, his own mistakes and his driving ego'. More than that, mere demonisation would absolve us all from the responsibility for this chapter in German history. The confrontation with Hitler as a human being brings us much closer to him and forces us to deal with him in a much more direct and intimate way. Approached in this way, Eichinger's film can be seen as an attempt to force audiences to explore the identificatory processes at work at the time with the figure of Hitler. The process of gradual separation from someone who was, after all, a 'father' to a whole nation never took place. The lack of detailed research of and confrontation with Hitler as a person resulted in a lack of coming to terms with this part of German history, and in turn allowed the continued identification with, or mystification of, him and his regime on the part of many of his followers. [6] Does this mean that Eichinger provides a rather belated 'cathartic' experience for the German people? Or is anything relating to this dark chapter of German history really history by now? If so, is the film really relevant other than as a spectacle?

The issue of the 'readiness' of Germany for such a depiction of Hitler was hotly debated, mainly in Germany, but also abroad, around the time of the film's release. It is aptly discussed in an article written by Sir Ian Kershaw, a British historian who is one of the greatest living authorities on National Socialism outside Germany, in an article written for *The Guardian* newspaper:

I had often thought that it was no more than a matter of time before Germany produced a feature film about Hitler. Only a few years ago, this would probably still have seemed too daring. But making such a film is a part of the continuing, gradual, but inexorable process of seeing the Hitler era as history – even more important, feeling it to be history. The dictator has always, understandably and rightly, tormented German historical consciousness, and still does. What happened under his rule and in his name has, perhaps permanently, destroyed any possible positive relationship to the past in Germany. And it might be added that the way the country has struggled to cope with its troubled past has often been commendable. But distant events necessarily become viewed differently over time. They become a part of history. This is the case in all societies. It will be the case even for Germany.

Maybe, then, *Der Untergang* is part of the beginnings of a newly developing confidence within Germany as a nation, and in this sense, Eichinger would have been right in his assessment that German audiences were (almost) ready for this film. This view is not one shared by everybody – demonstrated by endless discussions on the internet.

A mainstream feature film, meant to be watched by a large audience and quite obviously seeking to be a box office success at the same time as enlightening its audience, needs to be entertaining. It needs characters with whom we can identify. Should this worry us in this instance? Can Eichinger's motives be trusted? And does that really matter as long as the film reaches its audiences, provides entertainment and enlightenment, and does not lead to extremists glorifying Hitler? In this context, we need to take a close look at Eichinger himself, the producer and screenwriter of *Der Untergang*.

Bernd Eichinger has a mixed background as a producer and director, working in both arthouse and mainstream cinema. His 'political inconsistencies' polarise opinion. He is beyond doubt one of the most successful German film producers today with an instinct for material that attracts audiences, for young promising actors, and similarly, for directors – in short, the ideal film producer. Initially he was linked to New German Cinema, and produced films by Wenders and Kluge. Interestingly, he also produced *Hitler – ein Film aus Deutschland*. Soon he went on to larger-scale, international productions. His recent work includes the three *Resident Evil* films (2002, 2004 and 2006), Tom Tykwer's *Perfume* (2006), and *Der Baader-Meinhof-Komplex* (2008). Some say he has abandoned any principles beyond those of being in the limelight and making money. Such critics would also have been the first to condemn *Der Untergang*, simply because Eichinger had written the screenplay and produced the film. It was also held against him that he had not lived during the Third Reich (he was born in 1949) and could therefore not be an authority on those times. Against all this, it has to be said that he is committed to German film-making. One of his explicit reasons for making *Der Untergang* was that he wanted to avoid a Hollywood treatment of the topic. [7] *Der Untergang* was made by a German studio (his Constantin production company) and with a German crew, including the actors.

His experience as a writer of screenplays is more limited than that as a producer. However, as mentioned before, he felt so strongly about the subject matter of *Der Untergang* that he took to writing the screenplay himself after the publication of Joachim Fest's latest book. They subsequently worked together on individual points in the text. One major problem, and this was picked up by critics, concerned the conversion of (reported) events to a screenplay. This is obviously a particularly sensitive issue when it comes to Hitler's own verbal transactions with others. We will never know what exactly was said, how ideas were put into words. Now we only have Eichinger's, Fest's and Junge's word(s) for it – the choices they made must be seen as partly fictionalised.

For a film that was mainly set in a bunker Eichinger needed above all a director who was able to translate the claustrophobic atmosphere of such a rarefied space into film. He approached Oliver Hirschbiegel, who had previously directed *Das Experiment* (*The Experiment*, 2000), a psycho thriller that conveyed a similar sense of isolation and claustrophobia. Moreover, *Das Experiment* dealt with the development of fascism in a contained environment. [8] Therefore Hirschbiegel is no stranger to such issues and to converting real-life events into fictional accounts. Hirschbiegel is also the director of several TV thrillers. His other speciality is making very intimate films, with one single character who narrates and/or acts out an inner conflict. Eichinger and Hirschbiegel were in agreement that they wanted a film that clearly differentiated itself from a Hollywood production. This meant that special effects were kept to a minimum and, very importantly, that in order to avoid emotional manipulation of the audience, non-diegetic music was not to be prominent.

With a budget of 16 million euros *Der Untergang* was a major project for a German production company. With these funds it was possible to film the outdoor scenes on location in St. Petersburg, some of whose streets apparently resemble Berlin's towards the end of World War II. The 'Führerbunker' was rebuilt in the Constantin Studios in Munich. The available funds also allowed Eichinger and Hirschbiegel to recruit some of Germany's finest actors. They all needed time to think very carefully about whether they wanted to take part in the film because they were all aware of the difficulties involved in playing such loaded parts, and thereby breaking a major taboo of German film history. They were also aware that in doing so the whole crew were inviting controversy. The most important female figures are Eva Braun and Magda Goebbels. Eva Braun was the woman who loved Hitler unconditionally and whom he married just a few days before the end. She is portrayed as something of a 'flapper', even though there are hints that she is hiding considerable horror beneath her cheerful exterior. Hitler had always refused to marry her, because he believed as the 'Führer' he should not be committed to any other human being. Eva Braun is played by Juliane Köhler, who is a well-known face from other major German films. [9] Corinna Harfouch, another well-known actor of stage and screen, is Magda Goebbels, the wife of Hitler's propaganda minister Josef Goebbels, played by Ulrich Matthes. They are both able to convey incredible intensity.

And then there is, above all, Bruno Ganz as Hitler. He prepared for his role by conducting extensive research into film footage and radio broadcasts of the man. He brings to the screen all the dictator's characteristics that are known to many of us, but most astonishingly, he is able to enact the voice so perfectly that several

critics who know it well have said the sound of it had made them shiver. Ganz manages to convey something nobody had achieved so far: he made us realise how it was possible for this ranting and screaming 'Führer' to make a whole nation believe in him and identify with him to the extent that they did.

As mentioned before, Traudl Junge, who was Hitler's last private secretary, provided the film-makers with details from her time in the 'Führerbunker' through her memoirs. She is played by the young actor Alexandra Maria Lara[10], a face known to German audiences from television, and is portrayed as the observer of the events in the bunker. Because of her confinement there she represents the 'inside' part of the film, the one that occupies most of the most screen time. The 'outside', the real world, is represented by a young Hitler Youth named Peter. This boy is a purely fictional character; he stands for all those young people who revered Hitler, after having been successfully brainwashed by early National Socialist 'education'. *Der Untergang* uses the narrative device of having Traudl and Peter meet at the end. The film itself is bracketed by two appearances of the real Traudl Junge, taken from an interview in an Austrian documentary.[11]

In old age Traudl Junge reflects on her past and wonders if she could not have acted differently. 'I cannot forgive this child...' she says, 'I could have said no. I didn't know where it would lead... and still I find it hard to forgive myself.' Thus the former private secretary of the great dictator is immediately set up as an identification figure. The device

of framing the whole film with her reflections is problematic, even manipulative: It distances the audience quite comfortably from the horrific events represented in the film proper and makes us all voyeurs instead of participants. The actual film opens with her job interview with Hitler, two and a half years before the end of the war. A cut to the events of April 20, 1945, Hitler's 56th birthday, ensues, and from then on most of the action is concentrated in the 'Führerbunker'.

The original 'Führerbunker' was situated under the old Reich Chancellery between Wilhelmstraße and Vossstraße in the centre of Berlin, where a previous bunker had been extended and deepened from 1942 onwards. By April 1945 it had not even been completed. The deeper 'Führerbunker' consisted of roughly 20 sparsely decorated and furnished rooms. The important 'conference room' in which all the 'strategic' decisions were made was situated next to Hitler's own rooms. Most of the bunker was destroyed during the final days of the 'Battle for Berlin', which means that both Fest and Eichinger had to rely on eye witness statements as to the layout. After a short period of 'bunker tourism' after the end of World War II the Soviets, who occupied the area, decided to blow it up. This was not completely successful, nor was another attempt in 1959. The bunker must have been unbelievably fortified. During the time of the Berlin Wall the bunker lay inside the so-called 'death strip', an area between two lines of wall, patrolled by East German border police. In the final year of the GDR, blocks of flats were to be built along Wilhelmstrasse, which is when the final dismantling of the bunker remains were planned, but not carried out. A few years later, suggestions were floated to open it up as a memorial. This idea was abandoned, however. It would not have been possible to put it into practice anyway, since the bunker is no longer accessible, with only rubble remaining. This means that anybody who wants to see it now has to go to the cinema!

However, 'seeing' the bunker is not quite the right expression for the experience that the audience of *Der Untergang* is subjected to – even if it is somewhat voyeuristic. Eichinger and Hirschbiegel have created a space that makes palpable the extreme conditions under which the residents lived. The setting, the script, the performances, the direction and editing all work together to bring to life the last few days of this dictatorial regime, the absurd decisions that were being made, and the events in all their detachment from reality. Reports are received, then either ignored or countered with orders given by Hitler, orders that bear no relation to what is going on in the outside world.

The contrast between 'inside' and 'outside', between unreality and reality, is set up in the film by means of several of Hitler's personnel as they enter and leave the bunker; either, like Schenck, the doctor, to help wounded civilians, or, like Hitler's generals, to reconnoitre and to gain information on the state of the various German armies defending Berlin. Through them, we become witnesses to the battle that is raging in Berlin's streets, to death and destruction, of young and old alike.

When confronted with the outside world, the first thing that strikes us is the unbelievable noise, first of bombs, then of gunfire and heavy artillery, all of which alternate with eerie silence in between attacks. In the course of the film the street battles get ever closer, until towards the end we actually see the enemy, the Soviets, first in their tanks, then on foot in the streets. The film-makers have left the silences as just that, without trying to 'paste' them over with swelling music.

The same approach was applied to the scenes inside the bunker. Quite often, there is complete silence, only to be disrupted by people walking about or by messages being passed. This lack of aural overlaying is complemented by visual downplaying: The bunker colours are monochrome, mainly grey with variations in the different uniforms

between grey and green. The confinement in the bunker is very effectively conveyed by the (handheld) camera's position: there is always a doorframe or jutting corner in the frame. This increases the sense of claustrophobia and at the same time it decreases the amount of colour in the frame. Magda Goebbels stands out, wearing a tailored red suit and a string of pearls.

Again and again Hitler is either in complete denial of the state of his armies and the positions of the enemy's forces, or he conjures up or convinces himself of solutions that are unworkable: He orders the movements of armies that do not exist any more, he speaks of attacking the enemy in a pincer movement of two armies that are unable to attack, that can hardly defend themselves any more, and so on. His orders get more and more bizarre as time goes on and the enemy has long laid siege to the outer areas of Berlin.

Quite early on in the film the 'Clausewitz' order (the above-mentioned 'Nero' order) is issued by him. This is a code for the complete destruction of all public amenities and utilities in Germany, in what Joachim Fest called Hitler's nihilism and his total contempt for the German population. In one scene Hitler is seen standing with his architect Speer in front of new plans for a grandiose capital. He calmly talks of the advantages of a Berlin in ruins, either destroyed by the enemy or by the Nazis themselves: 'It is easier to shift debris than to demolish buildings.' When one of his generals mentions the need to evacuate three million civilians from Berlin, we realise for the first time what he thinks of his people: 'We must be cold-blooded in war. Not worry about so-called civilians. There are no civilians!' In one of his meetings with Speer he once again insists that 'the enemy must find only a wasteland.' Speer replies that this would mean the death sentence for the German people and throw Germany back to the Middle Ages, to which Hitler replies: 'It's all the same if the people perish...Only the weak have survived so long anyway.' His own brand of Darwinism is revealed gradually in the course of the film. Later on he speaks of compassion being a cardinal sin and about his pride in having all but eradicated the European Jews.

The Hitler of the film focuses on his mad sense of utter betrayal by the German people in general, and by some of his high-ranking officers ('They are the scum of the German people') in particular. Again and again his outbursts in the 'conference room' are directed at them. 'Are you questioning my orders?' he screams when confronted with details about dwindling armies and ammunition. After an order of his to attack that could not be carried out because only a handful of soldiers were left he rants: 'It was an order! Who do you think you are! Everyone has lied to me. Even the SS.' The effectiveness of these rantings and ravings is heightened by the deadly silence that precedes them and the camera's relentless gaze on his face. Bruno Ganz conveys very convincingly Hitler's mannerisms and facial expressions, including the way he brushes a strand of hair from his forehead, and his progressing Parkinson's disease, which forced him to keep his trembling left hand out of sight or to steady it with his right. But most of all it is his voice that is so convincing, his strange accent with distorted vowels and spitting consonants.

There are mutterings in the corridors between the officers who occasionally question the Führer's sanity. However, nobody dares disobey him. Even after his death they follow his orders by committing suicide. 'We have sworn allegiance to the Führer!' Others keep fighting the hopeless battle for Berlin, now besieged by the Russians, until (and some of them beyond) the moment when surrender is declared on May 2, 1945.

His closest ally and the brains behind the regime all the way through the Third Reich is Goebbels, his propaganda minister. He echoes and carries on Hitler's ruthless stance against his own people, even after Hitler's death. He and his wife Magda are the strongest examples of unconditional loyalty to the cause of National Socialism. When Hitler has declared his intention to commit suicide, both Goebbels and his wife are ready to do the same. Moreover, Magda is absolutely prepared to kill her own children. In an exchange between her and Speer he says: 'The children have a right to a future.' She answers: 'If the idea of National Socialism dies, there is no future.' After Hitler's suicide she goes on to single-handedly administer first a sleeping potion and then cyanide capsules to each of her children. This is undeniably the most chilling scene in the film – made so effective by Corinna Harfouch's portrayal of Magda Goebbels. She hardly speaks, all her thoughts

and emotions are contained within slight facial expressions. Is she an evil monster? In all this, her only communication with her husband is via looks that tell us about a history between them that has left them with no love. It was known that Goebbels was a philanderer; he cheated on Magda throughout their marriage. Part of her total dedication to the Führer may be explained by this. In the film, Goebbels is often left standing outside closed doors by her. They do not speak a word to each other. When the time has come, he puts on his leather gloves in an all-too-practised gesture, they both leave the bunker, stand opposite each other in the garden, look at each other, he shoots her and then himself. Like Hitler and Eva Braun before them, they are burned to a crisp by their loyal underlings. Nobody knows exactly how these events happened. The film-makers again made choices: Have we been manipulated into believing the way in which they chose to represent them? All of us who have seen the film will probably forever have the images of the red-dressed Magda Goebbels murdering her children in our heads.

It has been suggested that Hitler was able to talk himself into something, his talking doing the thinking, so to speak, and this comes across quite well in the film. He vents his idea of committing suicide quite early, and several times more later on – it seems almost as if this idea grew on him. Just one day before his suicide, on April 29, he marries Eva Braun, who has been his companion for years. This is the clearest signal yet that he has given up. He dictates his testament to his secretary, giving clear orders that his and Eva's bodies should be destroyed. He does not want to fall into the enemy's hands at any cost. For this purpose, cans of petrol are requisitioned and are waiting for the bodies to be burned. It is true, their remains were never found. This led to plenty of rumours after the war that Hitler was not really dead – the myth was alive in the minds of many. It is certain that the suicides took place, on April 30, but their exact nature is not – statements of witnesses in the bunker vary. The film-makers resolved the issue by not showing their faces in death. This was also a conscious decision not to dignify them by showing them dead.

When Eva Braun writes her final letter to her sister, and when she stands in front of her mirror to apply lipstick for the last time, we hear a subdued and enormously sad piece of music played by a few strings: It is the most famous aria from the opera 'Dido and Aeneas' by Henry Purcell, 'When I am Laid In Earth', sung by Dido, Queen of Carthage. This opera has a connection with the theme of *Der Untergang*, not just because it tells of the fall of Carthage and of Dido's suicide. One of the themes that runs through it concerns the question of the predetermination of life and how to deal with it. According to the opera we as human beings are duty-bound to question everything that confronts us in the guise of destiny wherever it seems that we do not have a choice. For we do have a choice: we are free to make decisions as to how to deal with such events. However, such freedom of choice also means great responsibility – the responsibility for ourselves and our own actions. Given that this music accompanies Eva Braun during her preparations for suicide, could the question be asked whether it does not ennoble her in some way? Surely this cannot have been the director's intention?

All through the film the music is sparse and subtle. There are occasional strings to be heard, playing very softly, and the end, Traudl's and Peter's escape on a sunlit day, is marked by a subtle melody played on the piano, striking a somewhat more optimistic note.

It is no mean feat to tell on film, in 150 minutes, the developments whose end we all know, mostly set in a bunker, and to hold the audience's attention, especially in view of the fact that the full range of events and the bewildering number of personnel is not fully comprehensible for a non-historian. This story could only be told so convincingly by the tightest of direction, performances, cinematography, and editing. In order for us to be able to follow the bewildering set of personnel and events, the dialogue has been augmented by contextual references. For dramatic purposes, Traudl Junge has been given a more prominent role than she would have had in reality: She is witness to most of the relevant exchanges in the bunker. The dialogues themselves have been adapted, complemented and sometimes rearranged, again for dramatic purpose. The film seems to tell us that those final days contained in a compressed form everything that had already been present in the Nazis' 'vision'. This interpretation may be problematic, given that it is mostly based on one historian's analysis, and criticisms have been made. On the other hand, every historical film takes such decisions of selection and presentation. All in all, the film conveys believably the 12 last days (20 April to 2 May), which, by the way, correspond ominously to the 12 years of the Third Reich. The characters that make up these scenes, the naive, the fanatical, the deluded, the authoritarian, the manipulative, the mad, the monstrous, are well drawn and preclude any kind of sympathy. They may even be too well-drawn, as they are partly fictionalised.

Interestingly, as early as 1955, a now little-known German film was made that covered more or less the same ground, *Der letzte Akt* (*Hitler – The Last Ten Days*, G. W. Pabst). Pabst was a famous Weimar cinema director who had not left Nazi Germany but had rather gone into 'inner emigration'. This film is worth mentioning not because it was successful – quite the opposite – but because it was a very early attempt to represent the father/demon Hitler. It is also interesting for its own story: Pabst had planned to make the film since 1948 but was unable to obtain finance for it despite his pedigree. This may tell us a little about the attitudes prevalent at the time. The film was based on a book by Michael A. Musmanno, an American lawyer who had been one of the judges at the Nuremberg War Crime Trials in 1946. Pabst's aim was to work against myths that were forming around Hitler's death. He, too, sought the collaboration of Traudl Junge. The project was commented on with hostility by the German press. The producer, Carl Szokoll, had been a major in the German army and a member of a resistance group that precipitated the end of the war by betraying German defence positions to the Soviets. The screenplay writer, Erich Maria Remarque, was resented by the German establishment for his anti-war book '*Im Westen nichts Neues*' ('*All Quiet on the Western Front*'), which was made into what is probably the greatest anti-war film ever (*All Quiet on the Western*

Front, Lewis Milestone, 1932). The film was banned in Germany following deliberate Nazi interruptions of the screenings. Remarque emigrated, and his books were destroyed during the Nazi book-burnings in 1933.

Der letzte Akt showed a link with the aesthetic traditions of the 1920s. It was a realistic portrayal of Hitler's final days, employing the stylistic means of 'New Objectivity' (Neue Sachlichkeit), of which Pabst had been a major proponent in the twenties. All these ingredients provided an explosive mixture for a film project that came far too early for German audiences. It was received with a mixture of incredulous horror, laughter, uneasy questions – 'Was it really this crazy?' – and debates as to its authenticity. People were unable to rationalise what they saw, it seemed to come from a different planet. Critical reception was even worse: Responses were that it showed a distorted view of history, it was macabre, half document, half horror opera, half thriller and half commemoration, bad taste, propaganda... It was widely condemned, resented or pronounced boring. In Germany a film like this was unable to reach people without the necessary historical dis̶t̶a̶n̶c̶e. It was too early for a Hitler film: after all, he had been dead only 10 years. ̶oad it was a hit. In Germany it vanished quietly, almost without a trace.

You may remember the framing device that *Der Untergang* uses: Traudl Junge as an old woman speaking about her past. Placing her second appearance after the end credits gives her great authority. (It also serves to manipulate the audience, as detailed earlier.) She says that for a long time after the end of National Socialism she was shocked by the revelations of horrific deeds in the name of the Führer, her own boss. But 'I didn't make a connection with my own past... But one day I passed a plaque on Franz-Josef-Straße [in Munich] that commemorated Sophie Scholl. [2] I saw that she was born the same year as me and was executed the year I began to work for Hitler. At that moment I felt that being young was no excuse and it would have been possible to find things out.'

This final quote from *Der Untergang*, a film about the last few days of the 'Third Reich', links in with another film that can serve as a contrast and complement to *Der Untergang*: *Sophie Scholl – die letzte Tage* (*Sophie Scholl – The Last Days*, Marc Rothemund, 2005). A contrast because it shows the young Sophie's almost superhuman courage in fighting against the Hitler regime with very modest means: Distributing leaflets with messages urging the German people to end the war by offering passive resistance. Sophie Scholl was executed in February 1943, officially for high treason, but in reality more for her refusal to renounce her resistance and her loyalty to her comrades. A complement because it achieves a similar intensity and sense of claustrophobia during the interviews with the Gestapo officer Robert Mohr, played by Alexander Held, who also appears in *Der Untergang*. Made on a much smaller budget than *Der Untergang*, it was filmed on original locations in Munich and used original transcripts of interviews and court sessions from the archives, as well as Sophie's own letters. We strongly recommend these two films be seen together.

FOOTNOTES

[1] *Der Untergang* was chosen over *Gegen die Wand* (chapter 13) as Germany's submission in the best film not in the English language category.

[2] For this film in particular, it would be useful to broaden your perspective by conducting your own further research. The internet abounds with reviews, interviews and opinions.

[3] Nero, a Roman emperor, who allegedly had Rome burned to the ground in 64 AD.

[4] Melissa Müller (ed.), *Until The Final Hour, Hitler's Last Secretary.*

[5] The debate is still raging: in the summer of 2008, Hitler's wax figure in the new Madame Tussaud's in Berlin had its head chopped off by an outraged visitor.

[6] This was, of course, a charge already made by the Young German film-makers of the sixties and seventies, as described in the relevant previous chapters of this book. Their convictions led to the grotesque representation in Syberberg's film, as mentioned above.

[7] This reminds us of Edgar Reitz's insistence when countering *Holocaust* with *Heimat.*

[8] It is based on the famous Stanford psychological experiment. In the meantime, by the way, another German film has been released that exposes how easy it is for fascism to develop within a discrete group: *Die Welle* (*The Wave* (Dennis Gansel, 2008).

[9] Including *Nirgendwo in Afrika* (*Nowhere in Africa*, 2001) which won an Oscar in 2003.

[10] She also plays Ian Curtis' love interest in *Control* (2007).

[11] *Im toten Winkel* (*Blind Spot: Hitler's Secretary*, André Heller, 2002).

[12] Sophie Scholl was a young student and a member of a resistance group against the Nazi regime called 'The White Rose'.

CHAPTER THIRTEEN: CROSSING BOUNDARIES: *GEGEN DIE WAND* (*HEAD-ON*, 2004)

In this chapter we discuss a Turkish-German film. Our choice is informed by the fact that Turkish-German film-makers working from within Germany have made an extraordinary contribution to contemporary German culture in the last 10 years or so and are continuing to do so. We have selected *Gegen die Wand* (*Head-On*) because it marks a high point in a cinema that started out in order to explore the plight of 'guest workers' in Germany, but has in the meantime achieved tremendous popular and critical success. *Gegen die Wand* is the first 'cross-cultural' film that was received well in Germany and in Turkey, and amongst different, German or immigrant, communities within Germany. Besides focusing on *Gegen die Wand* we will also list other significant contributions to the topic.

As outlined in our chapter on *Angst essen Seele auf*, a significant number of immigrants have made Germany their home within the last 50 or so years. Many of them came from Southern European countries because they were invited by the West German government from the 1950s onwards in order to make up for a shortage of labour in post-war Germany. Within the immigrant population of Germany as a whole the Turkish immigrants have formed the largest proportion. For obvious reasons they migrated mostly to the conurbations, and nowadays Berlin, Frankfurt and Hamburg are the cities in which most Turkish immigrants live. With their status as non-European citizens and their cultural and religious differences from Germans they are also the immigrant group facing the most difficulties, legal and cultural. Children from a Turkish background, but born in Germany, must as adults choose to take on either German or Turkish nationality since German law does not recognise dual citizenship.

Immigration is a fact of life in Germany now, and Germany is a country that depends on immigration. But quite apart from the fact that immigrants fulfil important economic functions, Germany is their home. Many of them have never seen the country of their forefathers, or at least have never lived there. And now they are also making their presence felt through their contributions to Germany's cultural life. While Fassbinder was the first film-maker in Germany to turn to the subject of immigration, concentrating on prejudice and xenophobia among the German population, there is now a thriving film culture among immigrants themselves, mainly from film-makers with a Turkish background. This is perhaps not surprising if we consider that Turks not only form the largest number of immigrants in Germany but also that they experience the most clashes between their own culture and German culture.

In the mid-eighties the first Turkish-German film-makers started to represent themselves rather than being represented by others. Tevfik Baser is often quoted as being the first to make an impact with his film *40m2 Deutschland* (*40m2 of Germany*, 1985) and his subsequent *Abschied vom falschen Paradies* (*Farewell to a False Paradise*, 1988). In both films the focus is on Turkish women who suffer from their husbands' violence and take the first steps to make contact with other (German) women, in the first instance by learning the German language.

Not surprisingly, Turkish-German films tend to deal with biographies of life between/in/of two cultures. However, the stories and images are very diverse. When watching these films it becomes clear very quickly that there is no such thing as a 'standard' biography of 'a foreigner'. What also becomes clear is that there is social demarcation, exclusion and oppression not only between the different cultures but within the migrant culture itself. The films of Turkish-German film-makers, especially the earlier ones, deal above all with this oppression within the culture of the oppressed. Later films also tell stories of generational conflicts which tend to be conflicts between cultures at the same time. Scenarios include Turkish fathers who keep their daughters under a tight rein. In these films young people with Turkish roots (some also from mixed marriages) are trying to find new ways of life, new identities.

Since the 1990s the third generation of Turkish-German film-makers has been active. Fatih Akin, Thomas Arslan and Aysun Bademsoy are the most important names. In all their films they take as a starting point their own experiences and describe their characters' search for roots, for a new identity, and also do not rule out the possibility of a return to

Turkey. This reflects reality in that a number of third or fourth generation immigrants are considering, or have indeed gone through with, returning to their country of origin. In that group of films we find the most diverse biographies and complex ways of negotiating identity. In Thomas Arslan's first feature *Geschwister* (*Brothers and Sisters*, 1995) this variety of identities and their negotiation on a day-to-day basis is precisely the focus. Three siblings from a mixed marriage construct quite different life plans, including choosing between German or Turkish nationality. It is significant that the film does not focus on their 'problems' as immigrants, but represents them as young people for whom cultural diversity presents itself as an opportunity in the process of becoming adults.

Since the mid-nineties Turkish-German cinema has gone from strength to strength. This process of emancipation has probably enabled other, non-Turkish film-makers to raise awareness of other immigrant groups, in particular of asylum seekers and illegal immigrants in Germany. They look at life on the margins of society, their characters truly are victims. In the hierarchy of immigrant status they are the lowest of the low. One such film is the sensitive portrayal of two young illegal immigrants in Hamburg, a Kurd and a black African, in Yüksel Yavuz's *Kleine Freiheit* (*A Little Bit of Freedom*, 2004). In recent years German film-makers have also come to the fore again with the topic of immigration. To mention just two: *Ghettokids* (2002) is a TV production that focuses on two brothers of Greek-Turkish origin, while *Lichter* (*Distant Lights*, 2003) by Hans Christian Schmid is set on the German-Polish border and has as one of its strands the fate of illegal Ukrainian economic migrants on their way to Germany. These films show the perspective of the migrants as well as the German environment. *Knallhart* (*Tough Enough*, 2006) is a German film which focuses on the German perspective in its portrayal of 'multi-cultural' youth gangs in Berlin. In this renewed interest of German film-makers in the subject a direct link with Fassbinder's portrayals of immigrants in Germany (in *Katzelmacher* and *Angst essen Seele auf*) can be established, which makes his early contribution to this topic all the more relevant, even today.

After this short detour let us now come back to Turkish-German film. The German journalist and film critic Georg Seesslen assesses its significance in an article for the Goethe Institute's *Young Turks* series of films (2003): 'Turkish-German cinema has shown itself to be immensely enriching for the general film culture in Germany. In its mixture of familiarity and foreignness, of understanding and obstinacy, it allows us to take a close look at the social reality of the country, a look that German cinema in its core is in danger of losing.' This assessment was written before Fatih Akin's *Gegen die Wand* burst on to the scene, a film which was finally granted the recognition that the vibrant cultural expression of Turkish-German cinema deserves.

With *Gegen die Wand* Fatih Akin has been confirmed as one of the most exciting contemporary film-makers in Europe. At the Berlin Film Festival of 2004 the film won the Golden Bear, a huge triumph in two respects: After 18 years it was the first German production to win the Golden Bear, and it was a film by a Turkish-German film-maker.

Finally, so it seems, with the recognition of this film, immigration as a fact of life has been recognised in Germany. After Berlin the film won several German and European awards for best film. Since then Akin has been recognised as a constant among young stars of European cinema. The triumph continues: His subsequent feature, *Auf der anderen Seite* (*The Edge of Heaven*, 2007), was nominated for the Golden Palm at the 2007 Cannes International Film Festival, and won the Best Screenplay award at the same festival. It was Germany's official submission for the Best Foreign Language Film category of the 2008 Oscars. Although it did not win, Akin's continuing recognition, both by the public and by the critics, could not be given stronger expression than this.

Fatih Akin was born of Turkish parents in 1973 in Hamburg-Altona, a part of the city with a large immigrant population – 'a huge kindergarten where it doesn't matter whether you're black, white or yellow' (Akin). He grew up in this multi-cultural community and counted all manner of nationalities among his friends. Football was the common denominator between them. Very early on he started writing stories about his environment and his friends. They accepted the fact that he was 'a bit different', that he went to grammar school and wrote stories about them. This unique position – being part of the community and yet in a way separate from it – gave him the opportunity to study his neighbourhood very closely, with an ever-observant eye and great sensitivity. The authenticity resulting from this informs his work.

From an early age Akin wanted to be involved in film-making. While still at school he starting acting in school plays and writing his own screenplays, always based on his own experiences. Even then he felt very strongly that his experiences were not those of the ghetto and that he wanted to connect with the larger world. His first acting roles were on television, but soon he felt that he was made to act the 'token Turk' – the Turkish brother who defends his sister's honour with a knife, for example. These experiences prompted him to develop a strong desire to work against clichés of 'foreigners'. So he began to write his own parts because he felt it was the only way to counteract such stereotypes.

He studied at the Hamburg Academy of Fine Arts, and soon began to make short films. As a film-maker he is an auteur in the best sense: He is a director, screenplay writer, producer and actor. Amongst his influences he quotes 1970s' New Hollywood directors in general and Martin Scorsese in particular. This influence can be seen most clearly in his first feature film, *Kurz und Schmerzlos* (*Short Sharp Shock*, 1998), which is set in the multi-cultural neighbourhood of Hamburg-Altona. Like Scorsese's debut *Mean Streets* (1973), Akin's story of three young gangsters, or rather wannabe gangsters from different ethnic backgrounds (a Serb, a Turk, a Greek), features strong violence and an exciting musical soundtrack. As a 'counter indication' (his own words) to *Kurz und Schmerzlos*, his next feature film, *Im Juli* (*In July*, 2000), was a gentle romantic road movie. This and his next feature, *Solino* (2002), in which he used somebody else's screenplay for the first time, received mixed responses.

Music is an important part of his film-making, not just in his feature films, but also in his documentaries. In his documentary *Crossing the Bridge – the Sounds of Istanbul* (2005) he explores the music scene of that city. More and more he is drawn to the culture of the country of his ancestors, in both documentaries and feature films. His protagonists are attracted to it, too; some explore it, and others return to it. *Gegen die Wand* is a good example of this.

Quite clearly, Akin's background is important, but he does not make 'immigrant films'. The focus of his films is not his Turkish-German identity. As a confident 'zapper between cultures' he does not need pity, or guilty, embarrassed reactions from his audience, and didactic films about xenophobia are not his style either. This is a development away from the earlier representations of immigrants in Germany, in a similar way in which other recent film-makers of immigrant background have embraced more wide-ranging subjects, as detailed above. Arguably, though, he has gone further than any other German film-maker with an immigrant background. He sees himself as a film-maker who 'tells his stories straight from real life, directs them with courage, and does not shy away from the mainstream'. His self-proclaimed 'belief in cinema', which for him means complexity, a lack of compromise and the use of the spectacular comes across clearly in *Gegen die Wand*. This film forms the first part of a trilogy that Akin calls 'Love, Death and the Devil'; the second part is the above-mentioned *Auf der anderen Seite*.

Asked in interviews whether his identity is more German or more Turkish he answers that neither is the case. He is not *in* a certain culture or *in between* cultures: He is a film-maker with several cultures. Turkey as a geographical and cultural entity does play an important part in his life and his films. However, for him Turkish culture informs German culture and vice versa; the similarities are stronger than the differences. Someone's nationality is not what matters to Akin, he sees it only as a label that separates people. He wants to overcome separation and barriers between people and nations. The generational conflicts, for example, which are evident in his films, are not a specifically Turkish or German phenomenon, but a universal one. The causes and effects of Turkish immigration in Germany in the course of the last 40 years or so have taken constantly developing shapes and configurations. His awareness of all these permutations has led him to describe himself as a humanist rather than identifying with any one culture or nation.

Given that Turkey as a country, Turkish music and culture, feature strongly in his work, even though his films are released in Germany, it is also interesting to look at his reception in Turkey. In an interview he says that he is very popular in Turkey, but that it tends to be a different kind of popularity to the one he enjoys elsewhere. Turkish people often do not know his work at all. They admire him as they would admire a football star: simply because he is famous. Turkish newspapers celebrate him as 'the Turkish Tarantino' and *Gegen die Wand* as a Turkish film. Turkish immigrants in Germany celebrate Fatih Akin as their hero – for a brief time after the release of *Gegen die Wand* all the generations of immigrants, of both sexes, were as one in their praise. This extraordinary, hitherto unheard of and unseen effect cannot be overstated. Not only are Akin's films recognised as excellent in themselves, but he is also making history – German-Turkish cultural history. Time will tell whether this will have long-term consequences for the future of Turkish-German relations, or whether it is in itself a sign of normalisation, or both.

From the very first moment of the conception of *Gegen die Wand* Akin was determined to 'shoot the Bear' – the Golden Bear of the Berlin Film Festival. This determination persisted against all the odds encountered by his team during the film's production. One of those odds was a cross-national barrier: The male lead, Birol Ünel, a Turk with a Turkish passport living in Germany, was banned from entering Turkey because he had not done his military service there. Attempts to secure a German passport for him were unsuccessful – he was refused German citizenship for what Akin calls 'small misdemeanours' (mainly drug-related), although he had lived in Germany all his life, was trained in Germany, had been acting in the German theatre, and hardly speaks Turkish. However, since important scenes were set in Istanbul, it was paramount that he should be able to enter Turkey. Ironically, it was the Iraq war of 2003 that helped solve the problem: Turkey needed money to finance its part in the war, and a law was passed eventually granting amnesty from military service to Turkish males born in a certain year, which just happened to be Ünel's birth year, against payment of a sum of money. The amnesty for Birol Ünel was finally granted and he was able to enter Turkey unhindered.

The title *Gegen die Wand* refers in the first instance to the way in which the broken, self-destructive alcoholic Cahit tries to kill himself: In his drunken stupor he drives his car at high speed against a wall. This is, by the way, the German title of the film, literally translated as 'Against the Wall'. But he survives, and his journey begins. In the hospital where he is taken after the 'accident' he meets Sibel, who, like him, is Turkish, and who, like him, has tried to kill herself, by slitting her wrists. When she meets Cahit, her own journey begins. Both their journeys are full of pain and do not spare them anything in the way of suffering.

Sibel asks Cahit to marry her for convenience, since she is desperate to escape her traditional Anatolian Islamic home, represented by her strict father and her hot-headed brother. Her mother is much more sympathetic towards her daughter. Her family wants her to marry; she on the other hand wants freedom.

Because she sees no way out of this conflict she becomes obsessed with death as the only solution. After meeting Cahit she has the idea that a marriage of convenience might be another solution. Cahit just happens to appear on the scene at the right time. However, she is fully aware of the circumstances from which she wants to escape: The code of honour of Anatolian migrants is used as a weapon to keep women in check regarding the temptations of German cities. There is a hint here of the early self-representations of Turkish-German film-makers with regard to the fate of women in a strongly patriarchal culture, as outlined above. But times have changed: Sibel speaks perfect German, she has caught a whiff of freedom, and she wants more. Her motivation is an entirely hedonistic one. 'I want to fuck, lots of it', she says unequivocally. She knows what submitting to the male domination in her family means: In the past her brother broke her nose when he saw her with a boy.

Eventually Cahit agrees to marry her. In the scene in which he officially asks her father for her hand the film makes one of its many 'politically incorrect' statements: It is obvious what an unsuitable husband he is, but he is a Turk (although he hardly speaks Turkish), and so the family have to accept him. Here we have the most inconceivable and refreshingly 'non-pc' situation: A traditional Turkish background, a hedonistic Turkish female lead, an alcoholic, junkie Turkish male lead in a marriage of convenience! This is not the stereotypical Turkish ghetto: there are no head scarves in sight, and Cahit is

not the clichéd, diligent greengrocer next door – which is how Turkish immigrants in Germany were perceived for a long time. The film does not pass judgement on the lifestyles of the two protagonists, least of all Sibel's. She is portrayed sympathetically; her hedonism is shown as an unquenchable thirst for life.

Sibel moves in with Cahit and begins to clear out his sodden flat. She spends her entire dowry on refurbishing the place. Without realising it she 'cleans out' his life at the same time. Cahit has been married before. It is not entirely clear what happened to his wife although we assume that she died. It is obvious that he loved her deeply and that he has never recovered from her death or disappearance. However, while Sibel goes out to have fun, he gradually recognises the impact she is having on his life and begins to fall in love with her. Even more gradually, the same is happening to her.

A 'hard-core love story' ensues, which results from their respective volatility, their vulnerability, their tendency to self-destruct, and their great capability to feel passionately. In terms of genre, the film has been described as a romance or a melodrama. Neither term does it justice, since its doom-laden story, its tense atmosphere and its spiritual quality transcend both genres. And even though Cahit realises it earlier than Sibel, they both become each other's fate. They become embroiled in what is called *kara sevda*, 'dark passion', in Turkish culture.

A review of *Gegen die Wand* in the film magazine *Sight & Sound* offers an excellent explanation of *kara sevda* in Turkish culture: 'The word *sevda*, with roots in Persian and Arabic, referred originally to "a dark-coloured fluid that the body produces when one gets sick." It later came to denote intense passionate love: a prevailing theme of fables, music, cinema and poetry, *kara sevda* is an overwhelming condition experienced almost like an incurable illness, from which the "victim" can never recover and through which s/he will be forever transformed... It inflicts pain, yet supplies the strength to endure it. *Kara sevda* is both the poison and the remedy.'

Cahit's dark passion begins as soon as he realises that he is in love with Sibel. The manifest expression of this love is him getting drunk in a bar, shouting 'I'm in love!', smashing his glass and grinding the splinters into his hands. Such representations of violence hit us in the face and make for quite uncomfortable viewing. Cahit's dark passion continues with him lashing out at one of Sibel's lovers, who has insulted her, to defend her honour and to act out his own jealousy, and killing him unintentionally. He is sentenced to three years in prison. Sibel visits him, and for the first time she gives in to the love that she feels towards him and allows intimacy between them, thus giving up the personal freedom she has fought so hard to attain. 'I will wait for you!' she says. All the time he spends in prison this declaration and her letters keep him from total despair.

Because of the scandal surrounding the killing, Sibel's promiscuity is revealed for all to see, including her family, who subsequently disown her. More than that: Given the opportunity, her brother would kill her in order to save the family's 'honour'. Ironically, killing her lover makes Cahit a hero in Sibel's family's eyes: It is perfectly acceptable to kill someone in order to save somebody else's honour. However, Sibel is now in real danger of her life. In another ironic turn of the narrative, her only option to escape 'traditional Turkish family wrath' is to leave Germany and go to Turkey, to Istanbul to be precise, where her cousin Selma lives and works. Sibel cuts off her hair in an act that could be described as sacrificial. She has become aware of the emotional and spiritual ingredients of *kara sevda*

within her: the recognition of Cahit's strong attachment to her and her own attachment to him, her guilt with regard to his prison sentence, her despair at having to leave her family and Germany, and her despondency at having to wait for Cahit's release for such a long time.

The years she spends in Istanbul are her own personal journey through darkness. Selma has secured her employment as a chambermaid in the hotel in which she works. She accepts her new life at first. Then, immense depression sets in. In her letters to Cahit she writes: 'Istanbul is an energetic city full of life. I feel that I am the only lifeless thing in this city.' She finally gives in to her self-destructive impulses, tries and succeeds in procuring drugs, is sexually abused and ends up wandering through the less salubrious streets of night-time Istanbul, this time not inflicting physical wounds on herself as she did at the beginning of the film when she slit her wrists, but verbally provoking some Turkish men and willing them to kill her. She is stabbed with a knife and nearly killed. This is the most uncomfortable scene in the film to watch. It is also her own confrontation – gegen die wand – with the destructive side of *kara sevda*.

Again and again in the film the characters are driven to encounters with death or near-death, as seemingly the only way to overcome suffering. However, as outlined above, *kara sevda* carries within it salvation. Sibel recovers from her stab wounds, time passes and she finally meets someone else and has a child with him. Her life has really and truly changed.

Cahit's life, suspended in prison, has yet to change. When he is released, his first mission is to find out where exactly Sibel is. He is obsessed. He travels to Istanbul, meets Selma and is told that Sibel is now leading a different life. Still he needs to see her. It seems that Sibel needs to see him as well. When they finally meet in his hotel room, they are for the first time really and completely together. Cahit wants her to leave her present life, take her daughter with her, and live with him. His idea is to go to Mersin, the place where his ancestors came from. They agree to meet the next day at the coach station. In cross-

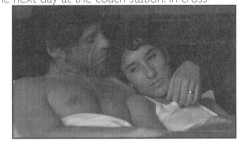

cutting we see her packing her suitcase and him waiting for her at the bus station. She changes her mind and never shows up. The final frames of the film are of him on the bus, calmly leaving for Mersin. They have let go of each other, both found peace in separate lives: the remedy of *kara sevda* has worked.

The narrative, though linear, is interrupted by several musical tableaux. These consist of the same view of Istanbul from the European side across the Bosporus to the Asian side of the city, resembling a picture postcard. Facing the camera is a group of

Turkish musicians in traditional costume, and a female singer at the centre of the arrangement, singing and playing popular Turkish songs. The image looks old-fashioned, like a scene from the fifties, and is quite startling and unexpected in a film whose visual style is otherwise edgy and completely contemporary. The quite obvious interruption serves to divide the narrative into chapters, an unusual device in mainstream film. The break in the narrative has a distancing effect on the viewer. At the same time the singer comments on the next 'chapter' in the story by telling us what emotional upheavals lie in store. She also comments on *kara sevda*. This pointing forward also has the effect of somehow foreshadowing the fate that the protagonists cannot escape, the nature of their obsession and the resulting development of the plot.

There are several scenes in which stereotypes are undermined or exposed quite directly: We have already mentioned the constellation of the protagonists and their respective character traits. Cahit represents for Sibel's family Turkish masculinity and yet is positioned outside the traditional Turkish value system by virtue of his life as a drop-out who is only marginally Turkish. He is therefore able to hold up a mirror towards male hypocrisy and double-standards. This is evident in one scene in particular: He has been invited to play cards with several Turkish men, family and friends, while the women discuss the relative virtues of their husbands in the next room. The men want to take Cahit to a superior brothel with specialist prostitutes. 'Why don't you fuck your own wives?' he wants to know. They are outraged and their reaction is fierce: 'Don't you ever mention the word "fuck" in the same breath as our wives,' they threaten him.

When Cahit has landed at Istanbul airport he is taken to the city by a taxi. His Turkish – though improved – is not the best as he tries to explain to the taxi driver that he does not know Istanbul at all and is just looking for a hotel. Quickly the taxi driver realises that Cahit is from Germany and launches into German, tinged with a Bavarian accent. It turns out that he grew up in Munich. They converse in German.

Gegen die Wand is an uncompromising film; it does not mince its words (or actions). The film tackles many cultural stereotypes and does so very directly, unexpectedly and sometimes humorously, hitting us with its representations of violence and of politically incorrect situations. It makes for quite uncomfortable viewing at times, and forces us, the audience, to question ourselves and our own attitudes towards what the film seeks to portray.

In an interview, the actress Sibel Kikelli talks about the film and her part in it and whether she thinks it has the ring of truth about it. Asked whether she thinks the story of a young Turkish woman marrying a Turkish man for convenience in order to satisfy her family, but also in order to be able to do whatever she wants to do, is conceivable, she says that yes, of course it is, but it would not be something she herself would do. She would not marry someone without loving him. The premise of this story is quite extraordinary. It provoked strong responses from the Turkish community, some negative, but, as detailed earlier, mostly positive.

There are certain parallels in Sibel Kikelli's life with the film, however. Sibel left her small-town life in southern Germany in order to be independent. In an extraordinary coincidence she was approached by a casting agent in a shopping mall in Essen, the town where she lived then, quite far away from Hamburg where the film was to be shot. She had never heard of Fatih Akin before, but said yes, she would give it a try, and was selected by Akin personally. Here was the new life. For her there is a very important statement made early on in the film (by the doctor who interviews Cahit after his attempted suicide): 'If you want to end your life, then end your life. But it doesn't mean that you have to kill yourself.' With the film she ended her past life without killing herself – she started a new life.

The reception of the film was overshadowed somewhat by the revelation that Kikelli (in her previous life) had taken part in porn films, a fact that was known to the makers of *Gegen die Wand*, who nevertheless decided not to make 'the scandal' public. A German right-wing tabloid, the *Bild Zeitung*, 'exposed' this fact on the front page: 'Film Diva A Porn Star'. Predictably, the revelation was a public sensation (which is why the paper used it in this way, of course), but, and this is much more interesting, many Turkish girls and women publicly stood by Sibel and said: so what, so she's made porn films, that's up to her, why should that make her a bad person?

The serious German press reacted very strongly against the 'revelations' ('*Bild* is a scandal!'), emphasising their irrelevance and praising the film and Kikelli's role in it instead. The Turkish Culture and Tourism Minister felt compelled to say: 'A politician can be held responsible for past deeds, but an artist should not be judged for such mistakes.' A columnist of the Turkish newspaper Hürriyet, which is published in Germany, wrote: 'I would even go further than that. If a politician neither betrays his country nor uses his influence unduly, if he does not steal, then he should not be judged in matters of the heart.' Even the conservative Türkiye said: 'What counts is the award.' [2] Thus the *Bild* incident backfired and promoted both the film and its female lead. It certainly helped to make Sibel Kikelli 'the most famous Turkish woman in Germany'. In her subsequent career in film acting she has managed to secure roles that have led her out of playing exclusively Turkish women. She refuses to be pigeon-holed. Thus her experience can be summarised as 'a successful story of integration' (taz) [3] It is more than that, though. Sibel Kikelli's self-confidence is so strong that it enables her to go her own way, beyond feminism or Islamism, just like her character in *Gegen die Wand*.

As we have seen in this chapter, *Gegen die Wand* in so many ways, textually and contextually, brings into focus different aspects of culture and recent history of Germany: the beginnings of serious discussions around multi-culturalism, including the issues of parallel worlds versus integration of immigrants, relations between Germany and Turkey, the role of the press (both Turkish and German, both tabloid and broadsheet), and exciting film-making.

Fatih Akin's vibrant film-making continues, and he has in the meantime made the second part of his trilogy project '*Love, Death and the Devil*'. The film carries the English title *The Edge of Heaven*, which is a somewhat hyperbolic rendering of the German title *Auf der anderen Seite* (*On the Other Side*). This title refers back to the film discussed here, the first part of his trilogy whose German title means 'Against the Wall'. The six main characters in *Auf der anderen Seite* are faced with death in their intersecting lives. Again, Akin's film is set across borders, from Germany to Turkey, and back again, and again he furnishes his film with intertitles that foretell death. However, *Auf der anderen Seite* is about much more than death. It is a profound exploration of love, loss, grief, and reconciliation. It is about transcending boundaries, building bridges across cultures, and finding our common humanity. While the characters in *Gegen die Wand* bash their heads, literally and metaphorically, against each other and against walls in a dark and violent story, *Auf der anderen Seite* has a much more peaceful, optimistic feel and outlook. Akin is not afraid to show big emotions; his narrative does not necessarily strive for absolute realism, but for a deeper understanding of humanity.

For Akin his continuing success is slightly ambivalent. It is a vindication of his constant effort against what he perceives as the 'token Turk' phenomenon in German film and TV, against not being taken seriously as a film-maker from an immigrant background. But at the same time it means a great responsibility to live up to growing expectations, not just within Germany, but equally within the country in which he does an increasing amount of his filming, Turkey. In his efforts to 'normalise' relationships between people from different backgrounds and between the two countries he is ably supported by a number of other Turkish-German film-makers, but he is currently the only one who achieves international distribution of his films. And he is only in his thirties!

The rapprochement between Germany and Turkey and their respective audiences was one of the effects of *Gegen die Wand* that Akin could have only dreamed about. However, that it was not a one-off event was proved on the occasion of my own visit to a German cinema to see *Auf der anderen Seite*, in central Munich, a city not exactly known for its radical politics. The audience consisted of a roughly equal number of Turkish and German viewers. There were younger and older Turkish women and men; there were groups of middle-aged German women, groups of Turkish men, and some single men and women of both denominations. If the composition of the audience on that Friday evening is anything to go by, Fatih Akin has achieved what nobody would have thought possible before: the beginning of a reconciliation between different cultures as well as between different age groups. Recognising our common humanity is one of the biggest challenges – if not the biggest – the world is facing at the present time, and Fatih Akin is meeting it: head-on.

FOOTNOTES

[1] Her epiphany is reminiscent of Bresson's *Pickpocket* (1959) and Paul Schrader's *American Gigolo* (1980), although both those films end with the prison scene.

[2] The quotes are a summary of an article in *Tagesspiegel*, a German daily paper, translated by the author.

[3] taz = *Tageszeitung*, a left-wing paper published in Berlin.

CHAPTER FOURTEEN: THE OTHER GERMANY: *DAS LEBEN DER ANDEREN* (*THE LIVES OF OTHERS, 2006*)

Das Leben der Anderen is the most talked-about German film of recent years, perhaps since *Lola rennt*. It has won 34 German and international awards, including the 2007 Oscar for best Foreign Language Film and the 2008 BAFTA award in the same category. It is shown and discussed in schools and colleges. Its topic of surveillance is specific to the former East Germany (the German Democratic Republic or GDR), where it is set, and at the same time universal, and therefore seems to strike a chord with audiences wherever the film is released, not just among those directly affected by it. Could it be that we are all in some way (directly or indirectly) affected by it?

The main relevance of *Das Leben der Anderen* lies in the fact that it explores the final years of the GDR, starting in 1984 and ending just after the reunification of Germany in 1990. Unlike previous post-unification films on the topic of East Germany this film tackles issues that proved to be decisive in the collapse of a state, and it does this without any parody or nostalgia. We have explored some important stages of GDR history in our chapters on *Die Mörder sind unter uns* and *Spur der Steine*. To remind ourselves, let us first reprise the basic historical facts and then concentrate on those that are relevant to our discussion of *Das Leben der Anderen*. The GDR (1949-1990) was a self-proclaimed 'dictatorship of the proletariat', ruled by a single party, the Socialist Unity Party of Germany (SED). However, the GDR was part of the Eastern bloc and as such always dependent on political developments in the Soviet Union, which could be more or less dogmatic and repressive at different times. Many citizens of the GDR believed in the principles of socialism, and accepted the necessity of hardship and restrictions that resulted from the development towards full-blown communism, even though it might mean extreme censorship and intrusion into their lives. However, others were critical of the 'real existing socialism' as found in the GDR, which, over the years, did not lead or even get close to the promised blissful state of communism where everybody is equal. Many GDR citizens fled or tried to 'flee the republic' towards the West, a punishable offence and made almost impossible when the GDR's first, external, weapon against 'defectors', the Berlin Wall and its extension along the Western borders of the GDR, was built in 1961. In high-profile cases the state silenced such critical voices inside it by forcing them to leave the country ('Zwangsausbürgerung', or forced expatriation). Most of these dissenters came from amongst the circles of artists or 'cultural creators' ('Kulturschaffende'), which included writers, film-makers, actors, and singers. These people were perceived as particularly dangerous by the state because they had great visibility within society and at the same time they were quite unpredictable in their opinions and in how they expressed them.

The dissenters, or 'others', threatened the state in two ways: they made their opposition known, thus undermining the system directly, and they also exerted a fascination on many who still followed the party line, thereby 'poisoning' loyalist citizens' thoughts and sowing doubt in their minds. This is how they became known as 'others', i.e. 'not part of the state'. In order to keep its citizens under control and to be able to punish its 'enemies', the state spied on them through a system of extremely sophisticated surveillance. This surveillance was the GDR's second, internal, weapon in the fight for communism, which was the programmatic aim of the Party. Surveillance was also a weapon against 'imperialist enemies of socialism', who were perceived as fighting this 'experiment' from outside the borders and who infiltrated the socialist state and supported so-called 'hostile-negative forces' within the state. The Ministry of State Security (MfS), or 'Stasi' ('Staatssicherheit'), the GDR's secret police, had an active involvement in the lives of those categorised as 'others' in order to beat them into submission by various means. These could extend to imprisonment, often for many years, blackmail, demotion to menial jobs, or by forcing them to work for the Stasi as informants, the so-called 'Unofficial Employees' (IMs, or 'Informelle Mitarbeiter'). The aim of this sophisticated and tightly controlled system was no less than the SED's surveillance of an entire society. Some figures may illustrate the extent of secret policing: about 100,000 full-time officers and somewhere between 250,000 and 500,000 civilian informants were employed by the Stasi to spy on a nation of 18 million! However, not all the informants had to be forced to work for the Stasi: Many did so voluntarily, with great pride and absolute belief in the system. And so it came about that neighbour spied on neighbour, family and friends spied on each other. Meticulous files were compiled and kept about every single person under surveillance. In the 1980s the neighbouring state of Poland developed politically more liberal attitudes, and a general loosening of doctrine. Gorbachev's political and economic reforms took the USSR in a similar direction. The GDR on the other hand became even more hard-line in response to the liberalisation of its neighbours; the Stasi became more and more active and its measures more repressive and sophisticated. In *Das Leben der Anderen* we see these mechanisms at work.

DEFA, the state-owned and controlled film production company of the GDR, was one of the cultural organisations that experienced the effects of the long arm of the Stasi, particularly in the 1980s, which is the decade in which *Das Leben der Anderen* is set. Therefore DEFA may serve as a good illustration of the climate in the country in those years. Projects at DEFA perceived as 'dangerous' for the system were not realised, film-makers were forced to turn to bland and inoffensive productions, and colleague was set to spy against colleague. In some cases this coercion was successful because people targeted as informants or their families were threatened with reprisals if they did not cooperate with the Stasi. If they had any weaknesses at all, the Stasi threatened to expose them. They could in effect only continue to work if they became informers. (We see this measure at work in *Das Leben der Anderen*.) Censorship measures were forced on feature films: within the narrative no individualist characters were allowed, and of course no criticism of dogma – socialist society and its achievements had to be in the foreground. The visual style of films had to conform to 'socialist realism' – extravagant, experimental or expressionist visual style was taboo. (See also our chapter on *Spur der Steine* and similar repressive measures in the mid-1960s.) As a result, only very few good, i.e. interesting or challenging, feature films were made in the 1980s. Many film-makers, especially of the older generation, knew that rebellion was futile; for them the socialist dream had ended and they surrendered. Documentary film production had slightly more freedom, which resulted in more and better documentary films in the GDR of the 1980s. In theatre limited freedom was possible as well. In the second half of the 1980s, just like in any other area of life in the GDR, discontent and criticism of the regime gained ground within DEFA, especially among younger film-makers. And yet many GDR artists still believed in the principle of socialism, even though the concrete reality in their country was not what they wanted. This comes across clearly in *Das Leben der Anderen*.

After reunification, in the same way as the political system was abolished, so the film production system of the GDR was completely dismantled. This meant that DEFA employees lost their jobs. As mentioned in the chapter on *Spur der Steine*, for many artists and technicians DEFA was more than a place of employment. It was their home, and their colleagues were their family. They believed that they were working together for the common good, for a better world, a socialist world: a belief that turned out to be an illusion. Therefore, being made redundant meant for the employees at DEFA that they were uprooted, not just from their jobs, but, even more importantly, also from their way of life and their political beliefs. In the early years of the reunified Germany the notion predominated that DEFA had been nothing but one of the executive arms of a dictatorial regime and it was therefore dismissed as a mere propaganda-generating machine. Everybody working for DEFA was judged along the same lines. Time has shown that this simplistic view was untenable and more balanced and differentiated reappraisals are now being conducted in Germany in respect of DEFA history (and indeed all of GDR history).

During the lifetime of the GDR already the term 'Stasi' became synonymous with the SED dictatorship's secret apparatus of repression of its people. After the collapse of the regime a heated debate commenced as to whether the files that the Stasi had kept on individuals should be made accessible to those affected by them. It was decided that access should be granted. Thousands of people were horrified to find proof of what they might have suspected before, namely that they had been spied on by friends, family members, or lovers. For many it was a liberating experience to finally be able to put names to those endless years of suspicion. In the meantime there have been calls (from the political left) to close the Stasi files for the sake of wrapping up that part of GDR history. To that end it is argued that by now the unfortunate past should have been overcome, that enough had been done to come to terms with it. The 'Birthler-Behörde' (formerly known as the 'Gauck-Behörde', after its respective directors), the authority that administers the Stasi files, refutes this claim and cites the numbers of people applying for access to their files: ׀ In 2006 the applications increased by 20 per cent compared to the previous year to more than 97,000. By September 2007 approximately 1.6 million people in total had asked for access to their files. Because public interest is undiminished, the authority wants to keep the files accessible until at least 2019, thirty years after the end of the GDR. These are legitimate questions: should bygones be bygones, or would you support the argument that people have a right to know, to be able to close a chapter of their own personal history, to grieve, for as long as they need to?

In the meantime there have been criticisms of the Birthler authority with regard to the perceived inefficiency of the administration of the Stasi files. There have been criticisms against the authority for withholding information, for (quite literally) 'blacking out' certain details in certain files. While there may be some justification for this criticism we must take into account that there are legal limits to the access to information contained in the Stasi files. There is also not always incontrovertible evidence against specific individuals as informers. Therefore access to certain details and certain files is restricted by law, and by injunctions taken out by suspected individuals against their 'alleged' or 'unproven' Stasi activity. Another criticism levied against the Birthler authority is the fact that it employs former Stasi officers and guards as porters – especially in view of the fact that Stasi officials on the whole were not properly scrutinised and punished in the process of dismantling the GDR regime. Many people feel uncomfortable or even outraged by this. However, it is argued that the Stasi files have to be interpreted by 'experts', otherwise they would not be intelligible because they are so bound up with the system that produced them and that is now defunct – the terminology used, for instance, would not be readily understood by the uninitiated. Apart from the 'Birthler-Behörde' there are other organisations with the task of handling aspects of the SED past, some conducting academic research, others offering practical help for victims of the GDR dictatorship.

After this excursion into the background of the issues raised in our focus film let us now examine the precise historical setting of the film. The main part of *Das Leben der Anderen* is set in 1984. This has a ring of George Orwell's famous novel (written in 1948) about it. However, it is just a coincidence, even if Orwell's predictions are remarkable, that this novel about a dystopian state that controls its citizens by total surveillance should be set in that particular year, which, in the real life of the Eastern bloc states, did indeed turn out to be a particularly repressive one. The main storyline of the film ends in 1985, on the day when Gorbachev's election in the Soviet Union is announced in the newspapers. Gorbachev's years as Soviet leader were, as mentioned above, characterised by gradual economic and political reforms, and continued until the eventual collapse of the Soviet Union and its satellite states in 1991, and in the case of the GDR even earlier, in 1990. With that background knowledge, when we see the relevant newspaper headline in the film we know it is not going to take very long for the regime to be deposed, for the Berlin Wall to come down and for the GDR to be dissolved.

Das Leben der Anderen is a remarkable film in its own right, even without looking at any context. However, when we take a look at the way it was conceived, and by whom, it becomes even more remarkable. The film's director and scriptwriter, Florian Henckel von Donnersmarck (aka Florian Henckel-Donnersmarck), was born in Cologne in 1973. He had quite a cosmopolitan upbringing, growing up in New York, Berlin, Frankfurt and Brussels, then living in Berlin. At present (after the success of *Das Leben der Anderen*) he resides in Los Angeles. Before embarking on a career as a film-maker he studied Russian in St. Petersburg, and Political Science, Philosophy and Economics (PPE) at Oxford University. He then went on to study directing at the Academy of Television and Film in Munich. At only 27 years of age, while he was still at film school, he began working on *Das Leben der Anderen*. Before that and while working on the film's screenplay he had already directed a number of short films which all won prizes. It is therefore not hard to see why he is already referred to as a 'heavyweight' in the industry, justified by his intellectual and creative as well as his physical stature!

Das Leben der Anderen is Donnersmarck's first feature film. How is a West German film-maker (and such a young one at that: at the time of the film's release he was only 33-years-old) qualified to make a film about the GDR? He points out that he did not set out to make a film 'about the GDR' as such. This focus developed later. Instead he initially came from the angle of classical music, Beethoven's Moonlight Sonata, to which he listened one night during his student years. Suddenly he remembered reading about Lenin who once said to Gorki that he could not bear to listen to the Appassionata (another

Beethoven sonata) because if he did he would never finish the revolution. Apparently the effect of the music on him was so strong that it made him want to 'tell people sweet stupid things and caress their heads' instead of 'smashing those heads in mercilessly'. Donnersmarck began imagining what would have happened if Lenin had been forced to listen to the Appassionata. And then the central image of a man with headphones, listening to beautiful music, formed in his head. The man was a 'professional' listener; he was spying on an enemy who loves music. Thus Wiesler, the central character of *Das Leben der Anderen*, was born. Within minutes the treatment for the film was written.

It was one thing to create a framework for such an ambitious film, but quite another to flesh it out with a story and with historically accurate details. A young West German director who has not lived through the time and the events portrayed in his film needs all the advice and support that he can get. Altogether the director spent nearly four years intensively researching and writing his screenplay. In this he was greatly helped by his historical consultant, Prof. Hans Wilke, who is the head of an academic group based at the Freie Universität Berlin researching the SED dictatorship. Wilke is convinced that in order to appraise a dictatorship and its end with clarity, a certain historical distance is needed, the distance of a generation removed from the actual events. This gives Donnersmarck a definite advantage! Much of the story was based on actual events in the GDR which we will discuss in more detail later on in the chapter. As for the details for fleshing out his characters, Donnersmarck interviewed many people on both sides of the Stasi divide, perpetrators and victims. He spoke to ex-Stasi officers in order to gain insight into the minds of those who staunchly defended their state because they believed in it, as well as those who did it for personal gain. He spent many hours talking to victims of Stasi surveillance about the effect this had on their lives.

In the press notes to the film the director says: 'I spent almost too much time with the realities. But in the end, I had reached a point where I knew that I would be able to create a fictional story that was somehow truer than a true story.' Wiesler is fictional, playwright Dreyman is fictional, the exact circumstances in which their story unfolds are fictional. They are 'true' in the same sense as the protagonists of, say, *The Deer Hunter* (1978) or *Dr Zhivago* (1965) are within their respective historical context. This realisation is key to accepting *Das Leben der Anderen* as it is meant to be: not a completely realistic story but, in the director's own words, a 'hyperrealist' portrayal which explores possible outcomes grounded in reality. It is a brave and also risky attempt which must inevitably lead to criticism from those who do not accept this approach and who therefore base their criticism on the presumption of absolute realism. Such views have been voiced by different people in different ways. The main point of criticism concerns the portrayal of the main character, a Stasi agent who develops a conscience and who manages to 'save' his victim against the sophisticated apparatus of the Stasi. This is indeed a highly unlikely scenario, since, if it was possible at all, why did not more Stasi officers act? Consider in this context Donnersmarck's assertion: 'I do believe that fiction can actually be richer in content than fact. But perhaps that is a very German thought. The German word for fiction and poetry is "Dichtung", which actually means something like "density". Thus he prefers to think of his film on a level somewhat removed from absolute reality – possibly a risky approach to a subject matter as sensitive and hotly debated as Stasi history. In this respect, Donnersmarck can perhaps be accused of having made the wrong judgement with his 'hyper-realism'. Some say he should not even have turned to the subject in the first place, considering his obvious outsider status.

With regard to the historical details and the technical aspects of Stasi operations that pervade the film, the film-makers insisted on the utmost accuracy. Very careful research of locations was conducted; wherever possible filming took place at original locations, such as the Stasi headquarters and the infamous Hohenschönhausen prison, which was the centre of Stasi interrogations of 'enemies'. Other interiors and exteriors were assessed as to their atmosphere and the 'deserted' look that could be created in order to resemble GDR times. Berlin has changed considerably since the 1980s, which meant that a large proportion of the film's budget (which was modest) had to go into the recreation of a historical Berlin. In order to achieve the final look of the film and intensify his message, Donnersmarck just slightly 'raised' reality. The overall mise-en-scène is strikingly 1980s' East Berlin (as verified by people who know it). For the representation of Stasi spying

techniques he insisted on using original equipment, which he was fortunate enough to secure from a private collector of Stasi listening devices. At the former Stasi headquarters we see a huge card-filing system that was used to record millions of names, all written by hand, in different colours with different pens. The machinery still exists, the cards do not.

Film-making is a collaborative effort. For *Das Leben der Anderen* we have already mentioned the academic historical consultant. Another invaluable source of information and personal insight came from the actor Ulrich Mühe who plays the Stasi captain Gerd Wiesler. Born in 1953 in the GDR and acting first in theatre and then more and more in film, he brought with him first-hand experience of growing up and working in precisely the environment that is represented in *Das Leben der Anderen*.

His biography may stand for many of his fellow GDR artists and is therefore worth exploring in some more detail. After an apprenticeship as a builder combined with A-levels (or high school diploma) – an educational path that we cannot imagine but that was quite common in the GDR – he decided to fulfil his desire to become an actor. He achieved considerable status as a theatre actor in his country and was even allowed to travel to the West, a privilege reserved for high-profile GDR citizens. His questioning attitude, his desire to 'disrupt' the superficially harmonious, got him into trouble with the

Stasi, who kept tight reins on him. However, he believed in socialism as a principle, and when the Wall came down he was disappointed at first, and later very annoyed with his own people who voted Conservative (CDU) in the first all-German elections. For personal reasons he moved to West Germany, and gradually, with hindsight, began to be more critical of his former country and the restricted life it had offered him (and others). On visits to eastern Germany he was not always welcome because of the openness with which he spoke about the former GDR, but mainly because of his obsession with proving that his ex-wife had spied on him as an informer for the Stasi. There was no conclusive proof. The hostility that he encountered among his former fellow-citizens was at least partly an expression of their own refusal to admit that they had lived in a dictatorship.

At home in the West, he began to leave his past behind him, until Donnersmarck approached him for the lead role in his first feature film. And although he had been on the side of the 'others' in real life (i.e. spied upon by the Stasi) he found it a challenging but worthwhile experience to think himself into the part of a Stasi agent. More than that, he became Donnersmarck's advisor, mainly in respect of the screenplay, for which he suggested modifications based on his first-hand experience of growing up and working in precisely the environment that is represented in *Das Leben der Anderen*. Ultimately, though, his acceptance of the role was based on his appreciation of Donnersmarck's professionalism, thorough research, and creative ability. The decisive conversation between the two men before Ulrich Mühe agreed to play part demonstrates this. Mühe said that one of the questions that interested him about the role was: 'For a large part of the film a man sits in an attic, listens to other people and is constantly moved. How do you act that?' Donnersmarck quietly answered: 'Maybe you don't act it at all.' After that Mühe agreed to take on the role.

For Mühe's portrayal of Stasi Captain Gerd Wiesler he won several 'Best Actor' awards. He plays Wiesler with such intensity and conviction that, having experienced his performance, you will be unable to imagine that any other actor could have achieved it. We are captivated by Wiesler because of Mühe's performance: Through him, particularly his face, we follow a distilled history of Cold War surveillance; we begin to empathise with him as his tight features begin to soften ever so slightly. At first, though, Wiesler believes unconditionally in socialism and in the necessity to 'help people along their way' to a better society. He is totally committed to the regime and is prepared to go to any lengths to fight its enemies.

How the state created and sustained the hatred of 'enemies' is effectively demonstrated in the first scene of the film. The scene is shot very tightly: there is not one superfluous gesture or word, everything counts. We see Wiesler at work, as he interrogates a suspect at the infamous detention centre of Hohenschönhausen, ruthlessly, mercilessly. He is a true professional. Every trick of the Stasi's trade is played out. This interrogation is cross-cut with a lecture Wiesler gives at the Stasi Training Academy in Potsdam to a new generation of recruits during which he plays them a recording of the interrogation as a perfect example of how to break a human being down and to reduce him to nothing but an enemy of the state. The 'crime' that is investigated by Wiesler in this scene is the act of 'unlawful border crossing', which was deemed a 'crime against the state', punishable by two years in prison, and which a friend of the accused has committed. Even the

preparation and the attempt at 'fleeing the republic' were punishable. When the accused man does not give any names, Wiesler tells him that his family will be implicated. The suspect then breaks down and starts to talk. In such political cases the Stasi played a decisive part within the judicial system of East Germany.

Two other representatives of the Ministry for State Security serve as examples of the corruption that was rife within the Stasi. Minister Hempf orders the surveillance of a couple, a playwright and an actress, not because they are suspected of being enemies of the state, but because he wants to have an affair with the actress and wants the playwright out of his way. Grubitz, who is Wiesler's commanding officer, is a careerist, who uses his position to further himself. For him socialism is just a means to his own ends; he would do exactly the same in any other system. He rules with shrewdness and intimidation over his subordinates.

Hempf gives orders for an 'Operative Procedure' (Operativer Vorgang, or OV) to be opened against Dreyman, the playwright, and supervised by Wiesler, who is to report directly to Grubitz. According to Stalin, whom Hempf quotes at one point, 'writers are the engineers of the soul' and need to be controlled and used by the Party. Self-determined human individuality had to be eradicated. The 'Operative Procedures' constituted the highest-profile surveillance of suspects and consisted of bugging their apartments and phones as well as spying on their movements. Wiesler does exactly that. After Dreyman's apartment has been bugged extensively, he installs himself in the attic of the apartment block, listens to every sound in the writer's apartment and reports on every detail meticulously in what is termed 'Operation Laszlo'. [2] These operations were meant to be 'preventative measures' against 'hostile-negative acts' in order to 'contribute to the continuing implementation of the policies of the state'. In Dreyman's case there was no need for surveillance: He is 'party loyal' and not interested in subversive actions, even though some of his theatre friends are more critical of state ideology. His partner Christa-Maria Sieland is a successful theatre actress; however, she has a darker side. She is not confident enough to believe in the strength of her art alone, and gives in to the advances of Minister Hempf, who uses his position to force an affair on her. She is also addicted to painkillers, which makes her an easy target for blackmail. This weakness of hers becomes important when Dreyman, through the suicide of a friend, is jolted into action, no longer able to reconcile his conscience with the knowledge he has regarding the issue of rising suicides in the GDR.

He decides to write an article about his country's suicide statistics, which had been repressed by the Party since 1977 because they showed an enormous increase, which was obviously not an advertisement for the social climate in the GDR. Dreyman writes this article for the West German weekly political magazine *Der Spiegel*. According to the GDR penal code this constitutes an act of 'espionage'; it was 'treasonable transmission of information'. The clandestine meetings in his apartment with the relevant *Spiegel* editor constitute 'illegal contact' with 'imperialist forces'. Dreyman is fully aware of the risks he is taking, but he is not aware of the surveillance of his whole life that is already in place. The *Spiegel* editor gives him a mini typewriter that can be hidden easily, because the Stasi will have long identified the characteristics of his own typewriter. Dreyman's activities are very close to real events that took place in 1960s and 1970s Germany: *Der Spiegel* did publish texts written by dissidents within the Eastern bloc and smuggled into West Germany. One case in particular shows close resemblance to Dreyman's article and at the same time links in with Wiesler's transformation. It is the so-called 'Spiegel Manifesto' which was written in 1978 by high level representatives of East German public life. This manifesto branded the Soviet Union politbureau's orthodoxy as reactionary, as inflicting its own power politics on its people, thereby ignoring international labour movements and the interests of its satellite states. Stalinism and National Socialism were described as 'twins' in the terror they exerted. Within the GDR the main attack was against the 'clique at the top' that used the country as a 'self-service shop'. We see how Wiesler, the dedicated communist, suffers because of the cynical careerism of his comrades, in this case Grubitz, who tells him that he, Wiesler, does not have what it takes to make it through the Stasi ranks. Wiesler also realises that Minister Hempf is using the Stasi surveillance of Dreyman for his own ends.

Just as Dreyman becomes a subversive activist (outwardly), Wiesler betrays his employer (inwardly). He develops a conscience and starts to withhold information and to falsify his reports. He protects Dreyman for a variety of reasons, not least because he is drawn to the lives of these 'others' that he is spying on, as through them he realises the limitations of his own life. Gradually, only in his mind at first, he inveigles himself into these other lives. The first physical crossing of the boundaries between observer and observed occurs when he enters the apartment in order to 'borrow' a book of poems by Bertolt Brecht which he reads upon returning to his own drab and grey flat. The contrasts between the two flats and the two lives have been made very obvious by the production design. Wiesler's life is characterised by sparsely furnished rooms with harsh lights and empty walls – whether it is his place of work or his flat. Just like his surroundings his appearance is devoid of colour and individuality: He is dressed in greys and grey-blues, even his face looks ashen. In contrast to this, Dreyman's flat and the clothes he wears suggest warmth and individuality: The flat is rendered in a range of warm colours, with comfortable sofas and warm, individualised lighting. Gradually, Wiesler begins to interfere in this other life:

Fortified by alcohol he approaches Christa-Maria in a bar and reminds her of her greatness as an actress and tells her to think of her audience. This is a plea for her to break off her liaison with Minister Hempf, for Wiesler is only too aware of the danger in which she finds herself. She does not realise who he is, of course. To her he is a genuine fan.

Two scenes provide a chilling example of the more 'informal', almost accidental, day-to-day workings of the Stasi. These scenes, from earlier and later in the film, also show how Wiesler is beginning to distance himself from the task of achieving total control. In the first such scene Grubitz and Wiesler enter the Stasi headquarters canteen and seat themselves at the same table as some more lowly Stasi employees. One of them is telling a joke involving the SED Party leader, Erich Honecker, who was indeed the butt of many jokes in those days. Upon the arrival of the two superior Stasi officers the younger man stops in his tracks, looking worried. He is well aware that telling jokes at the Party's expense is a treasonable offence. Grubitz amiably encourages him to continue. At the end of the joke Grubitz barks 'Name, rank' at the young man, who is now clearly very frightened, whereupon Grubitz breaks into laughter, which does, however, not have any liberating qualities about it. He lets the young man off and proceeds to tell his own Honecker joke. Wiesler is quite disturbed by the event (in much the same way that we, the audience, are). In the later scene, Wiesler enters the lift in his own apartment block, and a small boy with a football follows him. The boy stares at Wiesler and asks: 'Is it true that you work for the Stasi?' Wiesler is lost for words and answers: 'Do you know what the Stasi is?' To which the boy responds: 'They are horrible men who lock people up.'

That's what his daddy says. Wiesler, initially on auto-pilot, asks: 'What's the name of your...', with the intention of adding '... father?', but he corrects himself and finishes the question: '...ball, what's the name of your ball?' The boy tells him with childish contempt that balls do not have names.

These two scenes are further examples of Donnersmarck's excellent screenplay in which not a word is superfluous: We know with absolute clarity that the second scene marks a turning point in Wiesler's life.

To come back to the redemptive power of music that was the starting point of Donnersmarck's idea for the film, Wiesler is 'forced' to listen to the music being picked up by the microphones in Dreyman's apartment. Pivotal in this is the Sonata for a Good Man[3] which Dreyman plays on the piano and which has a strong influence on the player, his actress lover and on Wiesler alone in the attic, with his headphones on. At this point all three of them seem to be united as human beings and have the chance to become better people. Christa-Maria does not succeed: She succumbs to her weakness and is forced to become an informer, but Wiesler is able to interfere once again and to

sabotage the work of the Ministry of State Security. Dreyman does not know at the time who his 'guardian angel' is. He only finds out much later when, after the GDR has been dismantled and the Stasi files have been made accessible, he realises that it was a Stasi agent, 'HGWXX/7', who has become 'a good man'.

As mentioned earlier, some critics have pointed out that Wiesler's about-turn would not have been possible in reality. Yes, probably not exactly in the way in which it is shown in the film. However, there were, in the history of the Ministry of State Security, some officers, even high-ranking ones, who did indeed become sceptical of the state of their country, with which, of course, they were confronted in their daily work. Above all the paralysis within the Party and its refusal to acknowledge reality made them despair. In Wiesler's case, his questioning starts when he realises that the Party bigwigs do not believe in communism any more: Their objectives are not political any longer, but personal – privileges, personal enjoyment, and power. Thus they abuse the Stasi to their own ends. Wiesler is not strong enough for open revolt, but feels compelled to act 'behind the scenes' in order to make at least a small difference. In the latter stages of the 1980s such actions became more frequent in the GDR, ultimately leading to the peaceful revolution which brought down the Wall on 9 November, 1989. This is not to say that it was the insubordination of members of the Stasi that achieved this almost unimaginable feat – it is the groundswell of ordinary citizens' protests that was a major conduit – merely to point out that there were small acts of rebellion by people who had lost their belief in the system.

There have been a number of feature films in Germany in recent years that address German history. The best-known amongst them are *Der Untergang* (2004), discussed in chapter 12 of this book, about the last few days of Hitler, and *Sophie Scholl – die letzten Tage* (*Sophie Scholl - The Last Days*) about the most prominent member of a student resistance group against Hitler. Both are serious accounts of horrific events. In the meantime the first German comedy about Hitler has also been made. With regard to East German history, too, a few films have been made. A very early example of a film dealing with the GDR is *Verlorene Landschaft* (*Lost Landscape*, 1992) by the East German director Andreas Kleinert. It is told mainly in flashback through memory sequences of a German politician with an East German background remembering his isolated childhood in the GDR. In 1998 Kleinert made *Wege in die Nacht* (*Paths in the Night*) about a former East German company director who despairs about the present in which he has become unemployed and useless. These films deal with personal memory in a dramatic way. Later films about life in the GDR are mainly comedies: *Sonnenallee* (*Sun Alley*, 1999) and *Good Bye Lenin!* (2003), for example, belong to a wave of nostalgia for the old East, but they also started the process of opening up to yet another difficult chapter of German history: *Good Bye Lenin!* in particular has been termed a 'symbolic funeral'. However, the liberating laughter that greeted these two comedies is not possible in *Das Leben der Anderen*. Apparently it takes both, comedy and drama, to come to terms with recent German history. However, the best of such films must contain universal truths and therefore have an impact that goes beyond their own historical context.

FOOTNOTES

[1] One wonders whether the release of *Das Leben der Anderen* had anything to do with the rising numbers.

[2] Would that be a reference to *Casablanca* (1942), where the name of the political refugee from Nazi Germany is Laszlo?

[3] Bertolt Brecht, the poet and playwright whose poems are read by Dreyman and Wiesler, was a strong believer in the 'goodness' of human beings, according to the basic socialist principle that it is circumstances that turn people 'bad'.

CONCLUDING NOTES

While trawling through German film history and situating it within wider political, social and cultural contexts we have observed that it is a history of discontinuities rather than continuities. There *are* continuities, to be sure. However, they are much more difficult to find. The threads keep breaking off and are sometimes picked up again much later. This is clearly related to Germany's troubled twentieth century history: From Kaiserreich through World War I, via the Weimar Republic to a dictatorship that lasted 12 years, which unleashed World War II, managed to destroy artistic innovation and (nearly) destroyed the will to keep going among those who had not left Germany. The exodus in the early thirties of the highest calibre of representatives of Weimar culture is almost too depressing to even think about. Just imagine how German culture would have continued to thrive if people such as Fritz Lang, Erich Pommer, Billy Wilder, Marlene Dietrich and all the less well-known but equally important craftsmen and women of Weimar cinema had remained in Germany.

The history of Germany's most important film production company is a clear expression of these continuities and discontinuities. In the book we have included the various manifestations of UFA/DEFA in the relevant chapters. Here we would just like to give a brief summary of the history of this unique place in Potsdam-Babelsberg. During World War I already, UFA was for the first time in the hands of big business and government in order to produce propaganda material for the war effort. Brought forward 25–30 years, the same happened during the Third Reich, only this time with much more ideological control and technical sophistication. After all, cinematic production had moved on considerably in the intervening years: In Germany, film as art had developed during the 1920s. This was also a time in which the German film industry was more and more centralised; many small production companies were incorporated into UFA, which for a while was considered to be equal to Hollywood. During World War II the Babelsberg studios were all but destroyed, but reconstituted as the centre of film production in the new state of the GDR. The UFA was renamed DEFA, and, once again, came under state control, this time within a socialist regime. Through various ideological ups and downs the company retained its significance. After reunification DEFA became Studio Babelsberg – not just a name change, but also a changeover of this centre for national and international film production into private hands. Nowadays the German film industry is much more diversified, though, and Babelsberg is just one of the country's film production companies.

DEFA is now part of history. After reunification, there was no will to consider DEFA as at all valuable: All DEFA films were grouped together and dismissed as 'ideological', 'communist propaganda', etc. As if western films were free from ideology! In the meantime, however, there has been renewed interest in DEFA films: in 2005, the Museum of Modern Art in New York staged a retrospective of DEFA films. DVD give-aways in a magazine in Germany drew attention to GDR films in Germany itself, and in 2008 the Goethe Institut released a package of DEFA films to be shown all over the world for greater appreciation.

Coming back to the wider context of German film culture, it needs to be stressed again that after the twelve years of National Socialism the democratisation of the country and its people was first and foremost in the hands of the victorious powers, the Allied forces of the USA, Britain, France, and the Soviet Union (soon to be divided, though). Although this control of the media by outside forces is understandable, at least initially, one wonders what would have happened if the seeds of a new beginning from within Germany's cultural community had been allowed to sprout. Add to this the division of the country into two separate states in 1949, both of which were dominated by ideas outside themselves: In the FRG western, democratic and capitalist concepts were in themselves positive, but not free from the self-interest of the occupying forces, particularly America. For the film industry this meant Hollywood products flooding the West German market. In the eastern part of Germany, the Soviet influence was much stronger than anything that happened in the west. In the GDR another dictatorship took hold. Again we can only imagine what film-makers such as Wolfgang Staudte and G. W. Pabst could have achieved in a united Germany.

It has also become clear in the course of this book that in all the incarnations of Germany there were within film culture small voices of discontent, of dissent even, also of warning and of analysis concerning the contemporary political situation. Many of them were brushed aside at the time, or ignored altogether, attacked for being too political, or censored. They were often prophets who surfaced at the wrong time.

Truly independent cinema was gradually achieved in (West) Germany during the 1960s and 1970s through the efforts of the film-makers of New German Cinema. These film-makers took up the challenge of changing German cinema on many levels: political, educational, and stylistic. They were true rebels, and yet many of them sought continuity with cinematic traditions of the 1920s. Unfortunately, their films were never as well-received in their own country as abroad. However, it was never their primary aim to be commercially successful. This is the main difference between then and now.

The reunified Germany provided a challenge and an opportunity for East and West German film-makers. The 1990s produced several significant films that dealt with current issues on both sides of the previous divide, and a gradual interpenetration of awareness developed, which has resulted in films that show synergies between East and West German film-makers. This process is ongoing, as is the important process of cinematic representation of immigrants, the best-known exponent of which is Fatih Akin.

Presently, German cinema is in a relatively healthy state. There are large-scale productions, such as Bernd Eichinger's box office successes *Das Boot*, *Der Untergang* and, quite recently, *Der Baader-Meinhof-Komplex*, films that tackle topics of German history with new confidence, but also attract criticism. Such mainstream representations sit side by side with unspectacular, low-budget films such as those made by Christian Petzold, Valeska

Griesebach, Thomas Arslan and other film-makers from the so-called Berlin School. Two other names that deserve to be mentioned in this context are Hans-Christian Schmid (west German) and Andreas Dresen (east German), who have consistently added to the debates around present-day Germany, its achievements and failures, and who demonstrate that the old labels 'East' and 'West' are no longer quite so relevant. Another book needs to be written about them.

The previous lines are a good example of the limits of a book of this nature: it cannot possibly do justice to every important film in the German repertoire. However, we have tried to be as inclusive as possible by integrating within each chapter related trends and individual films that can be explored further. Therefore we hope we have provided enough material for further individual study. Our bibliography has useful pointers as well.

Within the chapters we have already given possibilities for further viewing on particular subjects or directors. Here are some recommendations for thematic and other connections between films in the book that could be exploited for focused study:

- Literary adaptations: *Der blaue Engel, Die Blechtrommel*

- Films that deal with German history: *Die Blechtrommel, Der Untergang, Das Leben der Anderen*

- Immigrants as subject-matter: *Angst essen Seele auf, Gegen die Wand*

- City (Berlin) films: *Der Himmel über Berlin, Lola rennt*

- Fairy tales, myths, utopias: *Metropolis, Der Himmel über Berlin, Die Blechtrommel, Lola rennt*

- Documentary tradition: as propaganda in *Triumph des Willens*; as 'truth-seeking' in Werner Herzog's films

- Different visual styles to be compared: Expressionist – *Nosferatu*; realist: – *Spur der Steine, Der Untergang*; hyperrealist – *Das Leben der Anderen*; realist and expressionist – *Die Mörder sind unter uns, Aguirre, Der Zorn Gottes*; postmodern – *Lola rennt*

There are many ways in which this book can be exploited for the study of German film. Whichever way you choose to apply it, we hope that we have touched your curiosity and that you will use it as a springboard for further study.

SELECTED BIBLIOGRAPHY

GENERAL

Fischer, R., Hembus, J., *Der Neue Deutsche Film 1960-1980*, Goldmann Verlag, Munich, 1981
The most important films of the New German Cinema, here specifically *Aguirre*, *Angst essen Seele auf*, *Die Blechtrommel*

Jacobsen, W., Kaes, A., Prinzler, H.H. (eds), *Geschichte des Deutschen Films*, Metzler, Stuttgart, 1993

Kaes, A., *From Hitler to Heimat: The Return of History as Film*, Harvard University Press, 1989

Pflaum, H.G., Prinzler, H.H., *Film in the Federal Republic of Germany – A Handbook*, inter nationes, Bonn, 1993
Not up-to-date (as is obvious from publication date), but very useful for developments in West Germany, concentrating on New German Cinema and beyond, including full filmographies of most film-makers

Vogt, G., *Die Stadt im Kino, Deutsche Spielfilme 1900-2000*, Marburg, 2001

www.filmportal.de
Information on German cinema in its historical context, on individual film-makers and films (partly in English)

www.bpb.de
Valuable historical information by the Zentrale für politische Bildung, all available free

www.film-kultur.de
A German website with excellent classroom materials for key films (only in German)

http://rogerebert.suntimes.com/
This is the website of Roger Ebert, the great film critic of the Chicago Sun-Times. Here you find reviews of many of the films discussed in this book. Browsing highly recommended!

Nosferatu, Metropolis

Eisner, L., *The Haunted Screen*, University of California Press, Berkeley, 1974 (revised 2008)
The classic analysis of Expressionist cinema

Elsaesser, T., *Metropolis*, BFI Publishing, London, 2000

Elsaesser, T., *Cinema of Weimar and After*, Routledge, London, 2000

www.kino.com/metropolis/
Good plot summary, restoration 2002, detailed, flashy info and images

Furness, R.S., *Expressionism, The Critical Idiom*, Methuen, London, 1975

Pflaum, H.G., *German Silent Movie Classics*, F.W. Murnau Stiftung, Wiesbaden, 2002

Shepard, J., *Nosferatu in Love*, Faber and Faber, London, 1998
F.W. Murnau's fictional diary while filming *Nosferatu*

Der blaue Engel

Mann, H., *Professor Unrath*
The novel on which the film is based

Marlene Dietrich, Her Own Song, DVD, Edition Salzgeber, 2006

Triumph des Willens

Benz, W., *Geschichte des Dritten Reiches*, Verlag C.H.Beck oHG, Munich, 2000

Riefenstahl, L., *A Memoir*, St. Martin's Press, New York, 1992

www.kamera.co.uk/features/leniriefenstahl.html
Discussion of *Triumph of the Will* and *Olympia* – documentaries or propaganda?

www.nybooks.com/articles/20258
Interesting reviews of two recent books about Leni Riefenstahl

Die Mörder sind unter uns

Netenjakob, E., *Staudte*, Edition Filme, Berlin, 1991

www.bpb.de
bpb (Bundesamt für politische Bildung) website, in German only

www.ikf.de (Institut für Kino und Filmkultur),
Study Guide to *Die Mörder sind unter uns*, in German only

Spur der Steine

Poss, I., Warnecke, P. (eds), *Spur der Filme – Zeitzeugen über die DEFA*, Christoph Links, Berlin, 2006

Documentary VHS video: *Es werden ein paar Filme bleiben*, made by the Goethe Institute
www.filmzentrale.com/rezis/spurdersteinekk.htm

Aguirre, der Zorn Gottes

Cronin, P. (ed.), *Herzog on Herzog*, Faber and Faber, London, 2002

Fischer/Hembus, *Der Neue Deutsche Film 1960-1980* (see above)

Prager, B., *The Cinema of Werner Herzog: Aesthetic Ecstasy and Truth*, Wallflower Press, London, 2007

Angst essen Seele auf

Fischer/Hembus, *Der Neue Deutsche Film 1960-1980* (see above)

Töteberg, M., *Rainer Werner Fassbinder*, Rowohlt Taschenbuch Verlag, Reinbek, 2002

Sight and Sound, 2, 1999
Article on Fassbinder

Die Blechtrommel

Fischer/Hembus: *Der Neue Deutsche Film 1960-1980* (see above)

Grass, G., *Die Blechtrommel*, Deutscher Taschenbuch Verlag, 1993

Heimat

Kaes, A., *From Hitler to Heimat* (see above)
Documentary Film on BBC television, 2005

www.edgar-reitz.de

www.dieterwunderlich.de/Reitz-heimat-1.htm

www.heimat123.de
Excellent website, originally in German, partly translated, which contains the complete screenplay of the Heimat Trilogy

Der Himmel über Berlin

Vogt, G., *Die Stadt im Film* (see above)

Lola rennt

Clarke, D. (ed.), *German Cinema Since Unification*, Continuum, London, 2006
Not quite up-to-date, ends on a pessimistic note with respect to German cinema today

Töteberg, M. (ed.), *Tom Tykwer: Lola Rennt*, Rowohlt Taschenbuch Verlag, Reinbek, 1998

Vogt, G., *Die Stadt im Film* (see above)

Gegen die Wand

Akin, F., *Gegen die Wand, Das Buch zum Film*, Kiepenheuer & Witsch, Cologne, 2004

Sight and Sound article, *Dark Passion*, 3, 2005
Excellent exploration of kara sevda, and discussion of film

Goethe Institute, *Getürkt – Young Turks*, Munich, 2003

Der Untergang

Fest, J., Eichinger, B., *Der Untergang, Das Filmbuch*, Rowohlt Taschenbuch Verlag, Reinbek, 2001

Das Leben der Anderen

Henckel Donnersmarck, F., *Das Leben der Anderen, Filmbuch*, Rowohlt Taschenbuch Verlag, Reinbek, 2007

Poss, I., Warnecke, P. (eds), *Spur der Filme* (see above)

Press Notes (Lionsgate)

INDEX

Note: German language films are listed under their original title, with English translation in parentheses.